And No Birds Sing

And No Birds Sing

Pauline Leader

Mara Mills and Rebecca Sanchez
Editors

Gallaudet University Press
Washington, DC

Gallaudet University Press
Washington, DC 20002
http://gupress.gallaudet.edu

Originally published in 1931 by The Vanguard Press.
All idiosyncrasies of diction, punctuation, and spelling have been
preserved.

Library of Congress Cataloging-in-Publication Data

Names: Leader, Pauline, author. | Mills, Mara, writer of introduction. |
Sanchez, Rebecca, writer of afterword.

Title: And no birds sing / Pauline Leader; introduction by Mara Mills,
afterword by Rebecca Sanchez.

Description: Washington, DC: Gallaudet University Press, 2016.

Identifiers: LCCN 2016023954 | ISBN 9781563686689 (paperback)

Subjects: LCSH: Leader, Pauline. | Women authors, American–20th
century–Biography. | Deaf women–United States–Biography. | BISAC:
BIOGRAPHY & AUTOBIOGRAPHY / Personal Memoirs.

Classification: LCC PS3523.E124 Z46 2016 | DDC 813/.52 [B] –dc23
LC record available at https://lccn.loc.gov/2016023954

Photographs courtesy of Daniel and Jonathan Brand.
Cover painting by Henry Lavarack, 1930.

Contents

Underdog Bohemia
A Biography of Pauline Leader

Mara Mills

It seemed to be a terrible thing for a girl to run away.
—Pauline Leader

In the 1920s, Hubert's Cafeteria in Sheridan Square was "the nerve center" of Greenwich Village, open 24 hours and attracting a wild-eyed crowd of artists and writers around midnight.[1] Who might be found under the bright lights, amid the hubbub there? Maxwell Bodenheim, "village bard," was one of the regulars. He was the drunk who Luc Sante says incarnated "the perpetually mendicant garret poet." Another poet, Luis Muñoz Marín, sometimes stopped by before heading to Georgie Yee's opium den at Mott and Bleecker; he became governor of Puerto Rico in 1948.[2] Joe Gould, who may or may not have been writing *An Oral History of Our Time* while drinking all day at a local bar, often walked in to pour himself a free bowl of ketchup and mustard. A young Kenneth Fearing, who later founded *The Partisan Review*, also patronized Hubert's. According to Richard Bruce Nugent, the "gay rebel of the Harlem Renaissance," this cafeteria was briefly the epicenter of Bohemia in the years following World War I.

The entire country was caught in a boom of prosperity, spending, and license. . . . Money was easily acquired and freely spent. Saloons closed in fanfares of maudlin guzzling, only to be reborn as speakeasies. Greenwich Village blossomed into a mad bohemia that outdid any of those on the continent. Harlem flowered into a unique amusement center, and Broadway extended itself into the many side-streets.

Love cults, theatre groups, and radical movements flourished in the "Village." That section of the city became the Mecca of practically every 'struggling' artist, pseudo-artist and hanger-on in the country. At Hubert's Cafeteria on Sheridan Square, the great, near-great and nonentities of the underworld, the stage, art, literature and society rubbed elbows as they ate cheap food. In the middle of all this hectic activity, fantastic characters came to life and frequently produced worthwhile works.[3]

The slummers from uptown flocked to the Village to take in the scene; at Hubert's they sat at the few tables reserved for wait-service. Djuna Barnes described this new pastime of the upper classes in a 1916 article on "Becoming Intimate with the Bohemians." At the corner of 6th and Greenwich, a few blocks from Sheridan Square, she had once been hailed by a wealthy uptowner and her children seeking directions to Bohemia:

> "I have heard of old houses and odd women and men who sit on the curb quoting poetry to the policemen or angling for buns as they floated down into the Battery with the rain. I have heard of little inns where women smoke and men make love and there is dancing and laughter and not too much light. I have heard of houses striped as are the zebras with gold and silver, and of gowns that – Quick, quick!" she cried, suddenly breaking off in the middle of the sentence and grabbing a hand of either child exactly like the White Queen in *Through the Looking Glass* as she hurried forward. "There's one now!"
>
> And so she left me in pursuit of a mere woman in a gingham gown with a portfolio under her arm.[4]

The "mere woman" Barnes mentioned could just as easily have been Pauline Leader, the deaf poet who fled Vermont in 1925, at age seventeen, to find a place for herself among the other outcasts behind the plate-glass windows of the cafeteria.

Pauline Leader in her late teens.

Leader lost her hearing in 1921 as an after-effect of meningitis. She found that she quickly became "crazy, a freak, a half-person, in the eyes of the people" (71).[5] Formerly a star student, she was expelled by Bennington Public Schools when she could no longer follow her teacher's oral instructions. Her mother refused to send her to a residential school where she might learn lip-reading or sign language.[6] Leader thus embarked upon her own program of self-education: reading health textbooks at the local public library, stealing coins to watch silent films at the local movie theater, and most of all, writing poetry. She pored over the Sunday papers, which were filled with anecdotes about Greenwich Village. After reading an interview with Maxwell Bodenheim, who was publishing alongside Marianne Moore and William Carlos Williams in the *Dial* and other literary journals, Leader sent him a letter. Bodenheim began tutoring her about poetry via mail.

Leader's parents, Jewish immigrants from Eastern Europe who ran a market (and later a rooming house) in Bennington, were mistrustful of their neighbors, much less a poet from New York; they soon interrupted this correspondence. Fearing for her safety, they often hid her shoes and jacket to keep her from going outside. When Leader did venture out to the library or the movies, she was persecuted by neighborhood children, who treated her like "a strange toy."

> They wanted to touch me, feel of me. . . . In the holidays I feared to walk on the streets during the day because of the children let loose. They were there on the streets, a pack of wolves, and I was the single sheep. No sheep in a land of wolves was ever more haunted than I. Small boys, in the winter, ran me into corners and pelted me with snow-balls and tried to lift my dress. (84)

Finally, to get away from *the people*—the citizens and the "upper-dogs"—Leader ran away. "Somewhere—in New York—there were people who were different from these people; there were people who were not the people. New York . . . my mind returned to the two words often" (129).

At Hubert's Cafeteria, which Leader stumbled across on one of her long evening walks, she found the "glamorous outcasts" of Bohemia.[7] Yet even into this mongrel group she could not be integrated: neither homeless nor slumming, but working class; a professedly asexual woman; a Jew averse to Judaism; a deaf outsider to the Deaf clubs that had been founded throughout the city. By day the cafeteria was populated by shopworkers, taxi drivers, and factory laborers. At midnight, Leader noted, a band of artists and *poseurs* "transformed or rather hid its ordinariness with their carelessness, their youth, their dreams" (162). If the bohemians resisted the standardization, efficiency, and family routines of industrial-era America, she was an alien among the alienated. Her own daily life took place in the little-known spaces below the "menial labor" line in the classified ads: she worked in one sweatshop after the next, earning less than her hearing counterparts; she lived in a windowless rented room; she stole scraps of leftover food from tables at automats. She was a bystander to the carelessness and gaiety at Hubert's, rarely having an exchange with anyone. She usually sat at a table by herself, with a cup of coffee, a roll, and a cheap notebook full of poems. Nevertheless, as she wrote, "My life really centered about the cafeteria. I never went there before midnight, and I never stayed more than an hour, but I received from it what I needed to keep me going" (170).

Leader found time to write at the end of punishing workdays and during periods of unemployment; she was frequently fired for misunderstandings related to her deafness. She was a keen observer of *the people*, from the rhythms of habitual bodily motions (ironing, preening, slicing meat) to the semiotics of glances, to patterns of subcultural affiliation and exclusion. In her own words, she was the consummate onlooker, not a sightseer but an eyewitness: "I–I was always the looker-on, intensely curious, but without courage to dabble in the pool" (180). Drawing on the

conventions of the Künstlerroman, she described the events surrounding her move to the Village in an autobiography, *And No
Birds Sing*, published in New York by Vanguard Press in 1931, in
London by Routledge the following year—and reprinted here in
its entirety. Her writing in this book is at once frank and surreal,
reflecting the youth, isolation, and stigma of her circumstances.
Always watchful as the child of immigrants, Leader's relationship to the world became one of intense speculation after losing
her hearing: "The world was but a million moving shapes, fish
mouths opening and shutting, lips moving busily, the contractions
of throat and cheek, the swallowing of Adams' apples. This was
the world; this was the way the world began and ended. The only
thing that could transform the strangely dead and yet strangely
living spectacle was my imagination" (183). Immediately after
its publication, *And No Birds Sing* was widely reviewed. Whether
they liked the book or not, critics acknowledged Leader for illu-
minating the psychology of hearing loss and immigration, the
conditions in reform schools, and the social milieu of Greenwich
Village.[8] She anticipated the social constructionist claims of late-
twentieth-century disability studies with statements such as "but
for the people I would not be deaf" (105).

Long out of print, and nearly impossible to find before this new
edition, *And No Birds Sing* has nonetheless made its way onto the
bibliographies of numerous scholarly histories of wayward girls,
working-class women, and Jewish immigrants in early twentieth-
century America.[9] *The Gallaudet Encyclopedia of Deaf People and
Deafness* names Leader among the best of the early deaf authors
to achieve mass-market publication. "Born ahead of her time,"
she was one of the few to address "the deaf experience," yet her
autobiography is otherwise nearly absent from D/deaf and disability history.[10] Similarly, as scholars recast literary modernism
by counting impairment among its ruptures with tradition—
tallying representations of disability in the works of Djuna Barnes
or neurodiverse literary production by the likes of Joe Gould—they

revisit the same ground again and again. There were the winners and the losers even among the outcasts of Bohemia: some with lives deemed romantic and canonized; some who published, fewer still with commercial success; and then there was Leader, working in a bookbinding factory or as an office correspondent, herself going out of print.

Unimpossibility: The Author as a Young Woman

Leader's flight to New York City was something of a return; she was born there on October 16, 1908, and moved with her parents to Vermont shortly afterward. She was no stranger to exile. Her father and mother, Isaac and Frieda, were part of a massive Jewish exodus from Eastern Europe that began in the 1880s. Even before she lost her hearing, Leader felt like a castaway from American society. "We were barbarians, square pegs in round holes, thorns in the side of respectable small-town folk," (51), she recalls in her autobiography. "We gathered our particular friends from the foreign population, 'outcasts' like ourselves" (51). She refused assimilation but internalized certain resident suspicions ("to be a good American . . . snicker at anything unusual," 103). Her deep ambivalence about her Jewishness drew equally from shame and from righteous indignation at the hypocrisies of religion. Nevertheless, the book is populated by diverse Jewish figures: the poet Bodenheim, the owner of Hubert's Cafeteria, the workers in the sweatshops, the smart girl in the reformatory. Critic Barbara Shollar classifies *And No Birds Sing* as an "exilic narrative" in classic Jewish tradition.[11] An opening scene finds a young Leader hanging around the Bennington train station, despite threats from her parents that she will be "sent away" to a reformatory for this peculiar behavior. She identifies with the disabled "bums" who watch the trains; she listens keenly but without comprehension to the sound of distant news coming in on the telegraph key.

Leader had long felt isolated within her own family, describing her parents as quick to anger—and frequently abusive—as they struggled to establish themselves in Bennington. Before the rooming house, her mother ran a market and a butcher shop, which the family lived above. Leader disliked the blood on the floors and the smell of cold raw meat that pervaded their clothing. She was a bookworm, and her mother was known to throw her library books over the refrigerator, insisting that she do something useful, like help in the market or watch her four younger siblings. Still, Leader admired her mother's physical strength, her shrewdness, and showmanship. Frieda held court in the market, picking up bits and pieces of the languages of the other immigrants who came in. She sawed bones and scraped ice, and she also took care of the household chores, working constantly.

> My mother snatching a few minutes from the market to iron clothes in the back room. Her hand, red, swollen from hard work, moved over the white expanse of sheet and pillow-case. After a minute, the rhythm I was watching for came, lifted me. I was sailing, far, far, over my mother, the red swollen hand, the white expanse of sheet; I was flying on the magic carpet of the rhythm, out of the market, away from the market-smell, over the clock in the jail-tower, over the post-office, out into the green, green fields where there was only freedom. Away from authority, away from sharpness, away from the perpetual puzzlement. Mother! Mother! Come! Come with me, Mother! Poor, poor victim. You can't really want to stay here, shackled to the market-smell, shackled to a husband and children. . . . Are you working like this so that your children will not be underdogs? How do I know what is going on in your mind? (21–22)

Seemingly from overwork, Frieda's stomach ruptured. She died at age 39, shortly after Pauline ran away to New York.

By comparison, Leader considered her father "lazy," an entitled patriarch who avoided housework, ate "the best part of the meat," drank tea, and visited with friends (131). She later told her son

Frieda Leader.

Jonathan, "We were the most deprived children in Bennington. We never had anything. My father wouldn't spend a nickel on ice cream cones. We never had a doll. We never had a bicycle. We hadn't any decent clothes. We didn't have a normal childhood."[12] Well-educated and formerly middle class, Isaac experienced dispossession and disappointment with the move to the United States. By 1923, however, he would become the rabbi of the first synagogue in Bennington—a detail not mentioned in the book. Leader characterizes him as suspicious and "sneering." She came to believe that he envied her. He had once written poetry himself; he "had tried to be 'gentle', and he had failed" (106). Eventually, he thrashed her with a strap for every small infraction.

After her hospitalization and hearing loss, Leader was even more cut off from her family, let alone the daily routines of her small town. She was beaten by her father if caught outside in the evening; she felt like a prisoner within the house. Discharged from school, at the very least she was allowed more time to read. She threw herself into writing. In the first months after her illness, Leader underwent a radical estrangement, by turns terrifying and enthralling, from her usual sensory relations to the world. One night, locked indoors, she accidentally killed a kitten with the runner of her rocking chair, repeatedly crushing it because she could not hear its mewls. Her conversion to deafness at once retrained her eye and the rhythm of her writing, compelling unexpected translations and analogies. She heard physiological and remembered sounds: the activity of her brain, aural memories of birds and the river. She soon realized that she "had no need to hear as the people heard" (104). The voice from her throat became a tactile musical instrument; her inner speech took the foreground. "I always wanted words, and I always had them. I would have been terribly lonely without them. With them always in my mind, I could not be truly lonely. I played with them; I set them to music; I achieved endless variations with them" (104). She placed words into the silently moving mouths of people on the street. She matched the cadence of her internal voice to that of the poetry she read in the library, or to the kinesthetic pattern created as she followed the pace of a boyish woman on the street. Thus she began to write poetry in earnest, despite ridicule from her family.

Isaac Leader.

Leader's deviant position enabled her to become an inside-out ethnographer of Bennington. She trained her eye on its corners, admiring the carefree rebelliousness and sociable exile of the "street-women" and "loafers." Sexual and gender norms, she observed, eventually dragged most of them back into society, into the factories, turning them into *the people*—"Two more free things caught."

> On Sundays I would sit on the porch and watch them pass. Did they care what the people said about them, their painted faces, their lovely slim bodies? They did not appear to. They guessed rightly that it was merely envy of their youth and joyousness.
>
> But a few years later they married and the streets saw them no more. Respectability had got them. Once a year, perhaps, when there was going to be a parade and the whole town turned out, one might see them. Then one saw with a shock that this was *she,* with a baby, and another one on the way. She looked tired and wore old clothes. Was she the bright happy girl I had seen only a few years ago? The people had got her, and now she was indistinguishable from them. (115)

She came to despise sexual relations as well as marriage. She believed that sex had taken an appalling toll on her mother. "It was not the children it had brought into being, nor the gross body—body that had once been slender and proud—*but what it had done to her mind*. It should never do that to me. I would sooner let it alone entirely" (118). Leader kept a few odd acquaintances in Bennington, such as an alcoholic lawyer who worked above the market and loaned books to her. Otherwise, her days were solitary. As she explained, "I was deaf—for that reason I must walk alone. I could not approach anyone, or find a friend. My deafness was a wall that kept me from everybody" (114). In many ways, she preferred the freedom of the outcast.

In those months after she lost her hearing, she learned something new about observation itself: namely, the operation of looking could become a mode of branding. Being given "queer looks" made one queer. Certain outcasts were "marked off" as freaks.

Leader noted that sign language attracted stares and hence stigma; deafness was not a branding in and of itself. Once, in the street, she came across another deaf person, a boy who "had been sent away to an institution for the deaf where he had been educated, taught a trade, taught to work like others—which meant that he worked in the mills, would always work in the mills. God, what a life" (139). He gave her a look and a gesture of recognition, and she stared back.

> To make those gestures at me—it was a public branding. It exposed me.
>
> I was deaf, deaf, deaf. Why couldn't I realize it? I was different, queer, strange now, according to the people. Only I knew that I was the same.
>
> The sign language—it was a symbol to me of all they were trying to make me into. They were trying to make me really deaf. (70–71)

The trick was to "pass unnoticed." Or to be a companionable outcast—but not a freak, not crazy, not queer.

Passing was nearly impossible in a small town. The *Bennington Evening Banner* had run an announcement about her illness in 1921—*Pauline Leader of North Street is seriously ill*—right above an advertisement for Leonard Ear Oil.[13] She later wrote an untitled poem (below) about the asphyxiating qualities of village life.

> small town
> where is your horizon?
> though I have climbed to the dome of the post-office
> and peered from the clock-tower of the jail
> your highest buildings
> I could not find it
> and the lack of one suffocates me[14]

At age fourteen, she began to work in the local factories herself, saving money to one day run away. "How could they do it?" she thought. "To have no other life except the life of the factory. To come, day after day, after day, after day, to come here, to sit down at a machine, to be released from the machine only when it was dark. Meanwhile, the world, the marvellous world, was going by" (108–109). These stints were brief: she was inevitably fired for some mishap related to her deafness, and returned to the sequestration of her home. Maxwell Bodenheim, with whom she corresponded when she was fifteen, told her to read Ezra Pound, write about everyday life, and hide her woundedness from her aggressors. At seventeen, deciding that she would not end up a shut-in, "one of those relatives whom people hide" (136), she left for New York with a train ticket and $20 in her pocket. She had never taken the train alone before. Adding to the distress of the journey, she could not hear the names of the stations as they were called.

Her first months in Manhattan were by turns exhilarating and overwhelming. She rented a series of small furnished rooms in boardinghouses and hotels in Greenwich Village. But no one wanted to hire a deaf girl. Only after agreeing to work for reduced pay was she able to find employment—as a dishwasher at a restaurant, 9 a.m. to 9 p.m., for fourteen dollars a week. The men in the kitchen pinched her while she worked; they hid the clock so she would stop stealing glances at it. She was soon fired. She wrote poetry and wandered around the city until she ran out of money and was forced again to seek out "HELP WANTED" signs. In a series of poems titled "New York: Impressions," written when she was living at 254 West 12th Street, she alluded to the hazards that proceeded from not hearing the city's roar.

TRUCKS

New York is a city of trucks.
It is empty except for the trucks.
The streets are made for them.
Policemen are made for them.
Almost, one day, I was made for them
but the policeman caught my hand in time
and together, the policeman and I,
held each other's hand tightly

and together we tingled with triumph—
we had outwitted a truck![15]

Leader's younger brother, Herbert, said that she lived on tobacco and rye bread that first year.[16] She also frequented the Automats. Joseph Mitchell, the famed journalist who moved to the city in 1929, once interviewed a member of the Union League of the Deaf, who told him, "The deaf prefer cafeterias . . . particularly Automats" because food could be ordered there "without ever uttering a single word."[17] When Leader had extra nickels, she bought apples and oranges, euphorically, from the Italian pushcarts in Washington Square Park.

Leader traced Bodenheim to the return address on one of his letters from two years before. He had moved to New York from Chicago in 1916, disgorging poems, novels, and plays at an astonishing rate. He cultivated a reputation as a drunk and a rake.[18] His novel *Replenishing Jessica*—about a woman who marries a "cripple" for spiritual replenishment after numerous sexual affairs—was subject to an obscenity trial the year Leader arrived in New York.[19] Bodenheim ("Bogie") was acquitted; the novel became a bestseller.

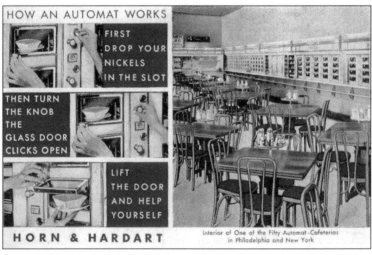

Postcard for the Horn & Hardart Automat chain that was popular during the years Leader spent in Manhattan.

According to the author John Armstrong, "The Village became the palace grounds of Bohemia's King Maxwell Bodenheim, and he walked surrounded by admiration."[20]

Leader went to Bodenheim's apartment and rang the bell with a notebook full of poems. As she recalled in an interview with historian Barbara Shollar in 1992, "He advised me to return to Vermont because in New York City I was battling against 'unimpossible odds.' I assumed he referred to my deafness. I didn't take his advice." Unimpossible is a contronym—a word that means both possible and impossible—an apt term for the wildness and unpredictability of Greenwich Village in the 1920s. "I didn't mix in social/literary circles with him and I had no relationship with him," Leader claimed. "I only met with him once."[21] If true, it was probably for the best—however, the extent of their involvement is not clear. Bodenheim wrote love letters to other teenagers, and in 1928 two more girls brought their poems to him. When they met with criticism, one drowned herself in the Hudson River, the other narrowly survived self-gassing in an apartment on MacDougal Street. Bodenheim's fortunes fell and his profligacy increased. He mobilized the unimpossibilities of disability, panhandling by faking blindness. In 1954, he made the tabloids for the last time when he and his third wife, passed out in a "in a ginsoaked stupor" in a squalid room, were murdered by her other lover.[22]

Leader began to frequent Hubert's, where Bodenheim could often be found at a back table, presiding over the Greta Garbo Social Club. Its members included the "millionaire playboy" Robert Clairmont, poet John Rose Gildea (who, like Bodenheim, was often called "the bard of Greenwich Village"), and poet Eli Siegel (whose "Hot Afternoons Have Been in Montana" apparently "swept the Village" as a barroom-recital favorite). The group's mission was "systematically seducing all unvirtuous innocents who bobbed like so many ripe apples in the liberated Village barrel."[23] In *Garrets and Pretenders: A History of Bohemianism in America,* published in 1933, historian Albert Parry described the Village of the prior decade—before the stock market crash of 1929—as an epicenter of free-love. The neighborhood spilled over with "love nests," nude fountain-bathers, pet parrots, men with long hair, Prohibition bathtub gin, and opium. A person with a disability, Parry commented, might also find admission; indeed, "it was only in Greenwich Village that he felt comparatively free from pity or ridicule. There, in appearance, he was equal to many other inhabitants. They were not often cripples, but they were freaks, what with their fantastic beards, exotic smocks, flowing ties, wide-brimmed hats."[24] Yet some disabilities befitted Bohemia more than others; the members of the Garbo Club cultivated madness, whether it was ultimately innate or elected, temporary or progressive. Gildea, for one, was committed to Rockland State Hospital in the 1930s.[25]

Leader spent her days working alongside other Jewish women in the dressmaking sweatshops of Soho or looking for employment if she was between jobs. For an hour each evening, she sat alone at Hubert's, taking in the spectacle. She recorded in her memoir, "One night a girl approached me, one of the girls I had seen flitting from table to table, laughing, always laughing. Her face was dark and small. Her body was small, and I imagined that its skin must have the same lovely dusky quality of her face" (164). The girl introduced her to a pack of others, poets and prostitutes, who conversed with Leader by writing in her notebook or on stacks of cafeteria napkins. "The cheap little notebook was soon filled with words, words, words. They replenished me as food replenishes a hungry man. Words, words, words, I was hungry for them" (164). Tom Boggs, another member of the Garbo Club, recounted in a biography of Clairmont that "the handsome Pauline Leader read her vivid verses which she could not hear" at Hubert's throughout that year.[26] Leader began to embrace "the queer wild being that was myself" (176), yet she continued to feel somewhat ostracized. She often sat alone. "Sometimes they came to my table, and sometimes they did not (176)." Many of her friendships were restricted to the cafeteria. Her mother died during this period, on the 31st of December, 1926.

She befriended the iconic Villager Joe Gould, a Harvard drop-out who claimed to be writing a multivolume "oral history" of everyday life based on eavesdropping and conversations with the "shirt-sleeved

multitude"—part of a broader modern fascination with field recording and interview.[27] He wrote, lost, and rewrote this oral history for
decades, ultimately publishing only a few fragments. His brand of
eccentricity and failure captivated poets, historians, and newsmakers
alike. He purportedly inspired Allan Nevins to found the first oral
history center at Columbia University in the 1940s.[28] He was memo-
rialized in a 1931 essay by poet Horace Gregory and in two widely
read articles by Joseph Mitchell, touching off a snowball effect of cita-
tions, biographical sketches, and films that continues to the present.[29]

For a short time, Gould and Leader occupied neighboring rooms in
the Bradford Hotel on 11th Street; she subsequently told her children
that they both also lived in the Chelsea Hotel.[30] While she worked in
sweatshops, Gould begged for money or food and collected cigarette
butts. When not residing in a cheap boardinghouse or commandeer-
ing a place to sleep on the floor of a friend's apartment, he was generally homeless. Whether loved or scorned, he was a fixture in the
Village. According to historian Jill Lepore, "He went to parties with
Langston Hughes. He dined with E. E. Cummings. He drank with
John Dos Passos. He was sketched by Joseph Stella, photographed by
Aaron Siskind, and painted by Alice Neel."[31] He introduced Leader
to the sculptor Gaston Lachaise and to many other artists and writers. She met his one-time girlfriend, who visited from Boston every
few months, bringing with her a baked chicken or some other sustenance. Gould also tried to sleep with Leader. When she declined, it
did not damage their friendship; they shared the tenuous rapport of
the underdogs. He recorded that Leader once said to him, "As long as
I live I will always be in trouble, and so I will want your friendship."[32]

Gould and Leader published in the same issue of *Pagany* in
1931. Gould's piece was an excerpt from *An Oral History* entitled
"Insanity," which extrapolated from the rule of sensory difference
to the relativity of mental health.

> Insanity is a topic of peculiar interest to me . . . I almost have
> first-hand information about it. There have been times when the
> black mood was on me. I needed every bit of self-control that I

possessed to refrain from shouting aloud or waving my hands in wild gestures that would have brought a curious crowd around me and eventually have landed me in the police-station. I could very easily imagine myself locked up as a maniac. Yet all the time, the real me was not in sympathy with these impulses. . . . The fallacy of dividing people into sane and insane lies in the assumption that we really do touch other lives. This is a matter open to serious doubt. Our physical senses differ so much with respect to sight, hearing and so forth that we have no certain means of telling whether any two of us live in the same tangible world or not.[33]

In May 1927, a competition was held for the best poem written about Hubert's. Bodenheim and Clairmont were among the judges, and they selected a ballad by Gildea for the $10 prize. The submission by Leader—"a struggling poet"—prompted them to organize a benefit dance for her at the cafeteria on June 7, with donations of 50 cents as the price of admission. The *New York Times* covered these events.[34] Leader recalls in her autobiography,

> All through the Village lately I had seen signs in the windows, signs that read, "Poet's Benefit Dance." So I was the poet for whom the dance was to be given.
>
> My coffee and rolls, and only coffee and rolls, had started the legend of my starvation. They supposed that I could not afford anything else, which was only half the answer. The other half was that I dreaded asking the counterman anything that would open up a lot of questions. (178)

She professed to be "lonely and miserable" during the dance itself: a looker-on yet again, "a freak who could write poetry" (178, 181). She was equally ambivalent about the money raised; it provided her with a period of freedom from work, but it also sparked jealousy—and unwanted overtures—from the other down-and-outs in the Hubert's set.

News clipping of Pauline Leader, 1927.

Her audience at Hubert's notwithstanding, Leader at first had difficulty finding an outlet for her poetry. She and Gildea tried to read their poems at the Troubadour Tavern one night that summer, but they were turned away. She wrote a letter to the editor of the *New York Times*, published on July 17, proposing that a gallery or room in Greenwich Village be dedicated to the exhibition of poetry.

> The two places I know in the Village where poetry may be read are practically closed to the unknown poet. The recitals are dominated by certain personalities who allow only certain poets to read. Besides, poetry cannot be read; the reading of a poem is itself a sensitive art. To fully appreciate it, one should read the poem. Typed and arranged on the wall, you take the poem or leave it.[35]

In response, printers Lew Ney (Luther Widen) and Ruth Widen donated space in one of their lofts, where anyone could pin a poem for a fee of ten cents and visitors voted on their favorites. Thousands of poems were submitted and, eventually, collected in scrapbooks that circulated to other cities, finally coming to rest in the New York Public Library. Bodenheim, Lola Ridge, Charles Henri Ford, and countless others participated. This "first national poetry exhibition" lasted for many months, moving to Susanne Strouvelle's Tiniest Little House tearoom (at 100 Bedford St.) and then to artist Lise Fulda's studio loft, accompanied by weekly readings. The exhibition was widely publicized in the papers. Prizes were awarded to those poems with the most popular votes, and in 1930 Parnassus Press published an anthology, *Whispering Walls*. Leader and Gildea shared second prize; Leader won for her poem "Broken Faces," written after her mother's death and reprinted in *And No Birds Sing*.[36]

As the summer of 1927 turned to fall, Leader became convinced that she was pregnant. She visited a clinic and was sent directly, without explanation, to a reformatory for "wayward" girls—the very consequence her parents had warned her about. She spent five days there, an experience that troubled her perhaps more deeply than any other in her young adulthood. Consternation ensued from the moment of her gynecological intake appointment: "She explored me as I had seen mother explore the insides of a chicken with a finger. I was shocked and revolted" (185). The "home" had bars on the windows, meager food, and separate bathrooms for the girls with syphilis. Walking the halls, Leader collected a new set of observations on the underdog in the circumstance of quarantine.

> I passed the open doors of the girls' rooms, and in the rooms where there were two beds I saw the two beds drawn up closely together, instead of with the width of the room between them as they were by day. The beds were noiselessly pulled apart when it was time for the police woman to cover her beat, but when she had gone again, I saw almost naked girls pull the beds together once more. I saw suppressed laughter, suppressed whispering, I saw strange distorted faces, unlike the passive faces of the day. (200)

Her period arrived, several days late, and she was abruptly allowed to leave, furnished with ten dollars sent by her father, who had been alerted to her detention. *And No Birds Sing* concludes at this point, with Leader's declaration, "I would never let myself be locked up again. Anything, anything, was better than that. Better to be cold and hungry" (214).

Another Free Thing Caught: Autobiography and After

Deinstitutionalized, Leader was released back to life as a Villager. Increasingly, her poetry began to appear in the "little magazines" for experimental writing cropping up in New York, Paris, and Chicago (not to mention countless small towns in between): *This Quarter, transition, Poetry*. Reformatted as prose, some of these poems—such as "Memory of the Ironing," published in the *Morada*—became part of her autobiography.[37] In Vermont, the *Bennington Evening Banner* ran an announcement about each new publication. The *Banner* even noted that Leader was "one of the few women writers whose work has been published by 'Blues,'" a short-lived journal launched by Charles Henri Ford that featured the likes of Ezra Pound, E. E. Cummings, William Carlos Williams, Louis Zukofsky, Kenneth Rexroth, and Gertrude Stein.[38] Pound wrote to Zukofsky from Italy in 1928, advising him to "form some sort of gang" that would dine and write and agitate together at least once a week in an "effort toward restarting some sort of life in N.Y." Pound offered to pay for the group's first two meals himself. "NOT too many women," he cautioned, placing Leader at the top of his list of possible invites. Ridge, Marianne Moore, and Jane Heap were alternates.[39] William Stanley Braithwaite reprinted one of Leader's poems in his *Anthology of Magazine Verse for 1929 and Yearbook of American Poetry*. In those years at the end of the 1920s, she later explained to Barbara Shollar, "I, too, became famous or 'famous.'" Her sister Mary wrote to let her know that "Papa believes in you now." No matter, Leader reflected in a 1991 conversation with her son Jonathan. "If I had seen him, I would have told him to go to hell. I don't want his belief in me. I don't give a damn about him anymore."[40]

In 1930 and 1931, she published a series of short stories about labor in the social work magazine the *Survey*, testing some of the scenarios that also appeared in her autobiography. In "Overalls," a sewing machine operator in a loft on Hudson Street, near Canal Station, is defeated by broken needles and piles of pants legs to seam; she is swiftly fired. ("Over-all, over-all, over-all. Who had thought up that word?") Much like Leader herself, the dishwasher in "The Girl Who Looked Too Much at the Clock" receives sustenance from peeking at the dial throughout an interminable workday.[41] She arrives one morning to find the cook laughing at her, the clock face removed from the wall.

Illustration by Alois Fabry that accompanied Pauline Leader's short story "Overalls," published in *Survey* in August 1931.

"No Laughter Allowed" is set in a book-binding factory where rows of women work under a sign that states "Talking Strictly Forbidden." The narrator gets into trouble for reading on the job because "a book was a product, not a book." She resists the imperative to "become more machine-like than the machines" through ceaseless exertion. Leader depicts the melding of the worker's body to mechanical equipment as a quandary of *rhythm*—a central category for modernist authors and artists, to which she brought her particular visual and tactile scrutiny.

The rhythm of the machine was staccato; the body of the worker moved in a constant staccato jerk, head and shoulders were brought up, brought up, brought up, and flung back in a never ending jerk in time with the machine. Until the worker got used to it, it was torture, for it involved not only the body but the mind. Words came out of jerked mouths jerkily. There was no getting away from the machines. The walls and floor of the room shook in little staccato jerks of anguish. When she left the factory for the side-walks, she had to learn all over again how to walk. Her body refused at first to obey a smooth rhythm.[42]

This bookbinder is ultimately dismissed for laughing. Leader published other short fiction in *Pagany, This Quarter*, and *New Masses*.[43] Edward J. O'Brien awarded her an asterisk in *The Best Short Stories of 1930 and The Yearbook of the American Short Story*, a convention reserved for stories that "possess either distinction of technique alone, or more frequently . . . a persuasive sense of life in them to which a reader responds with some part of his own experience."[44]

In 1929 and 1930, she published three articles in the *Sun* about her participation in classes for the deafened. *And No Birds Sing*, to the contrary, merely registers her failed attempt to locate a lip-reading school in the Manhattan telephone book. Parallel to Deaf clubs, dozens of social groups for deafened and hard of hearing people began to be founded in the city in the late nineteenth century. The Warren Articulation School launched lip-reading classes for adults in 1890; it eventually gave rise to the Nitchie School of Lip-Reading and the New York League for the Hard of Hearing.

Throughout her autobiography, Leader claimed detachment from the Deaf, hearing, and hard of hearing communities alike. Yet in the *Sun*, Leader related taking a lip-reading class (at an unnamed school) with a group that ranged in age from sixteen to seventy-five. She suggested that all modes of human communication are artificial and can be substituted by other forms of mediation: "The voice, the ear, and the eye are all bridges that people must cross to meet the man or woman at the other end. We [deafened] have the voice and the eye, but that other bridge—the ear—is, for us, a little shaky. Lip-reading is our substitute bridge." She also surveyed her classmates on the topic of "What Is Missed Most by the Deaf." Those who were not born deaf, but rather *lost* their hearing in industrial-era New York, pined for machine-made sounds as much as the human voice: acoustic cues like doorbells, ringing phones, the rumble of the L; entertainments like phonograph music or movie-going in the wake of the Talkies.[45]

In another piece, Leader gave an account of "Recreations for Those Who Are Deaf": dancing with one another, listening to radios outfitted with special amplifiers. "Here the deafened person's mistakes find tolerance instead of the impatience and exasperation he often meets with in the hearing world," she wrote of her group. Those assembled forget, "for the all too short length of the one evening every week we set aside to foregather in these attractive green and brown rooms that we cannot hear."[46] In 1931, she contributed a poem on the sensory independence of words to *Double Blossoms*, an anthology dedicated to Helen Keller.

"THE MYSTIC SENSE"

Helen Keller,
I would tell them of the identical dream within your
    mind,
I would tell them that to the few
The word with its assumption of form—
Image implicit only in the known escape of sight and
    hearing—
Can become meaninglessly too literal.

In this volume, she joined a celebrated list of contributors that included Countee Cullen, Clarence Darrow, W. E. B. DuBois, Robert Frost, Langston Hughes, James Weldon Johnson, Yone Nuguchi, and Rabindranath Tagore.[47]

In 1928 or '29, subsequent to the final scene in her autobiography, Leader began a relationship with Henry Lavarack, an industrial designer and painter she met at a poetry reading. She was nearly twenty; he, fifty. Lavarack was an English immigrant who worked for his brother Frederick, a wealthy railroad engineer and executive. He was married, with four children older than Leader, although he lived separately from his wife, who refused to divorce him. His own apartment was uptown, but "he often went down to the Bowery to get types to paint." He set Leader up in an apartment on East 14th, followed by another at 15 East 8th, with one of his subjects—a homeless man who had formerly been a sailor.

"I never had to do anything," Leader recollected decades after. "This guy who lived there did everything—cooked, cleaned, everything. I was badly spoiled." The sailor was worldly and a terrific cook: "He'd make things like curries I'd never eaten before." Lavarack also took her to "fancy restaurants." When they traveled by train, he booked tickets "in the best car." He passed notes to her; "he didn't mind writing down."[48] It was, perhaps, the only carefree period in her life.

In 1930, they moved to a cabin in Woodstock, New York, furnished with a wood stove and an outhouse. Joe Gould visited them there. On December 27, Leader gave birth to a daughter, Elinor. She also finished her autobiography that year. Originally titled *The Gnome and the People*, she submitted it to more than a dozen publishers before James Henle of the radical Vanguard Press accepted it. "It has been a long time since I have read anything that has moved me so deeply" he penned at the bottom of his acceptance letter in March 1931. He suggested that she change the title, and she chose a line from "La Belle Dame sans Merci" by John Keats. *And No Birds Sing* came out in June. It was dedicated to Lavarack. A painting he had done of her adorned the dustcover—likewise, the cover of this republication. By November, Leader received word that her autobiography had been selected as one of Vanguard's submissions to Columbia University for the Pulitzer Prize.[49] She was twenty-two years old. Routledge reprinted the book in London the following year.

Reviews appeared in the popular press and in specialty journals of social work and medicine. Annetta Peck, vice president of the American Federation of Organizations for the Hard of Hearing, wrote in the *Survey*, "Miss Leader's story is, aside from its high quality, its plain human interest, a case history valuable to the social worker, the otologist, and the psychiatrist."[50] Beyond the deafened community, many reviewers characterized the memoir as a "case report," although they disputed the nature of its evidence. The *Outlook* depicted Leader as a "victim" of deafness, poverty, stigma, family abuse, and misguided social service. Conversely, William Soskin, the literature editor of the *New York Evening Post*, perceived

Leader as "brave." She resented, he argued, "the efforts of society to make a 'patient' of her, to destroy the independence and intactness of her person. The benevolence of society toward an inferior she spurned." The poet and critic Horace Gregory called Leader a "powerful ego" who "defies all systems of organized society." In England, the *Week-End Review* took the autobiography to be a valuable "exposition of social conditions in New York."[51] The *Boston Transcript* offered instead an anti-immigrant and anti-Semitic reading: "The book is brutal in its frank egotism, in the primitive life it depicts among newly accepted citizens of the United States. It makes one wonder what can be done with all the Pauline Leaders and their parents who are knocking for admission to our land, as many of them have not her one redeeming trait of appreciation of beauty."[52] Several reviewers praised Leader for her objectivity and her unsparing self-analysis. Gregory described "the texture of her prose" as firm, the tone bitter and unashamed. English novelist and critic Hugh de Selincourt approvingly remarked, in *Everyman*, "Hideous things are related with a clean, relentless clarity, baldly and with no relish."[53]

Leader began to receive fan mail, which her neighbor in Woodstock—the early jazz critic Charles Edward Smith—encouraged her to answer. Millen Brand, an aspiring author and recent graduate of the Columbia School of Journalism, sent a letter of admiration followed by one of his short stories with a request for her criticism. She replied, thinking at first that he was a woman. They began to correspond about writing—she advised him to work on his characters' dialogue—and she invited him to visit her and Lavarack when they returned to Manhattan. "So he came to visit. So we fell in love." By 1932, she and Brand were married and he had adopted Elinor. Lavarack was apparently supportive and attended their wedding. He began a relationship with another deaf Jewish woman, Tillie, whom Leader knew from her lip-reading classes, marrying her when his wife died.[54]

Leader and Brand moved into an apartment at 32 Cornelia Street, next door to the painter Alice Neel. He took a job

copyediting for the New York Telephone Company. Despite its
renown, *And No Birds Sing* was not making much money. Rex
Stout, a friend, reassured Leader that it had simply been "published at a bad time"—the Depression. She introduced Brand to
life as a Villager, subdued as it was by the financial circumstances.
Their social circle included Kenneth Fearing, translator and left-
ist scholar Samuel Putnam, literary *salonnièr* Charles Studin, and
authors Muriel Rukeyser, William Saroyan, Sherwood Anderson,
Norman Mailer, and Kenneth Patchen.[55]

Leader soon became pregnant, and Brand decided they should
move to New Jersey, where he had grown up. They decamped for
Bloomfield, and the inexorable grasp of *the people* and their gender
norms began to contract around her. "I hated it there," she later pro-
claimed. "I wanted to move back in New York." Their son Jonathan
was born in 1933. Leader had to start cooking, a task she always disliked. Brand would wake at five each morning and leave early for the
office, guaranteeing himself a stretch of uninterrupted time to write.
In a stark role reversal, he took on the mantle of the Bohemian and
continued to attend salons and parties in the Village, even though
he had yet to publish a book. Talking to Jonathan in 1991, Leader
recollected that Brand "was never home. He always had a reception.
He loved that sort of thing. I hardly ever saw him."[56]

By 1934, they moved again, to Jackson Heights in Queens.
Leader's father died that year. Brand began to keep a diary. "It was
largely written for my wife who was stone deaf," he explained in an
entry filled with cross-outs, "and ~~because of the children—partly,
her deafness~~ on most of these occasions didn't go out with me.
~~Though some of the entries were written down even when she did
go with me in order to fill out gaps that would exist for her.~~"[57]
Once more, she found herself reading about the social exploits of
other poets and artists. In 1934, Brand wrote often about Augusta
Savage, then known as "the Negro Sculptress," for whom he was
sitting. She took Brand to events in Harlem such as Communist
organizer Angelo Herndon's prison release party. She invited

Brand and Leader to her openings, and she called on them at their home in Jackson Heights.[58]

Joe Gould was obsessed with Savage, an unwanted pursuit that entailed violent letters and obscene calls. Brand and Leader intervened on her behalf. In return, he sent harassing letters to them and to their son. In one from September 1934, Gould called Leader "a greasy neurotic Jewess with breath stinking of herring." Even if his oral history never took on heft beyond a few redrafted chapters, Lepore concludes that Gould did represent the American preoccupation with eugenics and the color line in his era.[59] He further tried to blackmail Leader with a distorted reminder of her all-too-few youthful flings.

> I gave you the utmost of loyalty without any censorship, although you did all sorts of unaesthetic silly things with all sorts of nondescript people when you were staying at the Bradford. You may remember that you asked me what I would tell my mother about you, whether I would say you were a good little girl or call you a nasty little prostitute and what I said. You are being filthier than any prostitute in what you are doing now.[60]

Drinking, begging, sexual affairs: whether the Bohemian life brought fame or defamation was often a matter of gender. Filtered through Gould, history itself was equal parts autobiography, obscenity, and New England men in shirtsleeves. Leader remembered a line that E. E. Cummings contributed to *An Oral History*—"He licked out her cunt with a spoon," the nursery rhyme counterpart to his memorializing poem that began "little joe gould has lost his teeth and doesn't know where to find them."[61] In the dollhouse Bohemia historians have constructed from these materials, the Negro Sculptress and the Deaf Poetess are *types* who accompany distinctive men. Cities have been drained of their masses—poor immigrants, factory workers—unencumbering the storylines of the upperdogs.

In 1935, Leader became close to Dorothy McCleary, whose first novel *Not for Heaven* had just won the Doubleday, Doran Story Prize Novel Contest.[62] McCleary was a familiar to poverty and disability. Now forgotten, she was anthologized three times in *The O. Henry Prize Stories* (as were luminaries like Pearl Buck, Truman Capote, and Dorothy Canfield). She frequently visited Leader in Jackson Heights, bringing along her lover, Alfred Mendes, who had moved to New York from Trinidad and was working on the novel *Black Fauns*. She was married, with one son, whom Brand described as "defective" and Mendes called "a mental case."[63] McCleary introduced Leader to a "perpetual pad," much like the Mystic Writing-Pad that so inspired Sigmund Freud. They used it to communicate. McCleary also fingerspelled, although Leader preferred to read lips or write notes.[64] When her children were older they sometimes spelled words in the air for her.

Leader had a third child, Emily, in 1935, who died of an unknown malady. She could not regulate her own temperature, and she had a cerebral hemorrhage at six months. Leader donated blood for an unsuccessful transfusion. The vase in which the baby's ashes were sealed would one day be stolen.[65] Somehow that same year, she also found time to complete a second novel, *The Natives*, about which little is known. The plot had something to do with bankruptcy and the loss of a farm. In a rejection letter, literary agent Elizabeth Nowell characterized it as too introspective and too heavy.[66] *The Natives* was never published, and Leader destroyed the manuscript. Without a "collection" of her own in an official repository, oddments remain from this phase of her life—whether or not she would have approved—among Brand's papers at Columbia University. These include letters that readers sent to her, the notes in her own hand that Brand chose to save, and his diaried perspectives on their marriage and eventual divorce.

Leader's last child, Daniel, was born in 1937. Brand published his first novel, *The Outward Room*, with Simon and Schuster the same year. It was a commercial hit, selling over half a million copies in multiple printings.[67] Newspaper interviews, radio shows, library events, and literary soirées followed in a rush. He quit his day job with the telephone company and was invited to teach fiction workshops at New York University. Leader was doubtless thrilled—she had encouraged and edited his writing for years—but Brand's success meant that he was even more often away from home. Her own public identity began to shift: she was increasingly dubbed "the deaf wife" of Millen Brand. "The rest, maybe I should call it the unrest, was professional jealousy," Jonathan Brand wrote in an unpublished reflection of his own. "Besides toiling at housework, Mama did double duty as Millen's subject and editor."[68]

The Outward Room tells the story of a woman's escape from a psychiatric institution. Brand claimed many sources of inspiration—Louise Young, a former love interest who became a psychiatric nurse; Alice Neel, who had been hospitalized for a year after a nervous breakdown; the sculptor Alonzo Hauser, who spent six months in a "mental hospital" and shared sketches from that period with him; written exchanges with a series of physicians and psychoanalysts.[69] But unquestionably, Leader was his principal guide and gauge. He dedicated The Outward Room to her. It duplicated numerous scenes and plot points from And No Birds Sing: a girl with a disability runs away to New York, is anxious about taking the train alone, lands at 14th Street, discovers the cafeterias and the Italian children in Washington Square Park, finds work cutting stray threads from seams in a textile sweatshop, and steals looks at the clock. Other scenes derived from Leader's life beyond her published autobiography. In the Bradford Hotel, for instance, a woman came in from the hall and slipped into bed with her one night. "She was just miserable or maybe she was drunk," Leader later reminisced.[70] In an early outline for the novel, then titled Escape to Life, Brand jotted several parenthetical asides to "see PL" or "ask PL" or "try room at PL's address."[71] Although The Outward Room is narrated in the third person, Brand—like Leader—interspersed delirious stream-of-consciousness passages.

In response to a fan letter from October 1939 that noted the thematic and "spiritual affinity" between the two books, Brand wrote in his diary, "Of course the relationship is not to Pauline's book but to Pauline, to the psychological difficulties that came with her deafness and her fight to ~~move outward, to~~ 'stand up' as she called it."[72] But unlike Leader's tale of stigma without redemption and independence at all costs, the heroine of *The Outward Room* is saved by love and literally healed by heterosexual sex. "She had accepted life," she realizes, after she sleeps with a man for the first time. She stops working to cook and clean for him. In an indictment of the characterization, as much as the character, a reviewer for the *New York Times* observed, "Only in the concluding pages of the novel, after months of washing John's clothes, cooking his meals and sleeping in his bed, does she assume some of the qualities of a living woman."[73]

Leader was not to share in Brand's triumphs. The family moved to Forest Hills at the beginning of 1938, and Brand began working on his second novel, *The Heroes*, as well as a theatrical adaptation of *The Outward Room* that director Sidney Kingsley opened on Broadway the following year (under the title *The World We Make*). He took time alone in "the country" that spring to write. In her letters to him, Leader described life in Forest Hills as "exhausting," "lonesome and blue."[74] She began to bracket her authorial self in quotes. "With children arriving," she subsequently reckoned, "'Pauline Leader' wasn't producing any books of her own." Otto Steinbrocker, a family physician, sent Leader a note telling her it was time to produce "a book rather than a kid!" Her publisher, James Henle, asked, "Are you making your life a gift to your children?"[75]

In April 1939, the seams of the marriage came apart. *The Heroes* was published simultaneously with Franklin Roosevelt's failed peace bid to Adolf Hitler and Benito Mussolini. The family moved to New Hope, Pennsylvania, situated in the region where Pearl Buck, Dorothy Parker, and many other authors resided. New Hope was also marked by "small-town anti-Semitism," as Brand reflected in his journal soon after the move. He was often in Manhattan while Leader and the children stayed behind. She began publishing articles on housework in "The Conning Tower," the *New York Post* column that featured Parker and Edna St. Vincent Millay. Brand kept a record of his heady activities. He drank scotch and soda with Sherwood Anderson on a Monday afternoon before teaching at NYU; he socialized with Dick Wright after the April lectures by W. H. Auden and Christopher Isherwood at the League of American Writers (founded by the American Communist Party); he attended a session of the World Writers' Congress on the theme "Can Culture Survive Exile," held in May at the World's Fair, and met Ernst Toller two weeks before his suicide; he accompanied the exiled photographer Lotte Jacobi to parties; he spoke on the fiction panel of the League's Congress at the New School in June, alongside Sylvia Townsend Warner, Dashiell Hammett, and Louis Aragon.[76]

Leader's brother, Herbert, disclosed near the end of his life that Pauline found contraceptives in Brand's pocket that summer.[77] By September 6, she and Brand resolved to separate. World War II had just been declared in Europe.[78] She moved with the children to Sunnyside, Queens the next month. She had in fact been working on another novel, *Roses Grow Deep,* which she sent around to publishers throughout late 1939 and 1940. Maitland Armstrong Edey of Random House responded, "You should be complimented first on the hard uncompromising reality which pervades this story. Unfortunately, we both know that it is not honesty which usually makes the most popular book."[79] She eventually destroyed that manuscript too.

In 1942, she decided to move the family back to Bennington until the war ended; she was assigned to work as an air raid warden, searching out chinks of light during mandatory blackouts. She drafted another novel, titled *A Song for My Land*, yet again unpublished and abandoned. In his rejection letter from 1941, Chester Kerr of the Atlantic Monthly Press complimented her writing, noting that the style was "curiously compact and effective." Nevertheless, reviewers deemed the manuscript unpublishable because of its pessimistic tone and plot. These critics, he told her,

> insist it is too serious a tale, unrelenting in its pressure, 'unsatisfactory' (I suppose to the Hilton or Cronin or de la Roche audience) in its conclusions, that we should get no thanks from

the booksellers or publishers for taking it on. I will grant I think its chances are less in these days of increasing concern with this wretched war, but I dislike seeing such writing go by the boards for the duration, believing as I do that this only fosters the more escape or war literature.[80]

Meanwhile, Metro-Goldwyn-Mayer began production on a film version of *The World We Make*, to which they had purchased the rights in 1939. The movie would never be completed; the female lead, Susan Peters, was seriously injured in a hunting accident, and Leader sued MGM, claiming rights as a co-author.[81]

After the war, Leader returned to Manhattan, to a cold water flat with a kerosene heater on 69th Street, near the edge of Hell's Kitchen, where she and the children lived until 1950. A young Marlon Brando stayed with his sister in the apartment below while performing in *A Streetcar Named Desire*. Leader's alimony from Brand in 1947 was $50 per month, a sum that ran shorter and shorter each year. He rarely visited the children, and he began to confuse their birthdays. Leader and Brand argued bitterly via post.[82] She picked up bureaucratic and ghostwriting jobs, such as responding to complaint letters for a logging company. She wrote a play that attacked Brand in cloaked terms, which she unsuccessfully circulated to Broadway producers. A friend of the children saw her sitting near the window one evening, writing in the fading dusk, the lights left off to save money.[83]

And so she returned to Bennington. Deaf, never having completed her middle-school education, she was compelled to work once again in the hated mills.

One saw with a shock that this was she (115).

She wrote on borrowed time, publishing occasional poems and letters to editors. She tried to release a collection of poetry with Vanguard, but Henle turned her down. On her art in this period, she told Barbara Shollar, "My 'obstacles' were my children. Also my jobs, I should add. I didn't have time for much else. After working all day in a textile mill or a shoe factory I was exhausted." She was opaque on the topic of her deafness: "If I hadn't become deaf, I think my life would have been entirely different." [84]

She took one year away from the textile mill to write full time.[85] The result was *A Room for the Night*, a series of sketches about the tenants of the rooming houses her parents had owned. It was funny and "light"; Vanguard accepted it for publication in 1946. *A Room for the Night* was extensively illustrated by Garth Williams, who became famous for his work on *Stuart Little*, *Charlotte's Web*, and *Little House on the Prairie*. Leader estimated that her long-awaited second book sold 3,000 copies in the first year.[86] She went back to work in the mills.

Over the next decades, Millen Brand published several more books, none as well reviewed as his first. Commentators on the most recent edition of *The Outward Room*, released in 2010 by NYRB Classics, call it one of the earliest "psychological novels" and highlight its distinction from his other works. Britt Peterson commends *The Outward Room* for its dazzling imagery: "Brand is at his best piling up the details of Depression-era New York, seen through the disorienting lens of the wandering and hungry stranger. . . . In Brand's later fiction there are too few moments like these."[87] Daniel Brand estimates that his mother wrote half of the novel—likely the half with these particulars about the female urban wanderer, which were intimately familiar to her.[88] Millen Brand subsequently co-authored the screenplay for *The Snake Pit*, an award-winning 1948 Hollywood film on the same theme of a woman with "mental illness." For a time, he was earning $1,000 per week in Los Angeles. Like Leader, he wrote for *New Masses*. In 1953, he was called before the House Un-American Activities Committee, chaired by Joseph McCarthy, and he was blacklisted as a Communist.[89]

Joe Gould died not long after, in 1957, in Pilgrim State Hospital on Long Island. Despite their terrible argument, Leader maintained a sort of loyalty to him. Of his many friends, Lepore says "none of them showed up for his funeral." But Leader was there, with her children. Jonathan took a photo of Gould in his casket.[90]

Pauline Leader in her New York apartment, October 30, 1957.
Photograph by Jonathan Brand.

She worked and the years proceeded. To put Daniel through the Massachusetts Institute of Technology, she took on an extra shift at a shoe factory, waiting outside at four in the morning for the bus that brought workers to the neighboring town. He remembers her as "a wonderful mother. What strikes me is her stamina and willpower; it was just incredible. She was fierce and determined, amazing and sad (given the tough circumstances of her life)."[91]

Leader died in 2001, at age 92, in Portland, Oregon, where she had moved to be near Jonathan. Would she have said that *the people* had gotten her? Contemplated after her death, Leader's youthful memoir is a record of short-lived hope, as well as burning grief and outrage. How bitter to accept that one can be exiled even from Bohemia. It is a place where books are made in sweatshop binderies and oral speech is an impregnable norm. The Bohemians and slummers are one and the same; glamorous exceptions bob on the labor of the strugglers. And the gingham-frocked multitudes? They are permanently gone, absent from the long-lost oral history of their time.

Acknowledgments

This introduction could not have been written without the passionate support of Pauline Leader's sons, Daniel and Jonathan, who rummaged in their attics and consulted with extended family to locate scattered photographs, clippings, poems, and letters. I am also indebted to Paul Hurlbut, a family friend who generously shared a draft of the biography he is writing for the Bennington Museum library in Vermont ("Pauline Leader: Bennington's Unsung Hero"). Finally, I walk in the footsteps of Barbara Shollar, who interviewed Leader in 1992 as part of her doctoral research. Shollar intended to reprint *And No Birds Sing*, but she was murdered by her partner before those plans came to pass.

Notes

1. Maxwell Bodenheim, *My Life and Loves in Greenwich Village* (New York: Bridgehead Books, 1954), 229.

2. Luc Sante, "The Invisible Man," *New York Review of Books*, May 10, 1984, 15. On Bodenheim as "the last Bohemian," see Kermit Jaediker, "The Last Bohemian," *New York Daily News*, February 28, 1954, 5. On Marín, see Nelson A. Denis, *War Against All Puerto Ricans: Revolution and Terror in America's Colony* (New York: Nation Books, 2015).

3. Richard Bruce Nugent, "Harlem," in *Gay Rebel of the Harlem Renaissance: Selections from the Work of Richard Bruce Nugent*, ed. Thomas H. Wirth (Durham and London: Duke University Press, 2002), 147.

4. Djuna Barnes, "Becoming Intimate with the Bohemians," in *New York*, ed. Alyce Barry (Los Angeles: Sun and Moon Press, 1989), 237–38. First published in *New York Morning Telegraph Sunday Magazine*, November 19, 1916.

5. Unless otherwise noted, numbers in parentheses following quotes refer to pages in this volume.

6. Frieda Leader did take Pauline to several ear doctors (see pp. 88–91).

7. Elizabeth Wilson, *Bohemians: The Glamourous Outcasts* (New Brunswick: Rutgers University Press, 2000).

8. For a survey of responses to the autobiography by contemporary reviewers, see Barbara Shollar, "Writing Ethnicity/Writing Modernity: Autobiographies by Jewish-American Women" (PhD diss., City University of New York, 1992).

9. Regina Kunzel, *Fallen Women, Problem Girls: Unmarried Mothers and the Professionalization of Social Work, 1890–1945* (New Haven: Yale University Press, 1993); Anne E. Goldman, *Take My Word: Autobiographical Innovations of Ethnic American Working Women* (Berkeley: University of California Press, 1996); Ann R. Shapiro, *Jewish American Women Writers: A Bio-bibliographical and Critical Sourcebook* (Westport, CT: Greenwood Press, 1994).

10. Eugene Bergman, "Characters Conceived by Deaf Writers," in *Gallaudet Encyclopedia of Deaf People and Deafness, vol. II*, ed. John V. Van Cleve (New York: McGraw-Hill, 1987), 175. Susan Schweik is one of the few disability studies scholars to reference Leader. See *The Ugly Laws: Disability in Public* (New York: NYU Press, 2010).

11. Shollar, "Writing Ethnicity/Writing Modernity," 404.

12. Pauline Leader, interview by Jonathan Brand, October 25, 1991, tape recording and transcript, in Jonathan Brand's possession.

13. "Bennington Briefs," *Bennington Evening Banner*, April 13, 1921, 8.

14. Pauline Leader, untitled poem, typescript, in Daniel Brand's possession.

15. Pauline Leader, "Trucks," originally published as "New York is a City of Trucks," *This Quarter*, Spring-Summer 1930.

16. Herbert Leader, "Pauline, Maxwell Bodenheim, Millen Brand and their Affairs", 1986, typescript, in Daniel Brand's possession.

17. Joseph Mitchell, *Up in the Old Hotel and Other Stories* (New York: Vintage Books, 2008), 220.

18. Ben Hecht tells an anecdote about Bodenheim eating his wineglass at a dinner party in *Letters from Bohemia* (Garden City, NY: Doubleday and Co., 1964), 120.

19. Or so argued Bodenheim's defense attorney, quoted in "Bodenheim Freed in Trial of His Book," *Reading Times*, March 22, 1928, 8. One of the lines quoted by the prosecution was "His fingers enveloped the fullness of her breasts quite as a boy grasps soap-bubbles and marvels at their intact resistance." See Ross Wetzsteon, *Republic of Dreams: Greenwich Village: The American Bohemia, 1910–1960* (New York: Simon and Schuster, 2007), 384.

20. As quoted in Jay Robert Nash, *Zanies: The World's Greatest Eccentrics* (Lanham, MD: Rowman and Littlefield, 1982), 35.

21. Pauline Leader, mail interview by Barbara Shollar, January 24, 1992, photocopy in Daniel Brand's possession.

22. Jaediker, "The Last Bohemian," 5.

23. Tom Boggs, *Millionaire Playboy: A Delirious and True Extravaganza of Inheriting a Fortune and Squandering It* (New York: Vanguard Press, 1933), 197; Jack B. Moore, *Maxwell Bodenheim* (New York: Twayne Publishers, 1970), 93–94.

24. Albert Parry, *Garrets and Pretenders: A History of Bohemianism in America* (New York: Covici, Friede, 1933), 327, 298.

25. "'Will' Held a Forgery: Document Disposing of Rosalind S. Gildea Estate Is Thrown Out," *New York Times*, November 17, 1936, 32.

26. Boggs, *Millionaire Playboy*, 54.

27. Quoted in Mitchell, *Up in the Old Hotel*, 58.

28. On the history of "oral history," prior to and including Gould and Nevins, see Charles Morrissey, "Why Call It 'Oral History': Searching for Early Usage of a Generic Term," *Oral History Review* 8 (1980): 20–48.

29. Horace Gregory, "Pepys on the Bowery," *New Republic*, April 15, 1931, 249–50; Joseph Mitchell, "Professor Seagull," *New Yorker*, December 12, 1942, 28–37; Joseph Mitchell, "Joe Gould's Secret–I," *New Yorker*, September 19, 1964, 61–125; Joseph Mitchell, "Joe Gould's Secret–II," *New Yorker*, September 26, 1964, 53–151.

30. Daniel Brand, personal communication with author, April 21, 2016.

31. Jill Lepore, *Joe Gould's Teeth* (New York: Knopf, 2016), 6.

32. Leader, interview by Jonathan Brand; Joe Gould to Pauline Leader, October 21, 1934, p. 2, Series II, Box 1, Folder "Gould, Joe 1934–35," Millen Brand Papers, Columbia University Rare Book and Manuscript Library, New York.

33. Joe Gould, "Me Tempore: A Selection from Joe Gould's Oral History: Insanity," *Pagany* 2, no. 2 (April-June 1931), 96–97.

34. "Girl Poet Misses $10 Prize," *New York Times*, June 8, 1927, 23.

35. Pauline Leader, "Poetry Exhibitions for Unknown Bards," *New York Times*, July 17, 1927, 9. Leader recommended Gildea to Charles Henri Ford for publication in *Blues*. Ford to Leader, March 24, 1929, in Daniel Brand's possession. Gildea was perhaps the person suggested by the following lines in her autobiography: "Once indeed I thought I found somebody. But he was unstable—and I too was unstable. I wanted no one who was so much like me" (182).

36. Ruth Widen, "The First National Poetry Exhibition: or, An Experiment and a Vindication," in *Whispering Walls: An Anthology from the First National Poetry Exhibition*, ed. Ruth Widen (New York: Parnassus, 1930). Pamphlet in the author's possession. "Broken Faces" was also published in the 1927 *Oracle Anthology of Poetry*.

37. "Miss Pauline Leader Receives Recognition," *Bennington Evening Banner*, November 16, 1929, 1. The *Morada* was a short-lived journal published in Albuquerque from 1929 to 1930.

38. "Miss Pauline Leader Writes More Poems," *Bennington Evening Banner*, March 19, 1929, 1.

39. Barry Ahearn, ed., *Pound/Zukofsky: Selected Letters of Ezra Pound and Louis Zukofsky* (New York: New Directions Publishing, 1987), 12.

40. Leader, interview by Shollar; Leader, interview by Jonathan Brand.

41. Pauline Leader, "Overalls," *Survey*, August 15, 1931, 471; Pauline Leader, "The Girl Who Looked Too Much at the Clock," *Survey*, February 15, 1930, 578–79.

42. Pauline Leader, "No Laughter Allowed," *Survey*, September 1, 1931, 514. For context on "rhythm" and modernism, see Michael Golston, *Rhythm and Race in Modernist Poetry and Science* (New York: Columbia University Press, 2008).

43. Her piece in *Pagany*, "Hired Girl," appeared in the same issue as Joe Gould's excerpt on "Insanity." Literary scholar Eric B. White argues that it "confronts the colour line at street level in a confrontational regional vernacular whilst reinforcing the sense of cultural mourning that inflects much of *Pagany*'s fiction. Yet by stripping the sentimental escapist exoticism from regionalist fiction, Leader's tale of interracial relationships challenges its model of social realism." Whereas other *Pagany* authors, such as Mina Loy, write about race with "modernist primitivism," White interprets Leader's story as "simultaneously destabilising, reaffirming and casting judgement upon the reductive binaries." Eric B. White, *Transatlantic Avant-gardes: Little Magazines and Localist Modernism* (Edinburgh: Edinburgh University Press, 2013), 200.

44. As noted in the *Bennington Evening Banner*, November 13, 1930, 3.

45. "Lip-Reading Bridges Nature's Slip," *Sun*, May 16, 1929; "What Is Missed Most by the Deaf," *Sun*, December 12, 1929. These articles were published anonymously, copies in Daniel Brand's possession.

46. "Recreations for Those Who Are Deaf," *Sun*, February 21, 1930, 18.

47. Pauline Leader, "The Mystic Sense," in *Double Blossoms: Helen Keller Anthology*, ed. Edna Porter (New York: Lewis Copeland Company, 1931), 37.

48. Leader, interview by Jonathan Brand.

49. James Henle to Pauline Leader, March 19, 1931, in Daniel Brand's possession; Alex Schlosser (Vanguard Press) to Pauline Leader, November 19, 1931, in Daniel Brand's possession.

50. Annetta Peck, *Survey*, August 15, 1931, 481. From a typescript digest of book reviews, in Daniel Brand's possession.

51. Quoted in Paul Hurlbut, "Pauline Leader: Bennington's Unsung Hero," unpublished manuscript to be deposited in the Bennington Museum library.

52. G.R.B.R., *Boston Transcript*, August 1931, 8. From a typescript digest of book reviews, in Daniel Brand's possession.

53. Quoted in Hurlbut, "Pauline Leader: Bennington's Unsung Hero."

54. Leader, interview by Jonathan Brand. The interview contains other details of her courtship with Millen Brand.

55. Ibid.

56. Ibid.

57. Millen Brand, "Sheet Journal," Series III, Box 76, Folder: "1930–1931," Millen Brand Papers. Although the folder is labeled 1931, the sheets therein clearly state, "I kept a record, mainly of meetings with friends, in 1934 and 1935."

58. A summary of Millen Brand's notes held in Series III, Box 76, Folder: "1934," Millen Brand Papers.

59. Lepore, *Joe Gould's Teeth*, 148–9.

60. Joe Gould to Pauline Leader, September 24, 1934, pp. 1–2, Series II, Box 1, Folder "Gould, Joe 1934–35," Millen Brand Papers.

61. Leader, interview by Jonathan Brand. Cummings' poem was originally published in *No Thanks* (New York: Golden Eagle Press, 1935).

62. Dorothy McCleary and Edward Anderson, *Not for Heaven and Hungry Men: Two Prize Novels* (New York: Literary Guild, 1935).

63. Series III, Box 76, Folder: "1935–1937," Millen Brand Papers; Michèle Levy, ed., *The Autobiography of Alfred H. Mendes, 1897–1991* (Jamaica: University of the West Indies Press, 2002), 94.

64. Dorothy McCleary to Pauline Leader, March 19, 1935, Series II, Box I, Folder: "1935," Millen Brand Papers.

65. Leader, interview by Jonathan Brand.

66. Elizabeth Nowell to Pauline Leader, May 27, 1935, Series II, Box I, Folder: "1935," Millen Brand Papers.

67. Peter Cameron, afterword to *The Outward Room* (New York: New York Review Books Classics, 2010), 236.

68. Jonathan Brand, "Whatever my mother told me, I listened to twice. (And No Birds Sing Again)," Unpublished manuscript, in Jonathan Brand's possession. Brand recalls editing some of his father's subsequent works.

69. See Folders "Young, Louise (1929–1930)" and "1930–1934" from Series II, Box I, Millen Brand Papers.

70. Leader, interview by Jonathan Brand.

71. Millen Brand, "Escape to Life," Series III, Box 49, Folder: "The Outward Room – plan," Millen Brand Papers. The exact quote is, "Might try [illegible] room at PL's address."

72. Millen Brand, "11/17/39," Series III, Box 76, Folder: "1939," Millen Brand Papers.

73. M. Brand, *The Outward Room* (2010), 128; Cameron, afterword, 236.

74. Pauline Leader to Millen Brand, n.d., Series II, Box 2, Folder: "Family 1938–39," Millen Brand Papers.

75. Leader, interview by Shollar; Otto Steinbrocker to Pauline Leader, Series II, Box 2, Folder: "1938," Millen Brand Papers.

76. Millen Brand, "July 27, 1939" and journal entries for April through June, Series III, Box 76, Folder: "1939," Millen Brand Papers. Leader was especially interested in details about Sylvia Townsend Warner.

77. Herbert Leader, "Pauline, Maxwell Bodenheim, Millen Brand and their Affairs."

78. Leader's uncle and other relatives in Europe died in the Holocaust.

79. Maitland Armstrong Edey to Pauline Leader, February 26, 1940, in Daniel Brand's possession.

80. Chester Kerr to Pauline Leader, August 20, 1941, in Daniel Brand's possession.

81. Jonathan Brand, "Whatever my mother told me."

82. On the birthdays, see Pauline Leader to Millen Brand, May 14, 1947, Series II, Box 2, Folder: "Family 1947," Millen Brand Papers. This folder contains numerous quarreling letters between Leader and Brand. On the alimony, see Pauline Leader to Millen Brand, March 5, 1947. I thank Professor Benjamin Harris of the University of New Hampshire for drawing my attention to this folder.

83. Jonathan Brand, "Whatever my mother told me;" Millen Brand to Pauline Leader, March 3, 1947, Series II, Box 2, Folder: "Family 1947," Millen Brand Papers; Ann Burrus, *Escape from Roxboro Road: A Memoir* (Lincoln, NE: iUniverse, 2006), 39.

84. Leader, interview by Shollar. The statements about "The Conning Tower," Henle, and her "obstacles" were all made in response to questions from Shollar.

85. Ibid.

86. Pauline Leader to Millen Brand, March 5, 1947, Series II, Box 2, Folder: "Family 1947," Millen Brand Papers.

87. Britt Peterson, "Two Therapies," *New Republic*, November 4, 2010, accessed July 8, 2016, https://newrepublic.com/article/77930/two-therapies-outward-room-millen-brand.

88. Leader, interview by Shollar. She informed Barbara Shollar, "We practically collaborated on it. He was always after me for 'suggestions.'"

89. Eric Pace, "Millen Brand: Writer and Editor Known for Works on Psychiatry," *New York Times*, March 22, 1980, 26.

90. Lepore, *Joe Gould's Teeth*, 143; Leader, interview by Jonathan Brand.

91. Quoted in Hurlbut, "Pauline Leader: Bennington's Unsung Hero."

POEM TO EMILY DICKINSON

To die by oneself, overnight, as the flower dies, requires
        courage.
Men of God! we die a little each time we chant a preparation:
At death, there is very little left to die.

To die and to take the silence with one—
We leave, jealous of the living,
So that it is almost as if it had not been:

This is the true immortality.

Pauline Leader

Originally published in *Poetry*, 36, no. 2 (May 1930), 85.

PART ONE

THE MARKET-PLACE

This is i, very small i, walking home from the market at night, walking through the dark, apparently limitless streets, leaving the stores behind, coming to the houses, leaving the houses behind if I walked far enough. Once I had done this, but the policeman and a posse had brought me back. They called me a bad girl.

To the market, home from the market, these were phrases I heard early. Home from the market—I saw my mother wheeling the baby carriage, myself walking on one side of the carriage, a sister on the other side. My father walked a little in back of us with my brother. In the carriage would be some other brother or sister.

I was very conscious of the streets and of the houses. There was one house in particular that we must pass on the way to the market, and pass again on the way home from the market. It was set far back from the street, in its own grounds. It was white—marble, I thought, for I liked the word marble—and it had pillars. I thought of it often.

The river ran by it. After a few years, when my chin could reach the bridge railing, I'd lean against it and watch the river. The stones in it made it like no other river, for no other river had such a strangely assorted bed of stones. Now and then I would turn my head and look at the marble house. If it was night, the river and the house looked silvery. But then, if it was real night, I hurried past, afraid of the silver and of something else.

Past the river, past the marble house, to the corner, around the corner, then a little way down, and home.

The railroad station was near home. I loved to watch the trains come and go, thinking up one-sentence stories about the people who got off, and wondering where those who got on were going. No nice little girl hangs around railroad stations, the people said. All the bums of the town congregated there, all the men who didn't work or were out of work, and all the men who had only one eye or one arm or one leg. I watched them by the hour, every time I could steal away. These strange creatures fascinated me as much as the trains. They came down, day after day, to watch the trains and talk. Like me, they seemed to have nothing better to do. Respectable people do not stand about all day and watch the trains, the people said. I pitied the respectable people. It was too bad that they did not take a day off now and then and come down and watch the trains. It was such fun! The arrival of a train, still far off, unseen except for puff-puff-puff of smoke, was such fun that it turned me giddy. It was too much fun. Thinking of it, still far off, but coming nearer and nearer, was even better than the actual awful sight of it coming down the tracks. Another attraction at the railroad station was the sound of the telegraph key. I stood hours listening to it. It was not so impressive as the sight of a train, but when at last I went home—perhaps my mother had sent someone to look for me, or come herself—it was the sound of the telegraph key that I took home with me, and not the picture of the train. The picture of the train was too big to take home. I was content to come to the station for it.

It was a train that nearly killed me. My mother and the baby carriage and I were on one side of the tracks waiting for the train to go by so that we might get to the other side. But the train kept making false starts. Calculating that the next one would be another false start, I ran across. I felt that I could not wait any longer. I must run across. But the next one was not a false start and the wheels barely failed to go over me. When my mother and the baby carriage finally joined me, my mother held threats over my head all the way home. The most terrifying of these threats was that I would be 'sent away' if I didn't behave. 'Sent away' meant, darkly, the reformatory. There was a boy in town who had been to the reformatory. Everybody knew it and everybody had invisible accusing fingers pointed at him as though he were a leper.

Sent away. . . . Why didn't I 'behave'? I did not know why I did these things, why I was different from other girls who walked in safe, proper ways, and were never threatened with being 'sent away.' Sent away . . . it could set my soul quivering. They were always saying it, so that I lived in a constant state of fear. I hated my father and mother for making me feel like this, for plunging me into this abyss of fear and uncertainty whenever they said the words. What had I done that I could not have helped doing? The policeman— the policeman was always shaking a finger at me.

Across from home was a second-hand store, the windows of which I would often explore. There was a grocery store which had everything that grocery stores have, and other things which the more up-to-date grocery stores on Main Street did not have. It was a general country store, one of the last of its kind in a village rapidly becoming a town. But best of all, there was the ice-cream store on the corner. Whenever I found any money in my mother's pocketbook, or in the jars, I took it and bought ice-cream. One time I found so much money that I gave a party. All the girls in the neighborhood were invited. There was some ice-cream left over and this I took to my father and mother.

"Where did you get the money?" they asked.

"I found it in the jar."

"Thief!"

"I found it!"

"Thief!"

I saw that they did not understand. They were not perfectly natural themselves so they could not understand perfect naturalness in others. They called me a thief when I had only been natural in obeying my impulse to get money for ice-cream, the more money the more ice-cream.

What did the people mean by 'thief'? What had I done that was wrong? The people were the strange ones, the crazy ones, with their cries of 'thief! thief!'

"There was some ice-cream left over. Here." Patiently I explained.

"Thief, you come with me," my mother said. My mother was the one who was always ready for action, I'd noticed. My father was lazy. He never did anything until my mother stung him with her words.

It wasn't being called 'thief' that hurt. Such a word meant nothing. It was their inability to understand. Their refusal or inability to understand meant that I was to be dragged through the streets to the ice-cream store and humiliated before the lady who sold the ice-cream. The lady would ever after have that knowledge of me in her eyes. I would have to go elsewhere for my ice-cream. I could not bear to face her, look into her eyes, after that.

In the store I hung my head in shame. I was ashamed, ashamed, for my mother's sake as much as for my own, to be thus exposed before everybody's eyes. My mother wanted the money back. I was a thief, she shouted to the lady; I had stolen the money to buy the ice-cream.

Thief! Thief! Thief!

What was the lady thinking? Laughing at my mother. Dirty foreigners! Wops! Kikes! Yids! Polaks! Don't know how to act civilized. See the way she looks in that dress! And shouting! Did you ever hear such shouting? Don't know enough to give her brats handkerchiefs when she sends them to school. The teacher has to give them pieces of paper. Stop picking your nose. You dirty Yid! You dirty Kike!

Ice-cream. I was sick of the whole thing. I wanted to vomit.

"Ma. . . ."

But my mother was oblivious. "I want my money back," she shouted.

I ran out and left my mother to it alone. I felt dimly that she was enjoying herself. She was a fighter. But all she could see was the lady from whom she meant to get her money back, while I could see inside the lady's head and inside the heads of the spectators, and I could not stand any more.

On Sunday I was an outcast. I did not belong with them, the American little girls, all dressed up in their hats and gloves.

"You have to wear a hat in church." I had heard this told importantly by a school friend. I never forgot it. Hats came to symbolize the difference between myself and the American little girls. I never wore them, and they did. And never more so than on Sundays did they wear their hats. So that on Sunday, more than on any other day, I sensed the difference between myself and the people. It was more than a racial difference, although it was that too. Sunday was—Sunday, the Lord's Day, as the little girl who had explained to me—the heathen—about the hats importantly continued. Sunday was a day of rest for them, a day of going to church, a day of wearing hats and gloves. Is there anything more beautiful than a small town on Sunday morning in the spring or summer time, everybody dressed up, everybody going to church? I could feel the beauty of it, and I wanted to be part of the picture. But Sunday for me was like any other day, except that the market was closed. There was no rest, no going to church. My mother on her one day off from the market spent the day cleaning the house.

I was an inferior being. At school I might have the highest marks, the teachers might praise me, but how much did that count after all? All the time I was an inferior being. The little girl who had told me about the hats and the Lord's Day had a subnormal intelligence, but nevertheless she was superior to me.

I ached to dress up too. I wanted to mingle with the people. I did not want to stand out. I wanted a clean dress, perhaps silk with ruffles, a hat and thin gloves, and I wanted my mother to have a silk dress, a hat and thin gloves, so that I might go out and walk with her. I would not fear comparison.

Instead, my dress was dirty. I would get a clean dress for tomorrow's school, but today was Sunday when my dress was dirtiest of all. I was ashamed to go out on the street in it.

"Ma, can I have a clean dress?"

"What for?"

I could not reply to this, because I didn't quite know myself. Or if I knew, I could not explain it to her. She would not understand. I knew the hopelessness of trying to make her understand. I felt defeated even before I began.

I went back and sat on the stoop and watched the people go by. Everybody looked different. It was as if, miraculously, out of the week-day people, a new people had been created. Tomorrow, the sullen lines, the impatience, would come back, but today, miraculously, there was only beautiful peace in their faces. Sunday peace.

It was Sunday and there was peace everywhere except in my mind. I hated Sunday because Sunday was beyond my attainment. I wanted the people, the child-people in this case, to nod to me as though I were an equal. They might pretend that I was an equal on weekdays, but today they went past me without seeing me. Even the Wops were above me today, although on weekdays we were united in a common cause. But even for the Wops, Sunday was *the* day. They went to the Catholic Church. They wore hats and gloves. The Wop mother might be unable to speak English well, less well than my mother, but what did that matter today? I could see the steeple of the synagogue and I hated it. What did it mean? It meant nothing. Did the Jews close their stores on Saturday as the Americans closed theirs on Sunday? Yet Saturday was the holy day of the Jews, but Saturday was also too important a day for making money to close the store. And not content with that, they kept their stores surreptitiously open on Sundays, many of them. This offended me. I hated Jews.

I wanted something. I wanted a symbol, too. I wanted a clean, sweet Sunday dress, a hat and thin gloves and white stockings and shoes. But it was more than that. I did not want to be an alien in all this Sunday beauty. I was terribly lonesome on Sunday. I was not a Jew—I knew I was not a Jew—and yet I was not a goy either. They would not accept me as one of them. I hated and envied the little American girls. To go about with such a *right* to Sunday, *their* day. I had no right to even show my face on this day.

I wanted to be like them. I did not want to be different. At night, when everyone was asleep, I clasped my hands together and said the Lord's Prayer. I had come upon it in the Wop's catechism book, and learned it, liking the rhythm of it, without bothering very much about the meaning of the words. I said the words in emulation of some hundred other little girls because I did not want to be different. Besides, there might be some magic in it. What did it mean? What did it awaken? After saying the prayer, I always waited a little to see if anything would happen. At the very least, I should be struck dead, but not even that happened although my father always said that something terrible would happen to me if I ever had anything to do with the 'goyim' and 'their ways.' My father, I knew, considered himself one of 'the chosen people', and this knowledge of his superiority helped him in his retaliations. But I was a realist. We might be the 'chosen people' way off somewhere 'in Jerusalem', but this was America, the place where I lived, and where I suffered savagely whenever I was called dirty Jew.

The Ledger. The cover was greasy and so were the pages. The hand that held the pencil and turned the pages had not long before grasped a lard paddle, a forequarter of beef, a leg of pork. My mother, resting her side on the counter as her pencil made entries in the Ledger.

The Ledger—the word was capitalized on the cover, and it was always capitalized in my mind—contained the names of three-quarters of the town's inhabitants. Bleak American names, New England names frosty as a winter morning, written out in Yiddish, becoming strange, un-New Englandish things, smacking somehow of witches' numerals. Or in place of names, there were nick-names, peculiarly apt, coined by my mother. In the market they would be henceforth known by their nicknames. My mother would use that nickname in speaking of the person to my father.

When I was eight, we moved from the house by the railroad station to two rooms over the market. There was a room back of the market where we lived and played. The two rooms upstairs were used only for sleeping.

Living so close to the market, in and out of it twenty times a day, I could not help but hear many strange things.

There was Anna, a heavy phlegmatic Polish girl with a red, coarse pored face. When my mother and father prospered and bought the first of what was to be known later as 'the houses', Anna took a room in the house.

Everybody considered Anna a good girl. (Who would look at that heavy body, that coarse bloated face?) It was a surprise, then, when one night she almost had a baby in the bathroom, but was taken to the hospital in time.

It was market talk for days.

"I always thought she was a good girl, didn't you, Mis' Lasher?" my mother said. "And I never even guessed! Did you?" My mother fairly smacked her lips.

"No, I didn't."

"You go way," my mother said to me. "This talk isn't for little girls." But I hid behind the refrigerator and continued to listen.

When Anna left the hospital and came to the market, my mother said to her, leaning back against the cash register, her arms folded:

"Anna, I can't keep you up at the house now."

"Yes, ma'am," said Anna.

"Who did it, Anna?" My mother was without mercy.

"Oh, nobody you know. He's a soldier."

"Well, Anna. . . ." My mother, cheated, was getting angry. "You see how it is . . . you'll have to go."

"Yes, ma'am."

"I'm sorry, but you know how it is, Anna. The house would get a bad name. . . ."

"Yes, ma'am."

"Ma, I wrote a story."

"What kind of a story?"

"A love story."

"And you only nine!"

"Can I read it to you, Ma? I passed it around in school and the girls liked it."

"All right, but hurry up before a customer comes in."

My mother leaned back against the cash register, her arms folded on her misshapen belly—belly that had borne six children—and listened while I read the love story I had written. When I could not think of anything else to do with my hero and heroine, I would rush them into hectic embraces. My mother, leaning back against the cash register, arms folded on her misshapen belly, belly shaking with laughter as I read my love story, one eye on the story, one eye anxiously on my mother, watching her reactions, and still another eye got from somewhere watching the door for any possible customers, praying that none would come until I finished my story.

Miss Bottome ran a boarding house and traded at our store. One summer school vacation when I was ten, I worked at the boarding house waiting on table. I met Julie who worked in the kitchen. Nobody knew Julie's age. Miss Bottome paid her six dollars a week, five of which Julie paid out for the support of her daughter. The daughter was raped as soon as she grew old enough, and everybody said what a shame after Julie had spent so much money on her. How many years had Julie been in Miss Bottome's kitchen? How many years, Julie? Oh, I've lost count. How many years of getting up before dawn and going to bed after midnight? How many years of putting on the oatmeal the night before?

How many years in that little back room with no windows that Miss Bottome allowed you? Oh, I lost count.

Miss Bottome tripping into the market of an evening. ("Damned Jews, I know they make a pretty penny out of me.")

"How would you like to work for me this summer? You're a big strong girl."

"Can I, Ma?"

"Sure, you're ten now. A big girl old enough to make some money instead of doing nothing but read all the time."

Four dollars a week all my own.

So I went to work for Miss Bottome. It was more out of curiosity than out of any desire to make money. I was curious to see how other people lived. I did not think that everybody lived as we did.

"Decent people wash their hands after going to the toilet," said Miss Bottome.

"This is the way to set a table," said Miss Bottome.

"You can't eat out in the dining room. Your place is in the kitchen with Julie," said Miss Bottome.

"Don't you know enough to knock on the door before you come in?" asked Miss Bottome.

"If I wash the base-boards in the dining room today instead of tomorrow, I won't have to wash them again tomorrow, will I?"

"But Miss *Bottome*, I washed them yesterday, and you said. . . ."

"Want to go for a ride some evening?" asked a boarder.

I learned about manners and life at Miss Bottome's boarding house.

The man who had the law office over the market was about fifty when I first knew him. I remember vividly being afraid to go up the stairs to our two rooms because he was in the hallway reeling drunkenly. There were two men, and from somewhere I got the knowledge how to adjust myself to both. I did not confuse the drunkard with the man. When he was drunk, I hurried past him, head averted, so that I might not have a too clear picture of him, but merely the knowledge that 'he drank.' When he was himself, the man, I brought him all my respect, forgetting, or truly deeming as nothing, 'the drunkard.'

The lawyer was sometimes in his office, but more often he was in the saloon across the road. Drink had made his eyes bleary, his hands unsteady, but beneath the wreck was the defeated idealist who consoled himself with detective stories. Beneath the detective stories, beneath the wreck, was the man who disdained, or was not sharp enough, to compete with nimbler wits. Law had become a business, whereas he still thought of it as a high profession with something of the savor of the arts about it. He liked to tell me of the few lawyers he respected, men of an older day.

The lawyer walks down the street, lurching. He has just come from the saloon, it is evident, and he is trying to get back to his office without falling down. He almost sinks down before the market door and I hear my mother and the customers laugh. Damn them! I look the other way. I do not want to see the appeal in his eyes. To show his soul thus before the people. I am ashamed for him. But I am with him as he climbs the dirty stairs to his office. I know just how he falls against the walls. By now he must have gained his office. He is away from the people's eyes and the people's laughter. I feel lighter. It is as if I have borne him on my back, up the stairs, to let my burden down only when I have reached his office.

I go up that hallway myself at night. I do not go up often because I am afraid. I know that the hallway has a bad name. I know that the offices that line either side of the hall are the offices of broken men, defeated men, men like the lawyer. I know that things happen in that hallway, nameless things. I am afraid of the very walls. Sometimes the fuse burns out and then there is no light. I am afraid that sometime, someday when I am walking through the hall at night to our two rooms, the fuse will suddenly go out and I will be left in the awful darkness. The lawyer will perhaps come lurching through the darkness. Someone will come up from the street and go to the dirty toilet, some bum, some drunkard. This is my fear. I tell no one, but I have nightmares about it.

Lena was a widow with seven children. She worked in the factory. One day she fell eleven stories down the shaft.

"Have you heard about her oldest daughter?" my mother asks. "Ever since her mother died—a good woman if there ever was one—she's been taking in boarders, and the neighbors say she sleeps with them." My mother's eyes glisten as she tells this tit-bit to her women customers.

I feel there is something wrong. I want to say to my mother: is it right that Lena who was your friend, who helped you many times with the care of your dirty brats, is it right that you should pay Lena back after she is dead by spreading evil stories about her daughter?

In reality, I say nothing. I have learned that one does not say such things.

I hear later that Lena's children have been driven out of town by this gossip. I wonder: do they hate my mother as I hate her sometimes?

It took Mis' Levretts five years to pay her bill. Every Friday night she paid something down on it. Her husband 'drank'. Her daughter bought fur coats on the installment plan and left it to her mother to pay for them. The daughter was sixteen, bigger than her mother, and she could have got a job in the mill where her mother worked, but she preferred to spend the day lounging about the house in a flowered wrapper that always looked dirty. Her room, which sometimes I penetrated, was heavy with the scents coming from the jars and boxes on the dresser table.

Mis' Levretts supported her husband and daughter. If she ever complained about her lot, no one ever heard her.

When her daughter got married, Mis' Levretts was unexpectedly called away the day before the wedding, and did not get back until it was all over.

The wedding night, the guests put the bride and her husband to bed in the bride's scented room. Everybody was there, everybody except Mis' Levretts. When Mis' Levretts returned home, all that remained of the celebration was a ten-cent celluloid doll. Mis' Levretts never got over it. On Friday nights when she paid something down, she would always say to my mother,

"My own daughter's wedding, and I wasn't there. . . ."

Why couldn't I be like other girls? Why couldn't I live like other girls? Be—American.

"Ma, our class is going to have exercises tomorrow. Can I have money to buy gym bloomers?"

"Gym bloomers! Gym bloomers! Think I've got money for such crazy things?"

"I hate you," I cried. "I hate you. I wish you were dead. I never have anything like other girls. They laugh at me. They say my coat stinks of the market. They hold their noses when I come near them. I hate you. I hate you. Damned dirty Jews." I turned on my mother with *their* cry. "Damned Jews!" I said.

I wanted a home like other girls. I didn't want a market, and two rooms upstairs. I wanted a home that was a house by itself. A house with a hallway in it. I dreamed of that hallway. It was a symbol—like Sunday. I did not want a place that led right into the bedroom or kitchen. There must be a hallway first.

I did not want to be always stinking of the market. Didn't my parents realize that we children were ostracized because of the market, and because of them?

What rottenness and meanness and cheapness was necessary to make money anyway, I thought as I watched from my corner near the refrigerator. How could people sink so low?

The country magazine, although it had only a few pages, was as interesting as a general country store. Like the store, it had a little of everything. One day there appeared in the magazine a full-page advertisement which read: Sell subscriptions to our magazine, and to the one who sends in the most subscriptions we will give, free, a pony, or a phonograph, or an automobile racer for children. The pony, the phonograph, and the racer were illustrated. I could not take my eyes off the racer. An automobile racer for children. It sounded marvellous. It sounded so un-markety. I looked at it, and felt a hundred miles from the market. That the advertisement might not be true, that there might be a catch somewhere—such questions did not trouble me. I set out to acquire the racer.

Who would buy subscriptions? A year's subscription to the magazine was twenty-five cents. I collected four subscriptions— one dollar. Obviously four subscriptions were not enough, and I wanted that automobile racer for children as I had never wanted anything else. Yet, although I rang one doorbell after another, no one would give me another subscription. In desperation I signed the names of everybody I knew. The money I sent in with these names I took from the cash register in the market when my mother was not there. It was like the ice-cream incident of not so many years ago. I wanted money badly; except that this time I wanted it to get the beautiful automobile racer instead of ice-cream. And this time, instead of hunting for the money in jars, I took it from where it was most likely to be—the cash register. My mother's and father's cries of thief! thief! meant nothing to me. Without think- ing, without analyzing, I simply obeyed my instinct: to possess the beautiful automobile racer. But before I could possess it for my very own I must get more and still more subscriptions. As I could not get any more names from the people themselves, I must make them up myself. The money to fit the names I would get from the cash register. It was beautifully simple to me.

I went about in a dream. The racer. . . . I went about telling of the subscriptions I had got. I'd rush into the market gleefully, waving a dollar bill and crying, "Four more subscriptions, Ma!" Yet not an hour before, when my mother's back was turned, I had extracted the dollar from the cash register, which I knew how to open noiselessly so that there would be no tell-tale ring. But I forgot all this, or rather it was of no consequence. The four names I had just written down I had truly received from the four people, along with the dollar. I would have said so, and believed it myself. I did not stop to disentangle the puzzle because there was no puzzle to me. I was headed, straight and true, for my beautiful racer. I saw nothing else.

But I was careless. The paper with the names on it I never hid. After adding more names I would slip it under the linoleum near the cash register. I saw no reason to hide it. I had no feeling of guilt—therefore why should I hide it?

One day my parents found the paper. It seemed that they had been suspicious for some time, although I had not noticed it, so absorbed was I in my dream of the racer and the lust for thinking up more names to fit the steady stream of money coming from the cash register. The paper gave me away. Sometimes there had been a dearth of names—even my willing imagination was forced to stop now and then—and I had copied the same name over and over again in my hurry to get nearer and nearer to the beautiful racer.

"Thief! Thief! If you don't behave, I'll send you away. . . ."

A piano was another symbol of that world where there were no markets, no two rooms, no dirty public hallway, no stinks, no drudgery, no impatience, no sharp words, no smaller brothers and sisters always to be cared for. When I saw a piano in somebody's house I went over to it timidly as soon as I entered the house. Finally, my father bought one. A country school-house had one for sale cheap, my father had heard. I went with my sister to see it and test it—although neither of us knew anything about tone.

The piano seemed marvellous to me. I thought of it upstairs in our two rooms. It would mean more crowding than ever, the beds ever closer together. Caressing the piano, I did not pay much attention to my sister's bargaining.

"How much do you want for it?" my sister, always practical, asked.

At this point I broke in. I would have given anything for the piano. I forgot that my father had said not to go over ten dollars.

"We'll give you fifteen dollars," I said rashly.

My sister, a true child of her parents, glared at me.

"Ten dollars," she said stubbornly.

"All right. Ten dollars," the woman said.

When my sister and I returned home, my sister made haste to tell of my fifteen-dollar offer for the piano.

"Fifteen dollars," my father sneered. "You fool!" How I hated his sneer! It held all the bestiality of the world for me.

I never heard the last of it, and somehow after that there was no more pleasure in the piano. I rarely touched it.

"Always with your nose in a book," my mother, fretful, fault-finding again. Her eyes were tired from nights of sewing on buttons and darning stockings after the market was closed. But I did not think to search for the causes of her constant fretfulness.

She grabbed my books and threw them over the refrigerator where I could not get them.

"Those are library books," I screamed at her. "You'll go to jail. I hate you, I hate you. I wish you were dead. . . . I wish you were dead." It was a phrase that was often in my mouth. I ran out of the market. I would run away from home. . . . I got as far as a mile and then weariness and fright overcame me and I turned back. I remembered that I was only eleven. Only eleven. What could one do at eleven? All the world seemed to be against me, on top of me. Oh, God, why couldn't I live like other girls? Why couldn't I get away from the market, from the market-smell that pursued me everywhere. The market-smell that stuck to my clothes, that I took with me into the classroom. A smell of cold meat, of cold pork, a peculiar raw smell—the market-smell. I could not get away from it. Everywhere I went it went with me. It ostracized me.

Why couldn't my father have a decent store? A drug store. The druggist's children smelled beautifully. They did not smell like me. Nobody refused to play with the druggist's children. But then, the druggist was also not a Jew, a dirty Jew.

To have a home like other girls, not two crowded rooms over the market, a home to which I could invite people. Who would want to come to two rooms at the end of a dirty hallway with a bad name?

My mother, my father, I judged them. Did they know better than I? Honor thy father and mother—but who and what were fathers and mothers? Some were kinder, more understanding than mine were, but essentially they were all the same. Who were they to set themselves up as authorities? What battle had they won, what great problem solved, to set themselves up with such magnificent shingles? They had no nobility so far as I could see. My child's way was straighter. They were fools who were always making a mess of things. I was too 'strong-willed', they said. My will must be broken, they said. Who were they to break me? It sounded like a crime to me, this breaking a person's will, this breaking of a person, but evidently they liked the idea. They were always speaking of it in relation to me. They were always speaking darkly of sending me away to a place where my will would be broken all right if my mother and father could not do it. Did my father really think he could break me with the lashes of his strap?

Another Jewish family had moved to town.

"Why are you always up there?" my mother demanded.

"I like to play with Rosie," I said.

"Rosie! You mean her brothers. You keep away from there, you—"

The slimy depths of my mother's mind. I took a look and ran away, sickened. She could not get away from it—that thing she meant. She saw it in everything. She was always running after me with it. She would not let me alone. She would not let it alone.

It was in nearly all her market talk with the women customers. They, like her, seemed to be interested only in it.

What did she mean? Whatever it was, it must be evil. Her barest gestures and hints about it were evil and I wanted nothing to do with it. Her words would blacken my mind if they could, if she was successful in drawing me into the arms of it. She herself was in the arms of it, and now she was trying to draw me into it. She was trying to make her thoughts my thoughts. I struggled and fled, but I could never flee far enough. Her hints were a million evil tongues whispering into my ears. Mother and daughter relationship, the teachers and the ministers were always saying. I did not want that relationship. I wanted to go my way, free of such evil. I wanted to mix with boys and girls without evil. I did not want to listen to the evil she was always hinting about, or warning me against, or even accusing me of. She could not believe I was free of such evil, she herself was so permeated by it. She could not believe that I saw no evil, that I was innocent.

Yet my mother was a good woman, they said. She was always screaming at me that she was going to send me away. And everybody would take her word for it—that I was bad. No one would believe me or even trouble to understand, for was she not a good woman, a hard worker, the mother of children, all nice docile children except for the eldest, who was a crazy one?

"I wish you were dead, I wish you were dead," I said over and over again in my soul with an intensity that frightened me.

There was a man in our town who had once been a brilliant doctor. 'Drink' had got him, and now he slept in cellars and took care of furnaces. The lawyer over the market had remained his only friend, giving him small change now and then and allowing him to sleep in his office.

He should have been miserable, but he wasn't. As he walked about the streets in his old clothes I was afraid of him. His eyes were too brilliant. They made me uneasy.

When my parents bought the first of 'the houses,' my father let him sleep in the cellar in return for taking care of the furnace. The cellar of the house was like a gnome's underground home in which I, a mere child, was not small enough nor quick enough to find my way about. When I imagined that I had finally found the door to the way up and out, I had found only the door to another musty labyrinth hung with cobwebs.

One night I accompanied my father and the former doctor to the cellar. My father was to instruct him in the various meanings of the furnace, and then we were to leave him. I came because I seized every chance I could get to come here—with someone, that is. I was afraid to come alone, afraid I might chance upon a gnome scurrying around like a mouse. What should I say to the gnome if I met him? For I was very shy. Only in rash moments when I was angry, and in my thoughts, was I bold. The gnome might be as shy as I was. Therefore, to avoid a mutual embarrassment, I never came without a grown-up. I knew too much about gnomes not to know that they would remain in hiding when one of the people was around. They liked the people as little, and trusted them as little, as I did.

My father had to go out for a minute and I was left alone with the former doctor and his too-brilliant eyes.

I stared at him. I could not take my eyes off his strange appearance. Then—he began to fumble. Oh, I knew that gesture! Hurrying down dark streets, I had seen that gesture made. I had heard voices behind me, telling me to stop and look. I had heard voices calling me from behind every tree on a dark street, it seemed to me, as I hurried, hurried on, but never able to hurry fast enough. The first time I had heard the voices I had stopped and turned my head, all unsuspecting . . . . and I had seen! Ever since, it had always been pursuing me, around corners, from behind trees, but I had escaped it, it had never succeeded in coming close to me again . . . . until now.

Somehow I found the right door up and out.

Was my mother right? Was there only this evilness in the world? Did everything return to it? Could one never get far enough away from it since it might find one even in the gnome's cellar?

The door between the two rooms was closed. Strange sounds were coming from the other room. I lay and listened. My sisters, in the bed with me, were asleep. Stealthily I picked my way over their bodies and put my feet on the floor. I crept to the door. It was open a crack, and, peeping through, I saw my mother, naked except for a short shirt, writhing on the floor. There seemed to be a lot of women there; the room seemed to be full of women, and they were all gathered around my mother on the floor. I recognized the women as being by day store tenders along with their husbands, as my mother was store tender along with my father. I had known them only as store tenders. Now I could hardly recognize them in their role of just women, apart from the counters of their stores. They grouped themselves more closely around my mother and seemed to be trying to get her on the bed, but she was waving them away. I could see the back of my father as he stood by the brass railing of the bed, his arms folded. The room seemed aglare with light, and the light looked strangely hard and forbidding. I began to cry softly. I could not be so brave as my mother, who was writhing without sound on the floor because she did not want to wake up the children in the other room. She rolled on the floor in her soundless agony, to the accompaniment of my soft animal crying which did not reach her. If she had heard me, she would have cried out sharply as was her wont, "Go back to bed, you'll catch cold!" Yes, even in her agony that made her so strangely remote from me, from the two rooms, from the market, she would have scolded me sharply for standing on the floor in my bare feet.

I continued to watch. She seemed to be somewhere else, where all was agony and a fierce bestial struggle, and from that somewhere else she was wearily, impatiently, warding off the efforts of the women to get her on the bed. Let me alone, let me alone, her hands said.

I wasn't sure, but I thought that this was having a baby. This was the aftermath to those pink and white baby clothes in the bureau drawer which I had fingered only this morning. I stared without feeling, without understanding, and therefore without my usual imaginative response to something moving, and then I crept back to bed, to my place near the wall, moving softly over the bodies of my younger sisters so that I should not awaken them. I felt dimly that what I had seen was not for them. Besides, my mother seemed to have enough on her hands without the addition of a pack of frightened children. I was very conscious of being the eldest. Should I tell my mother I had *seen*? No, I must keep a secret. I fell asleep. My last conscious thought was: all would be right in the morning. My mother would be my mother again in the morning. My mother would be her usual sharp self in the morning. Thinking thus, I felt at peace, and what I had just seen was forgotten.

My mother snatching a few minutes from the market to iron clothes in the back room. Her hand, red, swollen from hard work, moved over the white expanse of sheet and pillow-case. After a minute, the rhythm I was watching for came, lifted me. I was sailing, far, far, over my mother, the red swollen hand, the white expanse of sheet; I was flying on the magic carpet of the rhythm, out of the market, away from the market-smell, over the clock in the jail-tower, over the post-office, out into the green, green fields where there was only freedom. Away from authority, away from sharpness, away from the perpetual puzzlement. Mother! Mother! Come! Come with me, Mother! Poor, poor victim. You can't really want to stay here, shackled to the market-smell, shackled to a husband and children. Why do you bow your head? If you do not want to give of yourself, then do not give, mother. What has it all gotten you? You were beautiful once, there is your picture. This is the way the world ends, mother. It ends at night with the market-smell, and in between, your clothes, your thoughts, are never free of the market-smell. See yourself, mother. But you cannot. You are the under-dog. The perspective was given to me, your daughter. It will keep me from being an under-dog like you. Are you working like this so that your children will not be under-dogs? How do I know what is going on in your mind? I think you are less clever than I am because you cannot read or write English. But you have a shrewdness, a tenacity that I cannot help but admire. I long ago realized my father's incompetence, that the whole weight of the market falls on you, that without you it would be nothing.

But—leave it all. Leave him to his fate. You are the lost child crying in the wilderness. *You* are the lost child, not I. I have my hardness, I do not care. And you care, mother. You have given yourself away by your caring. You have let yourself be caught.

What does it all mean, mother? I search for a meaning as I watch you from far away, your red, swollen hand moving over the white expanse of sheet and pillow-case. I would like to come near you, but I am afraid of your voice that is always sharp, always hurried. You have not time to bother, you say. You must go into the market. You leave your dinner half eaten because a customer may be in the market. Or a customer may be on the way, coming, coming. And you must have his money. Do I not know that there are bills to pay? Where are we going to get the money? You almost hate me because I am not bothered by such thoughts, because I do not lie awake half the night worrying over where the money to pay the bills is to be gotten from.

I can only be near to you in secret, as now when there is this rhythm to send shivers up and down my spine, this rhythm that carries me away from the market-smell, that makes all things beautiful and possible—except the market-smell. I hate it! I hate it! It is the most hateful thing in the world. Come, rhythm, come! Hurry, mother, hurry! When the rhythm will come from out of your red, swollen hands, from out of the white sheets, it will carry us away on its magic carpet, away from the market, away from the market-smell.

It was a long time ago. In one half of the barn are the horses stamping in their stalls. In the other half are broken-down buggy bodies, like tired old men who have sunk down at last. They should bury buggy bodies, I think, they look so much like tired old men who have sunk down at last. I turn from the buggy bodies. They make me feel creepy. Even in the daytime I cannot play on them as my sisters do. They do not see the old men, but I do, and I cannot play on the bodies of old men who have sunk down at last.

On the buggy body which looks least like an old man are my father and I. He has put the bags over the heads of the horses, and now that they are quiet, he has come to sit beside me. The door is open and we can see the stars. What are behind the stars? I ask my father. My father does not know. But he can tell me the names of the stars. I think my father wonderful. The horses noisily chew their food. There is a spider's web by the window. I can just make it out in the moonlight. My father and I talk about my favorite subject—a doll supposed to have been left, forgotten, under the bed of the hospital where I was born. Or is it only a dream I have made up to console myself for not having a doll? But my father answers all my breathless questions, so there must have been a doll. A grown-up would not make-believe. My father and I smile at each other, and rock back and forth on the seat, pretending we are riding.

It was a long time ago, but the picture will not leave me. I take it out sometimes and stare at it, not quite believing. I was a nobody then, without individuality, and I had got on well with my father and mother.

Another picture. This time was before the time of the phrase 'home from the market.' Yes, there had been even a time when it was not home from the market, because the market had been in the front room of that little house near the railroad station. It had not been a real market, of course, like the market we had now. Then, there had been only a little meat. Then, my father had scoured the countryside for cows, live ones, and led them home. Now we bought our meat from the packer's, 'dressed meat', as I heard my mother say. I liked the craziness of the phrase. It made me laugh. At unexpected moments I would burst out laughing, thinking of it, the absurdity of it—how could meat be dressed?

Then, too, we had not been as important as we were now. There had been no dressed meat, there had been live meat.

One winter night, my father, who had gone out into the country almost at dawn to get some of this live meat, did not come home. He should have led the live meat home long ago.

My mother, taking me, started out to look for him. We found my father some distance from home where he had fallen, too tired and too cold to go on. The rope was still in his hands, and the cow stood over him, patiently nibbling at the brown grass.

Half carrying him, half dragging him, my mother got my father home. I followed behind them, the halter rope in my hands, the cow sometimes leading me, and myself sometimes leading the cow, depending on the fluctuations of my courage.

I had some bad habits. A perpetual sucking in of the lip, a wrinkling of the nose, a jerking of the shoulders, these were only a few of the bad habits, and they came as regularly as the seasons. Spring brought the itch to wrinkle my nose, summer brought the lip-sucking, winter brought the agonizing jerk, jerk, jerk, of the shoulders. They were visitations of the devil against which I was helpless. I was whipped to within an inch of my life, threatened with being 'sent away', but with no success. I would not, because I could not, stop doing 'those things.' But no one understood that I could not help myself.

Toward the end of winter, I would begin to anticipate the habit for spring; in spring, the habit for summer; in summer, the habit for winter. I was at the mercy of these habits. They made my life a hell.

My mother was constantly asking her women customers for advice about my bad habits, and the advice was usually to give me a whipping, which I duly received, but it did no good.

It was my birthday. There was, wonder of wonders! a box for me, just come by express, my father said. Everybody gathered around while I tore off the wrappings. At last I opened the package. In it was a pair of my father's old shoes. It was considered a good joke, and at the expression on my face, everybody roared with laughter. Blindly, obeying my instinctive impulse, I threw the heavy shoes into my father's face.

"I wish you were dead, I wish you were dead," I cried. "Damn you, damn you, you dirty Jew. I hate you. I'll run away."

"I want this side of the bed."

"You give it to me or I'll tell Ma. . . ."

"Oh, shut up! You tell and I'll hit you. Have your old side of the bed. I don't want it."

"Now will you do it?" . . . .

"Who's that coming? Ma? Quick, put out the light. . . . Make believe we're asleep."

"It wasn't anybody. . . . Anyway, let's play something else. Let's get the high-heeled shoes and make believe we're grown-up. When I'm grown-up, I'm going to wear high-heeled shoes all the time, and long dresses. What'll you be when you're grown-up?"

"Rich man, poor man, beggar man, thief; doctor, lawyer, merchant, chief . . ."

"I'm not going to be any of those. I'm going to write books."

"What's Providence the capital of?"

"What does three times four times six divided by three equal?"

"You've got to let Ma braid my hair first tomorrow or I'll tell . . ."

I'll tell . . . I'll tell. . . . We do not know why we think so, but we sense that it is a terrible thing. We never speak about it during the day, but at night we return to it stealthily. We use the exposure of it as a threat. . . . I'll tell . . . I'll tell . . . Life in the two rooms at the end of a dirty hallway, after my mother has put us to bed and gone downstairs to the market again. Perhaps it is Saturday night. I can imagine what the market is on Saturday night. I am attracted to the color and movement of the market on Saturday night. How I wish I was there. I am a little tired of the secret pleasures of childhood. . . . Why do I have to go to bed so early? . . . . I am going on twelve. . . .

I have what seems to me periods of childishness when I play with my younger sisters' dolls. They are not really dolls. Sometimes my mother will leave her thoughts of the market long enough to take a big handkerchief and after various foldings it will become a little old lady with a shawl around her head. She had no face, of course. Our imagination must supply the face, must put in the features in their right places. It was better than a doll with one set face. Yet— how I would have loved a doll like those I had seen other girls have, the dolls I had seen in store windows. But there was no money for dolls, my mother said. All the money went for more 'dressed meat.'

Since there is now no 'home from the market,' I do not go so often past the river and the marble house with the pillars. When I do go down that way, I do not stop so frequently to peer down at the river and distinguish each separate stone. The marble house no longer haunts me. I no longer spend hours around the station. Instead, I have a dress with a sash. The sash enchants me. It is the sash season. I tie and untie my sash, and turn and turn before the mirror. I love the bouquet the tied ends make, a bouquet that rests gently on my behind, a bouquet that bounces up and down on my behind when I walk. I even have a yellow dress with black velvet ribbons running down the front. In the trunk in the room behind the market is a pink satin dress somehow acquired. It is to be made over for me. It never was, but I got more than enough out of the pink satin dress, dreaming over it, seeing myself in it. I finger the pink satin lovingly. I have a pair of patent leather slippers. I have everything seemingly, and yet I have nothing because I am fat. Being fat spoils everything.

I am fat. No one has told about the misery of a fat child. A grown-up knows about diets, exercise. If he has any willpower, he does not have to remain fat. But a child! All a child can do is to remain fat. Because I could not wear ready-made dresses like my sisters, I had fewer dresses. I must wait until my mother finds the time to make a dress for me on the machine.

My father loved to taunt me about my fatness. It was his cruelest and surest weapon, for he knew that I was sensitive about being fat. The depths of my hatred for him. . . . Which did I hate most, my father or my mother? I could not decide. But I, too, had my weapon. Dirty Jew . . . dirty Jew. . . . Why did they appear to hate me so, my father and mother? I knew the answer. Because I was not docile like my sisters, who accepted the parental authority without question; because of my individuality which they called disobedience and selfishness. Because I had my nose stuck in a book when I should have been minding the baby—how I hated the successive babies! What right had my mother to push them on to me to take care of after they were born? Because—there were a hundred other things.

They did not like my friendship with the lawyer over the market. He gave me books to read, and let me learn to type on his typewriter. Time after time I was whipped for going to his office, but it never stopped me. They hate you because you are a gentleman in spite of all the drink, I would think, looking at the lawyer. They aren't gentle-people.

We talked about our favorite book characters, Buffalo Bill, Young Wild West, Nick Carter, The Gray Phantom. I had become as rabid a reader of detective stories and wild west stories as he was. After he had finished reading the paper books and magazines, he passed them on to me. He spent money on them that he should have spent on clothes and food. Sometimes he talked to me about a poet called William Blake. Meanwhile, the law books on his shelves grew dustier and dustier.

Even more than the library, the lawyer's office was my retreat and my escape from the market-smell and my parents. The lawyer could talk my talk, almost. But the antennæ my mind put out met no antennæ come half way. I realized it. I could find no real friend even in the lawyer. It was not the almost forty years difference that separated us, nor yet the difference in up-bringing. I realized beyond those chasms. But the lawyer could not come up to where I was.

Still, we could meet. It was a great deal to have some place to go, even if I must pay for it afterward in humiliation and tears; even if I must listen to my mother trying to draw me into her net of evilness again.

I took the books off the shelves in the lawyer's office, the books that hid behind the law books. Unfamiliar names were on the covers, Swinburne, Coleridge, Shakespeare, the Bible, the William Blake he talked about. I did not dare take them home for fear they would be thrown over the refrigerator, or into the stove. No, I did not dare. I read them in the office, laying them down on the table heaped with legal documents, pipes, Nick Carters, Buffalo Bills, burnt matches. After I had read them, I put them back and returned to the latest Nick Carter.

The lawyer, a figure in black, relieved only by the white hair, would sit in his huge rocking chair and smoke and read Nick Carter. He paid no attention while I read or used up his best paper learning to type. The typewriter usually needed a new ribbon, needed a new ribbon very much. Why did I not say to him, I who always spoke my thoughts aloud, "Why don't you buy a new ribbon, Mr. Angel?" But I was silent. I too could be silent. My delicacy could not match his, perhaps, but humbly I did not see the drunkard, the dirty curtains that divided the office from the part where the bed was; did not see the bed that was seldom made, that always showed dirty sheets and pillow-cases, and a blanket that was insufficient protection against the cold.

I kept my eyes on his fingers and head, and did not see, or passed over as being without meaning, the blurred eyes, the twitching mouth. For was he not Mr. Angel, the lawyer? All the rest of the people in the town were just the people, but he was himself. He had individuality. He could not equal that something in me, but in other ways he was my superior, and my father's superior. Sneer as my father would behind Mr. Angel's back, to his face he was always respectful. Yes, he was superior to my father, and that was why my father sneered.

In every new grade that I entered there were boys and girls who had been 'kept back,' as it was called, boys and girls who had failed to pass onward and upward with their own class, and who were now forced to sit, isolated, strange, sullen, among boys and girls younger than themselves. They could not adapt themselves to us, and we could not adapt ourselves to them. Sometimes, from boredom at doing the same work over again, they dropped out in a few months and went to work in the mills. There was shame on their side, and not a little contempt for their 'failure' on our side. Two or three in every class, they generally took no part in the social activities of the new class. The new class did not want these failures, these outsiders, and neither did their own class, the class from which they had been dropped.

Yet there was something disturbing about them. We could not wholly ignore them. They were generally three or four years older than we were. If they were boys they wore long pants while the boys in our own class still wore short ones; if they were girls they wore their hair up—some even had 'rats' in their hair—while the girls of our class still had pig-tails or bobbed hair.

But it was more than physical differences. We felt that they were concerned with different things, things other than our chief concern in life. School work for example. The ever-interesting question, "did you do your homework?" did not interest them. We would not have gone up to them and asked them such a question.

In my class were two girls and a boy who had been kept back. The boy was very pretty, almost girlish in the fairness of his skin and the silkiness of his hair. His body was soft and rounded and slender like a girl's. He was different from the boys I had heretofore seen, boys who were virile creatures and prided themselves on their virility, boys who boasted of their prowess in games, who attended the Y gym regularly, who considered that the greatest thing that could happen to them was to be noticed by the coach. But this boy did not talk about such things, did not even think of them, I guessed. He did not care for the Y and the gym and the coach. He even had for a name one that I had thought only girls had—Francis. It fitted him as no other name would have fitted him.

There were always secret glances passing between Francis and the two girls who had been kept back with him. The girls, who sat in the front of the room, sat with their bodies always half turned toward the back of the room where Francis sat. Sitting near the three of them, I was made use of as an emissary to pass notes to Francis from the girls.

I sat so near them that I heard the whispers.

"'Member last night, Francis?" one of the girls whispered down the aisle to him.

Francis would raise his eyebrow and smile. His smile was as sweet as a girl's—more sweet than a girl's. I had never seen so sweet, so winsome, a smile.

They did not seem to mind that *we* heard. They guessed rightly that we would not half understand the implications of their words.

It was the two girls who ran after Francis, not Francis after the two girls, I saw. He never wrote a note to them. He sat in his seat, spending the school hours smiling willingly at them, but never sending a note, nor replying verbally; only with his sweet smile that might say so much, and again that might have said nothing.

"Francis, will you meet me tonight?"

"Francis, it's *my* turn. You went out with Marion last night."

"*Will* you, Francis?"

"Do you like my hair like this, Francis? I did it for you. I burned my thumb awfully singeing my hair so it would be curly."

Francis smiled his sweet girl's smile, mischievous at the corners.

I fell in love with him. I did not dare look at him. I would have died before bringing myself to take the liberties with him that the two girls took. I did not even look at him as I passed their notes on without a word, not minding if they were interrupting me.

Each night I looked forward to the next day when I would be near him.

He was not clever. But I did not scoff at him as I scoffed, safe in my own high marks, at the others who were not as smart or as quick as I was. I could not judge Francis by such elementary standards as a quickness in arithmetic or grammar or spelling. That he was dull made him all the more charming—and all the more different from me. What need had such a marvellous being to be smart? That was for heavy people like me who could not shine otherwise.

I sat in my seat without turning and listened to confidences whispered by the girls to Francis. Some were so naked that I, brought up in the atmosphere of the market where life was as raw as the meat on the hooks, could not help but understand. Last night . . . a meeting somewhere, and now the memory of it made the drudgery of the school-day lighter. Dimly I realized it. They knew another world, a world entirely different from the world I knew. Francis and the two girls were tasting of the forbidden fruit. They had climbed the tree, while the rest of us in the class were plodding at the tree's trunk, counting the roots that spread and spread and would never be done spreading. This was called arithmetic, and we were told that we must do this first. It was boring! Boring! Francis and the two girls had finished with all the drudgery of this counting, if indeed they had ever bothered to begin it. They were higher creatures.

Francis was a forbidden fruit himself, the apple that hung highest on the tree, out of reach, bigger, sweeter, more tempting, than all the other apples. The girls came seeking it again and again, trying to get it for their very own. Yes, they wanted Francis. They wanted to capture for their very own that sweet lovely smile which held all the lightness, all the summer of the world, which had the power to make the world into something other than the common thing it was. To walk with Francis down a dark, endless street—but endless!—this was what they were hungry for. This was what would lighten the drudgery of the school-day, the drudgery of life. They could not have enough of him. They scorched their hair until each separate hair assumed strange agonized postures, to make themselves beautiful for him, to win a smile from him, to be able to say, "I burned my thumb for you, Francis . . ." To win a smile from him, an empty smile, I knew with my awful clearsightedness, but what of it? There was nothing back of the lovely blue eyes, but what of that too? He was halfway into another world. Who went with him would be taken halfway into that other world, a more beautiful world than this. I loved him, and I despised the plodding virility of the other boys, despised myself.

I had no thought of making him look at me. But sometimes when I 'spelled down' the whole class and looked to him for a tiny spark of admiration, I did not receive it. He might be looking, instead, out of the window. It was but right that he should look out of the window and be faintly bored.

Such a lovely creature, such a lovely bright thing . . . I held my breath. Could such a lovely thing last? I had a curious fatalism. A lovely thing never lasted. I was afraid for all lovely things. I knew in me that they did not last. All the hard and sordid and everyday and common things lasted, but not the lovely things. Perhaps it was better so.

Autumn went by and winter came. For a week Francis did not come to school. There were rumors that he was sick. Then one day the teacher announced that Francis had died, of pneumonia.

Perhaps one night when he had been out walking with one of the girls he had caught the cold that developed into pneumonia.

A little later the two girls left school to go to work in the mills.

Christmas meant a great deal to the Americans, but nothing to the Jews. The others in my family might escape the Christmas influence, but not I. As the weeks approached to Christmas, I became as intoxicated with the Christmas spirit in the air as any American. Why could we not have a tree, hang up our stockings? I asked my mother, although I knew just the expression her face would assume when I asked her one of my crazy questions. I would find no help in that direction. I determined to go about it myself.

We could not have a tree of course, for we did not have a house. We had only two rooms crowded with beds. But I could hang stockings on the chairs. The money with which to buy the gifts? There was no use in asking my parents, so I got it in the usual way. There was all the cunning of the world in my head, all I knew of cunning and slyness learned from the people around me as I watched them in their markets, their grocery stores, their clothing stores, doing 'business' and becoming prosperous, buying property. I had learned their methods for getting what they wanted—except that my method was cleaner, straighter, saner. I went straight to the mark—'stole it,' they called it—while they went to all sorts of hideously cunning and twisted ways to get it. By my method I kept my self-respect and they lost theirs, or should have lost it. How could one prostitute oneself so, abase oneself so? A child of my environment, I turned their methods on themselves (with that secret difference by which I kept self-respect) and did not understand their outcry of 'thief! thief!'

When I got the money I hurried to the five-and-ten-cent store. What I bought I hid away—no mean feat when there are only two rooms and a swarm of sisters ready to 'tell Ma' of any lapse from righteousness—until the night before Christmas when I filled the stockings.

I was a crazy fool. I saw it in my parents' eyes, and I saw it in the eyes of my sisters who were always quick to follow my parents' example. They could not see Christmas. They could not see the attempt toward a something. They made fun of the stockings and of the cheap toys. The spirit of other worlds meant nothing to them. They were tight in their own world.

My eyes and ears were wide open, more wide open than their eyes and ears were, and more attuned to other possible worlds, worlds other than the world of the market, the world of the Jew, the tight narrow world that we moved around in. It was I who brought home new ideas, and never received thanks for the trouble. Nevertheless, I continued to bring them home. My eyes and ears were full of the things they had seen and heard, new things, and I wanted to incorporate these new things in my home. My efforts were not appreciated. Even so, I could play with the new ideas in my own mind. In my own mind, I lived in those other worlds, the worlds away from the market, the market-smell, dirty Jew, the two rooms upstairs . . . a world where there was privacy, where people did not come too close to one without first asking, a world where people listened gravely to crazy ideas.

Mixed in with my hatred of my father was shame. I looked at him with the eyes of the Americans. He was a ridiculous figure. He did not dress well, he was not clean shaven, he had a beard, a thick growth of hair covered his face. Yes, he was ridiculous compared with the American men, who all looked alike, who did not stand out. I wanted that kind of a father.

One time in school each pupil had been told to give the Christian name of his father. The teacher had wished to distinguish for us the difference between Christian name and surname. As the pupils gave their 'William' or 'Fred' or 'George' or 'John,' I crouched in my seat, red with shame and misery. Soon it would be my turn to tell my father's Christian name, and it was not William or Fred or George or John. It was a Jewish name. How I longed for a father who was a William or a Fred or a George or a John. Now I would have to say his name aloud before thirty boys and girls.

"And now your father's Christian name?" the teacher asked me.

I sat dumb. The world held no greater misery than what I was experiencing at this moment with the teacher and the thirty pairs of eyes looking at me. They knew! They knew my secret! They knew why I wouldn't tell my father's name. The thirty pairs of eyes were full of malice and a monkey kind of enjoyment. They knew! Safe with their Williams and Freds and Georges and Johns, they knew why I would give no answer. Damn them! Damn them! Had no one any mercy? Why had I to say it? My soul cried out against saying it.

"Tell your father's Christian name or I'll call the principal," said the teacher.

"I don't know," I said.

A shout of laughter went up from the thirty boys and girls. She didn't know her own father's name! Hadn't they shouted it at me often enough? Well, after school I would have another opportunity to learn it, the thirty pairs of eyes said.

"I won't say it," I said silently to the teacher. "Not all the principals in the world can make me say it."

Why didn't my mother dress like other mothers, go out like other mothers? My mother never went out. She was chained to the market and the sort of uniform she wore in it. It was a round, shapeless apron covering her dress. She put on a clean apron every day. Sometimes she put on a dust-cap. All her vanity, all her coquetry went into the dust-cap. She would pause before the mirror to put it on, and let a few wisps of hair peep out over the ears. Now she was ready to lift forequarters and sides of beef as other women had need to lift only their babies. Now she was ready to saw through bones, and cut through flesh, to disembowel pigs and cows as other women had need only to clean out chickens. Now she was ready to enter the ice-cold refrigerator and grasp ice-cold meat.

Now she was ready to scrape the blocks with that long hard stroke that took her whole body, that used up her whole body. Now she was ready to scrape the blocks clean until their whiteness was a thing to marvel at when one remembered that ten minutes before they had been brown with caked blood. She must clean the blocks every day and there were four blocks, four long blocks, clean the blocks every day with that peculiar wired brush. Every day the blocks must be cleaned and the floor swept and fresh sawdust sprinkled over the floor. She took pride in her white blocks, in her fresh saw-dust floors, as other women take pride in their homes.

I hated my father. Why did he let my mother do these things? Why didn't he clean the blocks himself? Why didn't he sweep the market himself? Why did he lean over the counter by the cash register and read the Jewish paper most of the time? Why did he let my mother lift sides of beef from the hook? Why didn't he do it himself? I conceived a hatred for Jewish men. Jews let their women-folk work for them. American men were different.

And all the time life went on beneath my mother's market uniform. Life was created, nourished in the misshapen belly, delivered in one of the beds upstairs. A week later, she was back in the market.

"And nobody guessed it," she would say gleefully to Mis' Levretts.

The problem not to create life, the fear that there would be another baby, made her tone sharp.

Mis' Levretts and my mother talking. I listen, sitting on a cracker box and pretending to do my arithmetic while they talk. My mother in the attitude she loves, by the cash register, her arms folded over her stomach, and Mis' Levretts standing in front of her with the package of meat she has just bought.

Mis' Levretts gives my mother a little box.

"Try this. A woman up the mill told me about it. I've been using it."

I watch where my mother puts the box away and then when she is not around I look to see what is in it. But I can make nothing of the little bullet-shaped pieces that look like soap, nor can I puzzle out for what it is to be used.

My mother was the boss. She kept my father going when he, like so many Jews of his type, would have wished to sit back and drink endless glasses of tea and discuss the Talmud with another Jew. She was no spectator of life, but a fighting materialist. She gloried in battles. She loved the very smell of the market, the contacts with the people, the bargaining. All these she tasted with a gusto that was like no other gusto. It was almost like a meat gusto, a market gusto, a market gusto that is like no other gusto.

The market was my mother's parlor. Here, after the meat had been weighed and wrapped up and paid for, she held her chats with the customers who were all her friends. Friends, although she never went to their houses, and never met them any place except in the market. She knew everything about them. There was little that she did not know.

Especially were the foreigners her friends, the new immigrants, the Polaks and the Germans. For the Polaks, she alone kept the spiced bologna that they loved. She alone in the town could speak with them in their own language, learned over the counter. What could she not speak, I wondered sometimes, as I listened to unintelligible gibberish. She spoke Polish with the Poles who could not speak even the broken English of their kind yet. She spoke German to the Germans. She was even beginning to learn Italian. And she spoke a better English than my father.

It was to her that the salesmen from the meat packers and the wholesale grocers paid deference, kow-towed to. It was to her that they went for their orders and not to my father. When one of them came and found my father alone in the market, my father would say, "I'll call my wife," and send one of the children for her.

My mother came and immediately the market was a different place. The market had color and life once more. When she put her left foot forward in a particular way she had, and her right hand met the salesman's outstretched hand, we children crowded around her, happy and excited because mother was obviously enjoying herself.

The salesmen knew her. They knew her hunger for a little flattery. They knew just the right things to say, about the dust-cap, perhaps, or the roses that sometimes shown in her cheeks. My mother, only a few years over thirty, looked years older. Her eyes were tired, her cheeks sagged, her body was ungainly. Nevertheless, she was still susceptible to flattery. It was as if a little flattery could eradicate the tired eyes, the sagging cheeks, the ungainly body, and she was young again, young in body and spirit. If a salesman could provoke a pleased smile, it meant a larger order for him.

I could not dissociate my mother from the market, and the market could not have existed without her personality. I could not see my mother walking along the street, carefree, as I saw other women doing. My mother would never be carefree; she bore the weight of the market wherever she went. She would never be free of that weight.

The day when my father announced that he had bought a house. A house! A house! Now we could live like other people. But I soon discovered that it was not a house for us. It had once been a one-family house, but had been converted into apartments. My father and mother subsequently converted the apartments into flats. As for ourselves, we were to continue our life in the room back of the market and the two rooms upstairs. We have a house now but it really makes no difference. It does not affect *us*.

I walk with my mother to the house. It seems to me the most beautiful house I have ever seen, surpassed only by the marble house. It has three porches and big bay windows. I am in awe of those windows, windows that reach from the floor to the ceiling.

My mother goes into the house with her usual boldness. I envy her. She is afraid of nothing. I have refused to go in with her. I hover outside, instead. After a while I feel a little courage creeping through me. I want to go up and firmly grasp the door knob and turn it—but when I opened the door, whom might I not see? Would I find myself in a hall or in a roomful of people? For there are people living in the house. My father has bought the people in the house as well as the house.

But such a house would have a hallway, the hallway of my dreams. A hallway where you took off your things, where you coughed a little to announce your presence, where you made little noises, shuffling noises with your feet, where you hung up your things instead of flinging them wildly on a chair . . . such a house would most certainly have a hallway. Nevertheless, I am afraid of the unknown and I do not dare go farther than the porch.

My father bought the house, but it was my mother who paid for it. She it was who schemed to get the money when the interest on the mortgages fell due. She it was who sent my father out to find money. It was by her efforts that the house, and then the other houses, continued to belong to us. Time and time again it seemed as if the banks would have foreclosed except for her will.

We were growing prosperous. This was prosperity, then. My mother working harder than ever, my mother with a perpetual line between her eyes, her voice sharper and sharper. I could almost see my mother working herself to death.

I remembered that time, long long ago, when we had had just the little market on that little back street near the railroad station. My mother had not had to work hard in the market. She had had time to go for walks with us children. My father had gone too, sometimes. My mother had a serge dress. It had seemed to me the most marvellous dress in the world. It had a collar of lace, and there was a brooch in front. There were no lines in my mother's face. Her figure was plump and rounded, not heavy and misshapen. It had not been difficult for her to walk then—the days when she was daily to lift forequarters and sides of beef and finally rupture herself were still in the future, along with our prosperity. She could walk then, walk as freely and as lightly as the small hopping things beside her. We children were proud of her. We adored her. We sang the American songs we had learned in school to her. We basked in her admiration. We did the best we could to bring home the highest marks. There had been time for laughter then, and walking through the park on summer nights. Now my mother never left the market before midnight, year in and year out, and when she left it, it was only to climb the stairs wearily to the two rooms at the end of the dirty hallway. We had been poor then, I supposed, although that had meant nothing to us children, as our prosperity meant nothing to us now. We had always had enough to eat, and there had been cloth for my mother to make herself and ourselves dresses.

This prosperity, this house that had just been bought, what did they bring us? We were not so happy as when we had 'nothing.' My mother and father were no longer our friends and companions, we were aliens. We did not even speak the same language any more.

In that little market, we had been so happy! There was the buggy and the boy next door who would drive it for us. Often, on Saturday afternoon—Saturday afternoon, the busiest day in the week!—my mother and the children would drive into the country to a farm house where there was a phonograph. We would all sit around the phonograph and listen admiringly to the music. The lady of the farm house would change the disc again and again. Sometimes our mother changed the disc and then we would admire her with all our souls. Imagine being able to put the thing on, round and shiny, that made the wonderful music.

Sometimes our mother's elder sister would come to visit us. She was older and more tired-looking than our mother, who was young. She was not so well off as we were, we understood impressively. She had no market as we had. She had no horse and buggy, either. There may have been a touch of patronization in our mother's attitude as she took her sister for a drive through the town. We children sat on the back seat, our feet only halfway to the floor, and listened while our mother described the sights of the town. Wasn't she wonderful! In our passionate admiration at the fluency of her description—mixed in with a good deal of imagination, for she was a first-rate story teller and knew as well as anyone that reality is only something to build on—we almost fell out of the buggy.

There was that time when we had all gone to visit my mother's sister in her home. We had had to ride on the train to get there. Was it my first train ride? I could not be sure. I had taken so many train rides in my dreams.

My aunt's house was not as lovely as ours. It did not have a toilet in the house as ours at home had. You had to go out to a little house all by itself in back of the lived-in house. Once I lost a brand new shiny penny there and I cried the whole day.

It seemed to me now that we had all been terribly innocent then, my father, my mother, as well as we children. My mother and father had been the most terribly innocent of all.

Wonder of wonders, the market was to be sold. Why? I asked myself. Perhaps it was the competition of the chain stores. My mother told her customers that she was no longer able to do the hard work. Perhaps it was that. Perhaps the rupture that came and went was already making life a hell for her.

I was too young to realize the immensity of the change. I saw my mother sitting on a box in the market, in the midst of her ruins— the cans of groceries from the shelves taken down and spread on the floor. They were to be sold by the lot. Miss Bottome bought most of them for her boarding house.

My mother sat on the box looking across the street. What was she thinking? What were her thoughts? She was leaving this place after eight years. She had given all her young-womanhood to it. It had made an old woman of her at thirty-five. The hooks where the beef hung were empty now. The days when they had been so full, each hook with its side of beef or pork. And the gesture, the magnificent gesture with which my mother had taken a side or a forequarter from the hook and flung it on a block and dissected it. The sure thrust of her knife—as if she knew just where the knife would go—into the belly of a cow or a pig yet to be disemboweled. The swarming intestines dropping into the pail she held ready as she worked with her knife, the warm cloud of air issuing from the newly disemboweled belly of a pig. Once, hovering behind her as she slit the belly of a cow, I had seen a tiny calf, no bigger than a baby, hanging in the cow.

My mother could do all these things better than a man could, better than my father could. What other woman in town could do such things? The men had admitted her to their conclaves as an equal. She had proved her ability to be one of them. The whole town knew her. The whole town was entered in her Ledger. She knew everybody by name. She was a friend—if always with business, good business in her mind, for she was a business man first— she was a friend of the Poles and the Germans who had no other friend in the town.

But now she was going to give up the market. She was going to live on the rents from the house, the big house, as we called it. My father had bought a little house for ourselves, a little six-room house that connected with the big house by an alley. But even that we were not to have alone. Some of the rooms in the little house were to be rented. We could not afford to have the whole house to ourselves.

My mother sat on the box in the market. Now and then her hand went to her side with a now familiar gesture. That was where the rupture was, we knew fearfully, although not knowing exactly what a rupture was. But the word itself was terrible enough. Not a forequarter of beef, nor yet a can of some grocery, would my mother take away as a remembrance of her market days. No. Her souvenir would be the rupture.

We must be really prosperous, I decided, if we could give up the market and the market-smell, but why did prosperity include ruptures? And why did my mother look as she did, almost as if the world had come to an end. Then my mother's courage came back and she told me sharply to go into the back room. What was I doing in the market? It was cold. Go back where it's warm.

I was always in the market. I thought I hated it, but it had a fascination for me. I hated the colorless homeness of the two rooms upstairs with their beds and bureaus, and the room in back of the market. I was drawn to the color of the market, to the people coming and going, always coming and going, always new people. Why, anything could happen in the market, and usually did, and I wanted to be there when it happened. I was afraid of missing something. When I sat in the back room and minded the baby, I would think of the market, and of the things, *live* things, that were happening. I fidgeted and hated the baby for making me miss those things. What might not be happening this very minute, I would think.

To go into the market, to smell the clean, raw market-smell which I hated for its tenacity, which I hated because it had attached itself to me and would not let go, but which nevertheless I knew and recognized as I would never know and recognize anything else. The market-smell! The smell of the market! A smell that was like nothing else. A smell that was alive, that had taken its peculiarly pungent alive-smell from the dead meat on the hooks; as though the dead meat were oozing its last life-smell into the market room. The whole market was permeated with that life-smell. And I was drawn to it. Except when my mother was rendering lard in the back room. Then I remained away altogether. I could not stand it. My mind retched, as well as my stomach.

Sometimes on Saturday nights when the market was particularly full, I was allowed to put on an apron and help. But I was more of a nuisance than a help, getting in everybody's way. Finally, I would take off the apron and sit down on a box and watch the way my mother managed a market full of waiting impatient customers with her words and her smiles—she always had smiles for her customers, if for us she had only sharp words. And my father would follow her up with his deep laugh.

On Saturday nights my father would raise the register top frequently to see how much had been sold. If it was a 'good Saturday,' it meant a pair of shoes for somebody. That was why we children loved Saturday nights. We did our own shopping for the shoes. The shoe store was next door and we hurried over and got several pairs of shoes and brought them back for mother to pass on. We were as anxious as my father that it should be a 'good Saturday.'

Leave the market . . . leave the market. . . . No more delivering bundles before school, no more sobbing all the way to the house where I was to deliver the package of meat because I was afraid I would be late to school. No more of that. No more hearing the cold ring of the cash register. Why did even the cash register take on the personality of the market, become permeated with the market? The cash register in the drug store, in the shoe store, in the clothing store, had a different kind of sound, a warm sound. Our cash register rang out coldly, metallically. And no wonder, I would think, hearing its harsh sound even in the back room above the cries of the baby. It had stood for years in the market, a market that was always cold, winter and summer. The drug store was warm in winter. Why could not markets have stoves and warmth as well as other kinds of stores? Then my mother's hands would not always be blue-purple in winter, and she would always not be coughing half the time.

We are having dinner in the back room. Suddenly we hear a ring. It is the trick door bell. Someone has come in. My mother says to me, "Go and see who it is." I desire nothing better. I get up and run into the market.

I am back of the counter. What do you want, I say. I do not say, as my mother says, "What can I do for you today?", because

I cannot smile as she smiles, and those words unaccompanied by her smile are empty, meaningless.

My ambition is to make a sale all by myself. But all I can sell is frankfurts, for that is the only thing that is already cut. Will the customer ask for frankfurts? I wonder hopefully. Or will I have to call my mother as usual? Ah, if only I can make a sale by myself! But—I lift my voice to call my mother. The customer wants a steak, and a steak necessitates the using of a knife and saw to cut it off the hind-quarter. I am worse than useless when it comes to handling the knife and saw. Besides, they are so fierce-looking that I am afraid of them.

Too, I have another weakness. I cannot make change. My younger sister can do it better than I. I can make change in my head. I am the best arithmetic pupil in my grade in school and we have been taught how to make change with paper coins. I can do that very well. But when it comes to making change in real money, something goes wrong. I get too excited, and invariably give the customer back too much. The customer is usually honest and points out my mistake. But I am afraid of what will happen when my father hears of this. I am afraid of his sneers and of his "you fool."

Leaving the market . . . leaving the market . . . I think of the many times when I have stared at a clot of blood on the newly sown saw-dust. Nothing could possibly be as bright red as new blood. They have just brought in a freshly killed cow, or perhaps it is a pig, and there is a trail of bright red blood from the door to the hooks where the cow or pig has been hung to await disemboweling at the hands of my mother. In a half hour the bright red will be bright red no longer. It will be dark red.

My mother tells me to take a pail of saw-dust and sprinkle some over the trail of blood. The trail of blood is hidden now, but not for me. I know just where it is under the sawdust. I know just where it is. I could point it out for you, if you asked me. I restrain myself from shouting to my mother, "Ma, ask me where the blood is! I know!" You can't wipe out blood. All the saw-dust in the world will not wipe out blood. I know where it is.

We have a cat. All markets have cats, of course. The name of our cat is Daisy. We have had her since time began for us children. Daisy was forever having kittens. The kittens killed themselves almost as fast as they were born by drinking up the saucer of fly-poison which they probably mistook for milk. But Daisy survived always to have more kittens. Daisy was made of sterner stuff than her kittens. She had grown tough fighting the market rats.

I walk to the market. It is a cold, cold day. No day could be colder. I look at the windows of the market. They have been made opaque by the frost. I cannot see even the posters that sometimes hang high up in the windows, announcing a show.

I go in the market, and instantly I am closed in. There is no other world than the market. The opaque windows shut me in. There is no way out. I feel a little choked, and I want to run out again, but my mother has caught sight of me and that means I cannot slip out again. I am in for a whipping or a scolding because I am late. I should have come straight home from school to mind the baby. Instead, I have gone to a girl's house. I love to go to other girls' houses because it means glimpses into other worlds. It is not often that I become friendly enough with a girl to go to her house. Who would play with me? And if a girl offers me her house, I cannot offer her my house because I have no house to offer. But this girl is a new girl. She does not know perhaps that I am a Jew. She does not know of the market, perhaps. So she has taken me to her house.

I won't go into the back room as my mother orders me to. I sit on a box of crackers and stare at the opaque windows. I am safe while there are customers in the market. My mother will not make a scene before them, so I am safe until they go. She glares at me, but I continue to sit on the cracker box. I have an uneasy suspicion that my father is in the back room, and I am afraid to be alone with him. He has a terrible temper. He becomes insane at times. My mother knows when to stop in her beatings, but he does not. If my mother did not interfere when she thinks I have had enough. . . . Once he has almost killed me. I cry out. My mother comes running and tells him what has happened to a Jew across the way who whipped his son . . . the policeman has come. And my father stops hitting me with his arms. He is afraid of the police. My father is a bully, but he is afraid of the police.

So I remain sitting here on the box with my mother's glare on me, and stare at the opaque windows. There is no way out, the opaque windows say. I feel shut in, closed in upon, as my mother will close in upon me when the customers have gone. There is no way out through that opaque. I hate the market when the windows are like that. I must have windows through which I can see, out out out. . . . I must have freedom.

I do not wonder any more why I am beaten so much. I accept it as belonging to the blind order of everything, the fate of childhood, of belonging to child-dom. Perhaps my mother sees in me what I am not yet conscious of myself. She is trying to drive it out with her beatings. But she cannot. No one can, whatever it is that she sees.

I think of the subscriptions that were to get for me the automobile racer for children. They have not trusted me after that. When I am sent to the bank on Saturday mornings to change a ten- or a twenty-dollar bill into little packages of nickels and dimes and quarters, they carefully count the nickels and dimes and quarters to see if I have stolen any. They hide all the money from me. I want to tell them . . . but I do not know what it is that I want to tell them. So I say nothing. But I am very conscious of this atmosphere of distrust and suspicion.

Other girls have 'allowances.' In school, they brag of their allowance. I have no allowance. I have never had an allowance. I never will have one, so, as I must have money even at twelve, I evoke all my cunning and slyness to get the nickels and dimes I feel I must have to buy candy, to go to the movies, which, like the lawyer's office and the library, is an escape from the market.

I stare at the opaque windows and think what it would be like to have a father and mother who are Americans, who understand about allowances. Then I would not have to steal, as they call it.

In one of the two rooms upstairs my baby brother is being circumcised. There is a doctor there, and there are a great many Jews whom I arrange in my mind as the owners of the various shoe and clothing stores around the market.

The rooms have been rearranged. All the beds have been put in one room. The other room has a table with wine on it, and the chairs and the piano. My mother is in the room where the beds are. I want her to come out into the other room. I want her to taste the wine. Has she not made it herself, after midnight, after the market is closed? Why then should she not come and taste it? Why should my father be the fêted one? My mother has not only made the wine, but she has also made the baby. Why then does she hover in the bedroom away from the light and the laughter? My hatred for my father deepens. I would like to say to him . . . I would like to say so much to him that I can say nothing. I would like to say to him . . . but I give it up. I can only nurse my hatred for him. This was a world for men, apparently. Are all men like my father? I wonder. Not American men, I am sure. American men are different. It is only Jews who let their wives work in ice-cold markets, who let their wives lift sides of beef until they rupture themselves. It is only Jews who sit in front while their wives sit in back. I want my mother to come out in the other room where the feasting is going on. Why does she hover in the background? She it was who has been so sick not long ago, who has had to stay in bed for two weeks, not my father. But the way they are acting toward my father, you would think . . . And my father accepts it all as his right. Damn him! Damn him! I will not marry a Jew. Never! Never! I will marry an American. I would not marry a Jew if he was the last man on earth. Somewhere I have acquired a strong sense of the ethics of living, and I know that the way my mother works is wrong, wrong.

But my mother waits anxiously in the other room. There is a strained look on her face, as if she is listening for something. She asks me what they are doing with the baby. She is anxious about the baby. She is afraid that perhaps they will drop it, that it will roll off its pillow. There is a terribly anxious look on her face.

Suddenly it comes. A cry. My mother's face seems to break into little pieces. It is a cry from my baby brother. They have done something to him. What they have done I do not know, except that it involves having a doctor. I sense that my mother has been waiting for this cry. I see the cry go through her. I see her body shake, echoing to the cry. My baby brother does not know why he has cried. Has he felt any pain? My mother feels his pain for him. She would rush to him, take him away from those men, I can see from her face. But she restrains herself. She walks up and down the room, her face in little pieces.

Sometimes we keep chickens in back of the market. Then I must go to the grist-mill to buy feed.

The grist-mill is a wonderful place. On the ground floor I go to a cage where a man is and tell him what I want. He writes out an order for me which I must present to the man upstairs.

Upstairs. But to get to the second story I must ascend a flight of stairs, the slipperiest flight of stairs I have ever walked up. I am afraid every minute that I will slip. I am terribly afraid, but nevertheless it is thrilling. Upstairs I give my slip of paper to a man and then I wait while the order is being filled. While I wait, I look around. I must stick my nose into everything. I look at the different kinds of grain and meal. I even take a ride on the little railroad. The little railroad is even more thrilling than the stairs, for if I do not watch out, I will go right through the open side of the wall from which they lower the bags of meal to the buggies and cars beneath. It is very thrilling.

When the order has been filled and there is no more excuse for me to stay, I descend the stairs. Descending the stairs is even more dangerous than ascending them. Now I am genuinely afraid. The stairs are almost horizontal, as well as being slippery. I expect any minute to tumble head first.

Nevertheless, when feed is needed, it is I who volunteer to go to the grist-mill. I love the little building, standing in its own grounds, almost across from the marble house with the pillars.

And now we are going to leave the market . . . leave the market . . . I do not realize how much it has meant to me until now when the words go through and through my head . . . leave the market . . . leave the market . . . My mother sits among her ruins and scolds me when her courage comes back. When my mother scolds me I know that she is herself again, and I am not afraid any more as I am when her face looks as if the world has come to an end. My own courage comes back.

With the market will go our notoriety in the town. That is always in the back of my head, and I am very glad. We will become just like any other family.

But when we left the market and took possession of the little house, the first thing my parents did was to have a sign painted and hung outside the house. The sign, painted in black on a white background, advertised furnished rooms to rent, and it could be seen from one end of the street to the other. How I hated it! We were to have no privacy after all. There was to be no diminution of our notoriety. My mother was still a showman. I—I longed to be a nobody, like other nobodies. I knew what notoriety was, and I hated it. How foolish I had been to think that now, the market gone, we would live like other people. I did not know my mother and father. I would never pass unnoticed on the street. First it had been the market, and now it was 'the houses.'

The street protested against the sign. Our house must be another example of smooth small-town mediocrity and unaliveness, or there would be trouble, the street said.

My mother said to the street, "Go to the devil."

In that street, we children were barbarians. We would make noise from morning to night. If we felt like yelling, we yelled. We gathered our particular friends from the foreign population, "outcasts" like ourselves, and raised hell on the porch. At least we had a porch. That was an improvement over the other life.

It was a street given over for the most part to middle-aged men and women. The children who lived on the street appeared to be middle-aged also in their staidness. They had been what is known as properly brought up, and we had escaped being brought up. Our mother and father had been too busy to pay any attention to us, except to administer whippings when we were too exuberant. Not even the school teachers had been able to insert the bit between our teeth. So we were barbarians, square pegs in round holes, thorns in the side of respectable small-town folk. They could make nothing of us, phenomena from a crazy, unsmall-town world, and the sign that my mother hung up was the final outrage. Such a sign had never before appeared on the quiet, well-kept street. Rooms to rent, yes, but only a neat almost indistinguishable card in the window.

With no market to take any of her energy, my mother proceeded to set her stamp on the houses, as she had set it on the market, on her husband and children.

When the houses were bought, they had been occupied by old maids and their mothers, business people without children. Each had his own comfortable roomy apartment. My mother raised the rents, and the tenants, disturbed in their quiet, moved. It was not only the higher rents, but my mother who could never mind her own business, or leave well-enough alone, started to pry into their affairs. She wanted to make changes. She considered that they were getting too much for their money. The apartments were too big. She wanted to take away a room and rent it by itself, leaving the tenant with a mutilated apartment.

"They can go to the devil," my mother said, when the tenants began to move. "I can get more money for the rooms anyway."

Rapidly the houses were filled with men and women who were for the most part factory workers. People of a class or two below the original tenants. People who were quick earners and quick spenders.

"Never mind the kind of people," my mother said; "it's their money that counts. If they can pay, they're as good as anybody." My mother was a believer in democracy.

The character of the houses was 'lowered.' But my mother did not care. The money was rolling in. When a tenant fell behind with his rent, he was kicked out. My mother might have protested eternal friendship with him, but when the rent was not forthcoming, friendship flew out of the window.

The houses took the place of the market for my mother. She was not one of those women for whom the rôles of wife, mother, and housekeeper are enough. She had too much energy to be satisfied with such subservient rôles. She wished to be out in the world, fighting it. Without the houses, without some substitute for the market, she would have been unhappy.

She was very seldom at home. She was always 'up to the houses,' butting into the lives of the tenants, quarreling with them, joking with them, ferreting out their secrets. She had a great natural talent for life and living. That the talent was crude did not make it any less powerful.

The houses might be said to have taught us children the facts of life. People who lived together without being married were everyday occurrences. I saw every human comedy and tragedy acted, sticking close to my mother's skirts. Men who grew tired of their 'wives' and kicked them out; so and so who lived with a woman and was having children by her had a wife elsewhere. As for the men who took a room for a night with their 'wives,' my mother would say of such customers: "Their money is as good as anyone else's, and besides, the mills are slack and nearly half the rooms are empty." I liked Letty. Letty had an apartment by herself and didn't work, yet she dressed expensively. She had steady visits from a man. . . . The houses were full of the facts of life for us children. By the time I was twelve I was wise.

They were shameless, these people who lived in the houses. They did not hide as the other people in the town did. And the respectable folk could not forgive this omission, this almost Oriental display of freedom and frankness in a small New England town. The people in the houses were elemental people; sex was the beginning and the end of life. If a partner to the act was incompatible or became boring, get another. Sex, cards, the movies, food, drink, the real meaning of life was contained in these pastimes. After the hellish monotony of the factory, they took to these to forget the morrow and the seven o'clock factory whistle.

The houses were acquiring a bad name. But my mother did not care. And I—I walked behind her, refusing to be shooed away, refusing to go home. The houses were as interesting to me as the market had been. Saturday night was the best of all, as it had been in the market. I was ashamed of my mother's showmanship, but I could not help appreciate it on Saturday nights. She chucked the children of the tenants under the chin, she dandled babies, she laughed, she chattered, she advised. I envied her. Never would I be so unself-conscious. Never would I be able to give myself like this. Did she mean it? I would ask myself a hundred times. Or was she just playing? All the more credit then for her ability to act.

As I walked behind my mother, I would compare her with my father. My father, I knew, had read more books than my mother had; was the only one of the Jews in town who could read Hebrew. But I preferred my mother. My mother was a fighter. My father stayed at home and read books and drank too much tea and had to be stung into action. Yes, I preferred my mother.

One night I came home from school with a terrible headache.

PART TWO

THE GNOME

I was in the cellar of 'the house.' My half-guess had been right. The cellar was indeed inhabited by the gnomes. Only then, being of the world, I had not been allowed to see. Still, I had not been so wholly of the world but what I had seen was enough to awaken my suspicion that this was no ordinary cellar. But I had been afraid to explore; I had run, instead, to the door that led up and out.

The peppery silver dust I had smelled before and which had awakened my suspicion was not now in a teasingly small amount to be met with only in obscure corners, near a spider's web, to be sniffed at by the cat and me. The smell of the peppery silver dust was everywhere. I smelled it and I did not care if I never saw the door that led up and out again.

I walked around the cellar, or rather the labyrinths wound around me. Presently I came to a hole in the ground. I remembered having seen it when I belonged to the other world. It was a hole filled with water, crystal clear and cold.

"Kneel down and taste the water," a voice said.

I knelt down and tasted the water. It was wonderfully good.

"There is a ladder beginning a foot below the top of the water," the voice said again; "descend it. Your eyes are as clear as the water now, clearer than the water, so you will see it plainly."

I had no thought of disobeying, of timidity. The peppery dust took away one's fear. Down, down, down, I placed my feet on the rungs of the ladder, and I saw the marvellous water close over my head. Surely I should drown? But nothing happened. It was like descending through air which one could feel. Presently I ceased descending through the water and saw beneath me a hundred little men at their blacksmith forges. How red the flames! How red the shoes of the horses! I peered around for the horses, for where there are blacksmith forges, there must be horses. Did I not know! But I saw none, only the little men.

It seemed to me that I had been born with this picture, had known it always, for it did not seem strange or unreal to me. I descended the few more rungs of the ladder, and I was level with the little men in a room with gold walls, red gold, or it might have been the reflection from the fires. This room was their real home. The cellar upstairs was merely a place where they sometimes roamed.

I had seen! I had been the chosen one! The books I had read had all been guesses. None had told the marvellous truth about the gnomes, for none had really known the truth before me.

I turned to ascend the ladder. I wanted to go back now. I was heavy with my tale. I must tell it to someone, to the world.

But I was not to be allowed to return as freely as I had been allowed to enter.

"You must take him with you," said the one who appeared to be King, pointing to a gnome who laid down his hammer at the King's words. "Only on that condition will you be allowed to return to your own world."

"But I don't want to," I protested. "He is ugly."

"You need not have come here," said the King, and as he spoke, the hammers kept red time on the forges. "You need not have come here, you need not have come here. He must go back with you. Those who go down into the darkness always bring back with them, when they return to the world light, a sign which sets them apart from other men. The gnome goes with you. The gnome goes with you," the King said, and the hammers kept red time on the forges. "Only on that condition can you return to your world."

Now I could not see them any more. Now I saw myself tossing on a bed. Again and again I returned to the cellar, but the pool of water was opaque, forbidding. There was no voice to tell me to drink. The King of the Gnomes, his command, and then the darkness that hid them from me, I remembered those things. But the ascent through the water—how had that been accomplished? And had the gnome appointed by the King climbed back with me? I looked at the pool of water. It was stagnant. . . .

The gnome . . . the gnome . . . he haunted me. One day, a day broke as marvellously clear as the pool of water had been that time . . .

The gnome . . . the gnome . . . he haunted me. I opened my eyes and saw people around me. I made out voices around me. Then I listened more closely. There were no voices. The voices I had heard a second before I had heard only in my memory. The people around me moved without sound, except what sound my imagination supplied. I shut my eyes tight, to close my imagination away, to close the *within* sounds. I strained my ears to hear the sounds from *without*, the sounds the people made around me. Their mouths were opening and shutting without sound, like the mouths of fish.

I had heard the King of the Gnomes and the beat of the hammers on the forges in that gold cave where the gnomes lived. *That* had been the reality then, and these people moving around me so quietly belonged to the dream I had come back to again and again. I had half supposed *this* to be the reality.

Time went by. It did not touch me. I struggled between dream and reality, trying to achieve a balance, so that I might standup, stand still. More time passed and I continued to swing between the two worlds like a man swinging by his neck from a tree. Only with that man, the rope around his neck had broken the bond with reality. He was safely with the dream world, and he knew that it was the dream world. He was no longer perplexed, as I still was.

I must still struggle with the puzzle. Which was which? Which was dream, which reality? And how could I decide?

More time passed, and then another marvellously clear day came. I saw the moving shapes, I heard the voices. No! I did not hear the voices. I did not hear any voices. That was my imagination and my memory again. But I saw the moving shapes! I loved them, suddenly, even if I did not hear their voices, even if their mouths were the mouths of fish, for all the sound they made. I stopped puzzling out whether this was the dream or the reality. I did not care any more. There was something safe about these people, even if their quietness was unnatural. I wanted to hang on to them. I cried out to them, begging them to hold me. I did not want to swing any more between the two worlds. Only let me stay here, whether it was dream or reality. I was tired of this constant bewilderment. My head ached and ached.

The people came toward me. That was my mother. Her lips were moving, but I could not hear what it was that she said. The sounds I heard continued to come from inside my head. I laughed suddenly. I was at my favorite game of making up to fit. Then I grew serious. What was she saying? Why was she looking at me so strangely, so sadly?

All at once, it came to me. The gnome! It had not been wholly a dream, then. The gnome that the King of Gnomeland had decreed to return with me when I returned to the other world, the world of reality, he *had* returned with me. My mother was seeing the gnome. I saw the gnome in her eyes. I could not see the gnome myself, but I could see his reflection in her eyes. She did not appear to see me at all; she saw only the gnome and his ugliness.

"I am here still," I wanted to cry out. "Why do you look at me that way?" But I remained still and closed my eyes to shut out the sight of the gnome in her eyes.

More time went by. I was sick, I understood. This was the hospital. That was the nurse. The man who dropped in at intervals was the doctor. It was difficult to concentrate, but I worried my brain until I found a connection between all this and that last night of consciousness—the night of the awful headache.

Moving shapes. All was the same, and yet not the same. It was not that they had changed; it was myself. It was not that the moving shapes lacked tangibility, but I had lost . . . something . . . some key. I had lost the key to reality.

The gnome! The gnome! I could not see him, but they could. He was not invisible to them. He climbed on the lips of the people and snatched to himself the words that were meant for me, for my ears. In that way I was conscious of his presence. He would not let the words come to me, reach me. Thief! Thief! I cried at him in my heart.

One day, the nurse wrote on a piece of paper.

"I am going to talk to you by writing. You can't hear, but the doctor says you will hear again in a few days."

I stared at her. Didn't she understand, then? Didn't she know about the gnome? That it was he who was stealing the words away from me, words intended for me? . . . "You can't hear, but the doctor says you will hear again in a few days." . . . I thought over the words.

Even if they did not understand, still the doctor had said . . . Translated from their thoughts into mine, the doctor's words meant that the gnome would go away soon, in a few days. The doctor was stronger than the King of the Gnomes.

A few days . . . a few days . . . I watched the gnome at the lips of the people, stealing words, stealing my words. Thief! Thief!

I left the hospital and returned home. More than a few days had gone by and the gnome was still with me, would ever be with me, I had a presentiment. The King of the Gnomes was stronger than any doctor, I should have known in the beginning. What was a doctor compared with a King?

I continued to watch the gnome; whenever the people spoke to me, he would creep to their lips and steal the words meant for me. I did not really see the gnome, but I knew that he was always there. I knew him by the silence he left in his wake.

The gnome which the people with their usual lack of imagination named 'deaf' walked beside me, stealing all sound. He was
always with me, invisible himself, but his pranks on me were tangible. Everybody saw these pranks the gnome played on me. When
they saw me approaching, the eyes of the people would peer curiously around for the gnome. Their eyes could detach him from his
invisibility, so well, that I, meeting their eyes, saw that they had
forgotten me and were seeing only the gnome.

Strangely, the gnome never became as real to me as he was for
everybody else, although it was I who must live with him day and
night. If I were alone in the world, I would have forgotten him. It
was the people who gave him his power over me. Without them,
he would have had no life to make fun of me, he would indeed
have been invisible. But the people spoke to me, and the gnome
stole the words meant for me, and I was left helpless.

Once, I took the gnome with me into the forest and stayed there
all day. Under some tree—so I had heard—an aperture might
sometimes be found that led to Gnomeland. I did not believe that
the gnome would be refused readmission to Gnomeland, just as I
would not be refused readmission to the world of the people if I
applied without the gnome. It had been but a dream anyway that
had imprisoned us together in the dungeon which my body had
become for the gnome and myself.

All day I sat patiently under a tree, perfectly still, so that I
might not disturb him, or prevent him in some clumsy human's
way from leaving my body and rejoining the gnomes. At night
when I returned to the people, I would return alone. I was sure
of this.

But when I thought I had stayed in the forest long enough and
returned to the people, I saw by their eyes that the gnome was still
with me.

I began to shun the people. Surely, the gnome who could not
live without the people would shrivel up and die if only I withdrew
from their life-giving glances long enough? I went about with my

eyes to the ground, running from all mouths that showed signs of opening. But even this failed, and the gnome continued to steal my words, and the people laughed at the blunders I made in my silence and I was helpless.

The first few months that the gnome came to live with me I was too bewildered to hate him for the pranks he played on me. I tried to struggle to some sort of an understanding about myself and the gnome who never left me. He appeared to be greater than I. I was his prisoner. He loved to taunt me every time he could get an audience to watch him. He loved to have the people speak to me so that he might steal the words intended for me. I, hearing only silence, would not understand, and would answer wrongly and meaninglessly. The people began to laugh, and I could almost hear the gnome chuckle gleefully at their laughter.

I tried to be wise. If I was the prisoner of the gnome, so was he my prisoner. The gnome and I were inseparable. Neither could be left behind where the other went. The King of the Gnomes had singled him out to be the one near me night and day. In Gnomeland, he had probably been free as I too had been free before he came to live with me. Neither of us had had any warning that our freedom was to end until the King spoke.

At the King's words, I had begun a new life. Even before that, before the gnome came to live with me, I had known myself to be different from the people. Now I seemed to myself to be doubly different. The gnome, too, at the King's words, had begun a new life. In his previous one, no doubt, he had been happier than I had been in my previous life. That was why he resented his imprisonment more and continually played his pranks on me. Not that I hated him less than he appeared to hate me! No. When he had played one of his pranks on me, involving me in the deepest of blunders because I had not heard the words addressed to me, reducing me to helplessness, and all around me the people had stood with their open fish mouths laughing their silent fish laughter . . . I could have killed him.

I could not have endured it at all, the laughter, the curiosity, as though living with the gnome made me a circus freak, if there were not times when I could forget him. When I hid myself away from the people, hid myself in my thoughts who alone seemed to know that I was as before. There, among my friends my thoughts, I walked without the gnome. After a while, there came my poems also to conspire to save me from the gnome. The gnome had no meaning and no reality for them, my thoughts and poems, for they had too powerful a reality of their own. The gnome had shown himself to be of the people, and the people meant nothing to my thoughts and poems.

But in spite of all my efforts, I could not evade the people . . . When the people were around . . . when the people were around . . . I began to hate the people. If it were not for them, I would not be 'deaf.' There would be no gnome. I had always hated the people, had tried to be free of them, and now—now I felt that they had me in their power. The gnome was conspiring with them. From the first, he had declared himself on the side of the enemy. He was helping them strangle me and my freedom—freedom which the people had always called wildness and rebellion.

I could not hide myself always from the people. I must go back into the world whether I wished to or not, and I must take the gnome with me. It was the gnome and I now, not I alone. I had his battles to fight as well as my own, his blunders to overcome, or rather, by his pranks, the blunders into which I was always falling.

I was at home, but life seemed to be as it had been in the darkness of the hospital bed where my body had lain while I had fought between dream and reality, struggling for a stability—in either world, I did not care which, so long as the struggling and the perplexity ceased. Now with the gnome on my back, ever conscious of him, I struggled to adjust myself to reality, this reality, since it had been given to me instead of the dream. And this reality was a new and different world from what the old reality had been, the old reality of "before the gnome."

I felt naked, new born, timid. It was agony to walk down a flight of steps. I would not trust my feet. And there was the gnome's weight on my back. I was terribly self-conscious.

I lay in bed. My mother sat on the bed beside me. She was saying the numbers 1-2-3-4-5-6-7-8-9-10 and I said them after her, reading them from her lips. But she did not understand that I was only reading her lips, and not hearing her. And I only dimly understood it myself.

My mother was trying to come closer to me. I remembered when I had seen her in the hospital, that first clear day. Her face had seemed older. There were white hairs among the black ones—I could not remember having seen them there before. Her face was tired. She looked as if she had gone down with me into the darkness when I had gone down. Now she sat on my bed, trying to make herself believe that I could hear after all.

I was deaf. That was the gnome, as I more truly called it with my knowledge of what had happened when I had gone down, down, down. . . . When I lay in my bed and there was no one in the room, the gnome was not there; but the instant that someone came into the room and said something to me, the gnome made his appearance and stole the words intended for me, leaving me a blank and a silence. This was my explanation for the phenomenon of being 'deaf.' I did not tell anyone about the gnome. I realized that no one would understand. They would only look at me strangely as they had already looked at me more than once when I, wishing help, had spoken about my dreams—*had* they been only dreams, I asked? They seemed so real to me. And they had said, or rather written down, as the nurse had written down, "you must be still and not ask any questions. You have been a very sick girl." Which was not the answer I wanted. I wished help. I wished my questions answered. Only then could I be still.

They did not understand. It was useless. But—if only there were someone to help me, help me to puzzle out the tangled images in my head. I knew what they were thinking. Nothing had disturbed my mental clarity, my ability to see what they were hiding even from themselves.

"It has made her a little crazy."

And the doctor said, "She needs quiet and rest."

But what I needed was help, and that was not forthcoming.

I lay long days in my bed, alone with myself. I did not want anyone to come in, except my mother. Inevitably, when anyone else came in, the gnome came in too; only my mother was somehow able to circumvent the gnome.

There was no one in the room, and I prayed that no one would come in until I had worked out the puzzle for myself. I was going to expose my soul in the next few minutes, and no one must see. If I failed, I wanted no one to see the slight against my soul. Failure or success, I could no longer stand the uncertainty. I must know.

I got out of bed, and, holding the walls for support for I was still very weak, I crept to the piano—the piano that had been bought long ago for ten dollars.

I sat down on the stool, although sitting down sent needles up and down my spine. And then, breathlessly, I touched a white key with my little finger. Touched it and then firmly pressed it down. Was there a sound? Yes! Then I pressed again, uncertain. There was no sound. The sound I had heard had come from my own imagination, from my memory. I had merely deceived myself again. The sounds I was always hearing came from my own mind, storehouse of all the sounds I had heard and gathered—for the time when I would no longer be able to hear them at first hand.

I pressed another key. Ah! I knew just how it should have sounded! No one knew this piano as I knew it. That note—way up high, shrill, almost a screech. From my storehouse I supplied the sound perfectly. But that was not what I wanted. I wanted the reality, the firsthand knowledge. I did not want imagination and memory.

So it was with everything. I supplied the sound. I put sound into fish mouths, sounds but not words. I had the words in my storehouse, but which words to put in their fish mouths? That was the riddle, the great riddle.

I crept back to bed, and turned my face to the wall, away from the piano. I had exposed my soul to the piano and been rebuffed. If only from shame, I would not risk a rebuff again.

A few seconds after I had got into bed again, my mother came in. I saw her glance sharply from me to the piano—she at any rate heard—but I kept my face to the wall, pretending to be asleep. And after a while she went out.

That softening I had noticed in my mother's face in the hospital remained.

I knew bits of the Jewish alphabet. In that way my mother communicated with me, for she did not know how to write English. With her short stubby pencil that might have been used in the market, she wrote down Jewish hieroglyphics and I with my bits of knowledge translated them, letter by letter, into English. Each new hieroglyphic was a mystery that must be solved. I had to take each word she wrote to pieces before I understood its meaning. Was that a 'g' or a 'z'? Did 'g' turn this way or that way? Sometimes it took half an hour for me to understand a sentence, but my mother struggled on unweariedly.

"Oh, I don't know, I don't know," I would scream, as if she were submitting me to a torture.

"You do know," my mother would nod her head. "Once more. Try again." Finally I did know. I caught some of her fighting spirit.

I lay on the bed, my mother sitting on a chair near me, pencil and paper on her knee. Meanwhile, besides me, she took care of the other children, and the 'houses.' The rents must be collected, the rooms cleaned, arguments settled, more rooms rented. The houses had grown. A new one had been built. Each house had almost fifty rooms. And my mother, single-handed, took care of them all.

From the window near my bed I could see her going up the alley to the houses. She still wore the aprons she had worn in the market. There was a dust-cap on her head. She had not changed.

Up the alley to the houses . . . I waited with the fretful impatience of the sick until she came back. The food did not stay down when my father or sisters gave it to me. I must have my mother.

I could see the band from my window. I could see it even if it was still blocks away. As I waited for it to pass my window, I set it up, like a box of soldiers, in my mind. The conductor of the band, merely a factory manager in the everyday world, was transformed into a magnificent being when he twirled his stick so smartly. The leader of the band! How I went sick with delight whenever I saw him coming. *This* was his real life, I guessed. He lived only for these times when he could march at the head of all this music down Main Street, guiding it, almost bringing it into being.

It must be coming nearer. It had most certainly turned the corner. Pretty soon I would hear it and then I would see it.

Before I knew it, the band was passing by my window. It was going, going. The conductor in all his slender magnificence had gone, like the Pied Piper, into Elsewhere. The band had gone by; now it was the people who were going by . . . the children, and the more simple and childlike of the elders who would follow the musicians for blocks, untiringly. . . . And I, I had heard nothing. It was even more than that. I watched the band pass across my eyes, without the image making any impression on my mind. The gnome could create this double loss sometimes. All the imagination in the world would not help to fill the hole created.

I was deaf. Why didn't I realize it? I was deaf. Why did I forget so easily that I was deaf? The gnome whom I had forgotten was with me again. The sounds, the beautiful sounds, they could not reach me. I was deaf, deaf, deaf.

You can't hear any more. You can't hear any more. Because of the gnome, because of the gnome, you can't hear any more. The band! The band! I wanted to hear it. I did not want to be left out. I did not want to be left out!

I cried silently with my face to the wall. No one must find out. I hated the people following the band, hated them because I envied them. To be part of that crowd of simple people, if only I could be part of it! Why, lately, I had felt half-ashamed to follow the band, to be seen among such simple people as those who followed the band. But now I would have given anything to be of them, so long as I could hear and be drawn away from my home by the music. I asked nothing more.

A foot-fall. "I hear that," I said triumphantly to the gnome.

"Ha, ha," laughed the gnome. I could always hear him anyway, perhaps because he and I dwelled together in one body.

Then I realized it. I heard the foot-fall with my body, not with my ears. My body had suddenly become alive, or had it always been alive and had I been too busy with my eyes and ears to notice my body—aware of it as I should have been aware of it? I had heard the foot-fall with my body, it had reached me that way, and my body responded with a sensitive acknowledging tremor.

"Vibration," the doctor explained. I did not understand the word and returned to my own explanation and interpretation, as I did in almost everything else.

I made a discovery. If I pressed a key of the piano, one of the lower bass notes, I would fail of course to hear it—I had already proved that; but if I laid my arm over the piano, I heard the note with my body. It was not the same as if I heard it with my ears, alas, for my body did not seem to be alive enough, as my ears had been alive; but, nevertheless, I heard something, even if it was but the echo of a dead note.

But I stopped doing this after a while. I did not want dead music. It was too much like an eerie travesty of the real thing. And besides, they did not understand when I played the piano, holding my body against it as I played. They looked at me queerly as if I were crazy.

One night, unexpectedly, I returned to the gold cave.

"Will you take back the gnome?" I begged the King.

"I cannot do that," said the King. "He was decreed before you were born by an even greater King. I was merely to deliver him to you at the appointed time."

"Then it was all a scheme—even the headache and the sickness?"

"Yes," said the King. "Everything is a scheme. The beginning and the end are in us at birth. But I will grant you one wish that may be able to make life more bearable with the gnome."

"Let me hear music," I said instantly.

"You will carry music about with you wherever you go," said the King.

"I do not understand," I said, but before the King could say anything, it was morning.

I knew one thing anyway. It was only in this world that I could not hear. In that other world, the world of dream, I could hear perfectly. I had heard the King of the Gnomes. It convinced me that it was all the fault of the people. But for the people . . . but for the people. . . .

I waited impatiently until night came again. I must see the King of the Gnomes and get from him the answer to my question.

But instead of sleep coming to transport me to Gnomeland, there came a marvellous music. The most marvellous music in the world. It came not from the without, but from the within. I was more and more beginning to realize that there was a *within* world. I had not been aware of it before because I was too busy with the *without* world. Now the without world seemed far, far away, and the within world close, very close, to me.

I lay in bed and listened to the music that came from the within world. It carried me away to a land where gnomes were refused admittance, a land where one became whole once more because at the gateway to this land gnomes were thrown off as if they were heavy sacks.

As I listened to the music, I tried to describe it, but I had no words. I knew what the violin sounded like, but the violins in my head were as no other violins; no violins had ever had the sweetness of my violins; no organs had ever been so regional and yet so mythical as my organs; no orchestra in the world had ever attained such perfect unity as this orchestra in my head.

Where had all this music come from? Was this the King's meaning? Would the music cease? Aloof, I watched and waited. But the music did not cease.

The music was now wild, now soft; now the penetrating sweetness of a single violin. That must be a gypsy song, I thought, although I had never heard a gypsy song; yet, nevertheless, I *knew*. It was a gypsy song, a song to which all the gypsies of the world had danced for centuries. Now the music was on opera, although I had never actually heard an opera, and so could not compare. But I had no need of comparison. I *knew*.

Presently the music became softer and yet softer. This was a lullaby, the tenderest lullaby that had ever rocked a child to sleep. It was all the more tender that the child was deaf because it must go beyond silence. Presently, when I did not know it, I fell asleep.

Morning and then night again. I was impatient. Would the music come again? It came again. It was, if that were possible, even more beautiful than before. In the space of a day, my musicians had composed still more music. My music seemed to be capable of endless variations, although I would never have grown tired of it if there had been but one.

I loved my violin best, I decided. When it began—I could see the musician drawing the bow—I opened my eyes and stared straight ahead of me into the darkness. My mind and body quivered, listening to the almost too sweet sweetness. Time would pass. My musicians would give their whole repertoire before they would put the lights out and steal away until the next night. How could the rhythm in my mind die when I had such music to listen to, such music with which to compare my rhythm? My rhythm must measure up to such music; any false notes must be struck out of it. My rhythm must be as true as the rhythm of the music. The poems I would sometimes write I took to my mind and spoke over and over again until they fitted with the rhythm of the music, until there was no disharmonious note in the poem.

I ceased to dread the nights, for now sleep-time was the time when I could return to my wonderful music. I wanted to tell some-one of it—perhaps it might be possible to share the music with someone—but I remembered the queer looks I had received when I had mentioned other things. They would not understand. They would think 'crazy' again. I must keep this in my head, as I kept the other things, as I kept the gnome. The music in my head became a secret house of pleasure to which I returned every night.

My first walk was up the alley to the houses. But soon I was tired of the alley. One day, when I thought I could trust my legs, I stole out to the street. But the people I met on the street spoiled my walk. They knew! They knew! I could see the reflection of the gnome in their eyes. It was such a small town that everybody knew. I hated the curiosity in their eyes.

I walked far, far. My mother, when she found out that I was not in the house, would worry. I did not care. I had thought of this walk many times, and at last I must execute it. I wanted to walk until there were no more people and no more houses.

I saw a boy walking toward me. Suddenly he raised his arm. His fingers flew. The sign language. I cowered. Even the boy knew, then. I could feel my soul quivering. To make those gestures at me—it was a public branding. It exposed me.

I was deaf, deaf, deaf. Why couldn't I realize it? I was different, queer, strange now, according to the people. Only I knew that I was the same.

The sign language—it was a symbol to me of all they were trying to make me into. They were trying to make me really deaf. Thus I put it to myself.

To make me really deaf. That seemed to me from the beginning to be the battle between myself and the people. I wanted to go out into the world, by which I meant to go out into the streets as I had done before—before the gnome. The rift between myself and my mother came again. While I had been sick, I had been dependent, but now I was as well as ever again—except for the gnome. My mother attempted to keep me in the house when I wanted to go out.

"Give me my hat and coat!" I cried at her.

To prevent me from going out, her method was to hide my hat and coat, sometimes my shoes. I would go out into the world, even if I was deaf, even if I met nothing but ridicule and curiosity. Even if everyone on the street made the sign language at me. Even if I was crazy, a freak, a half-person, in the eyes of the people. I must go out. I was not made for a house existence.

My illness had imposed upon me a softness which was foreign to my hard independence. My mother wanted me to continue to lean on her.

"My hat and coat, my hat and coat," I looked all over the house for them, sobbing under my breath. I would go out. I would go out. My mother, everybody, are against me. They are trying to make me really deaf, really deaf, really deaf, I sob under my breath. My mother says I will get run over if I go out into the street. At every accident her heart palpitates with fear that I will be brought into the house dead. I see the selfishness behind this, this mother love. To save me I am to be kept shut up in the house. That is her love. But it is not the way; that is the worst way—to shut me up in the house, to make me a prisoner. I will die that way. I would rather die in the streets, run over by an automobile that I have not heard approaching, than stifle to death as she is trying to do with me. She fills my head with horrors that she has made up so that I will not go out into the streets, but remain at home under her eye. That is her love. I do not want it. If I do not take care, if I do not rebel, I am in danger of spiritual death. I know this by a blind kind of analysis, and blindly I strike out. I am in danger of becoming really deaf. I cannot get rid of that phrase. It sums up for me all the horrors in the world. My physical deafness is nothing; I can rise above it; but for someone, older than I and therefore with the whip-hand, to slowly shut away the world from me in order to protect me from being run over . . . no, that must never be. Complete annihilation lay that way. I would not listen to her stories of what lay in wait for me on the streets; I would not listen to her tales of the policeman who had said that I must not be allowed out. No, I would not listen to her, although I must read her words when my sister, at my mother's command, writes them out. My father threatens me with the strap if I do not read what my mother has dictated. He stands over me with a strap until I have read the cruel words. . . . It is possible that the policeman could have said that . . . that I must not be allowed out on the streets, that I was more than a little crazy? Or has my mother, from her 'love', made it up? I read and I listen. It is impossible to merely read the words with my eyes. They enter me. My soul begins to quiver. I become more and more timid, if that is possible. But, doggedly, I rebel. I must rebel, and keep on rebelling against them, against my mother. I no longer have first-hand knowledge. That is the terrible thing about being deaf, the most terrible thing, it seems to me. It makes me dependent, dependent on them, I who have always been fiercely independent. Now I am dependent on them. And can I believe them? Can I believe their words? I can no longer find out for myself, as I have always done before. I am shut in, shut in my tower of silence. I know my father, mother, sisters. I do not believe them. But nevertheless, a fear creeps in. . . . Is it possible that what they are saying is true?

Except for the attempts to chain me to the house, I was left alone with the gnome the first summer that composed the first months of my deafness. I had shunned the people for the most part, even the lawyer whom I had always gone to see at least once a week. I walked on the streets, alone, head down, so that no one should stop me and say something to me, which would immediately bring the gnome into being. This behavior had already drawn the attention of the people, and it marked the beginning of my reputation for being crazy.

The summer passed. September came. School was beginning again. It would be my first year of high-school—if I went.

I walked through the door of the high-school alone. But not alone! The gnome was with me. I had wanted one of my sisters to come with me, but they had all been too busy with their own 'first day' at school to bother about me. I had seen in my mother's eyes that terrible knowledge that had kept her from insisting that one of them should accompany me—if only to the door. She did not think I was good for anything any more. She thought it was useless for me to continue to go to school. I was useless for everything; I was good only to be kept at home. I must fight against that idea of hers; I must fight against that thought in her eyes, or it would inevitably get me. She would make me really deaf. Not only she thought me good for nothing any more. I saw it in everybody's eyes.

"You can't do anything," my sisters taunted. "You aren't good for anything any more. You're *deaf.*" Why didn't my mother stop them? But she did not. She thought the same thing.

That taunt. I could feel my soul quiver at its impact. I would talk to myself, to my soul:

"Sh-sh-sh, dear, sh-sh-sh. Stop your quivering. Stop your quivering, dear. *We* know. We have each other. You must not quiver, dear."

So I would talk to myself whenever the taunt came, and gradually my soul grew calmer, became quiet. The mad, frenzied swinging ceased. But I was never impregnable against their words. They came often, and then the quivering would start afresh. I could never run far enough from the words.

I could expect no help from anyone. I had been determined to continue with school, but I felt immediately that I did not belong here in this hall crowded with laughing boys and girls. I had a knowledge that set me ever apart from them. What did they know of shame, of hiding one's head from the eyes of the people, of being stared at? The terrible fear returned. Were they right? Was I useless? Should I have remained at home, hidden? Should I do as my mother wished? Should I let her hide me?

But I must not think such things. I must not. I must go out into the world. The gnome must make no difference to me, however much difference he made to others. Let them think me a freak! I would still go out into the world and get what I wanted. I must do that in spite of the gnome.

Fearfully, I stood by myself in the school-hall. That marked me out, but then, I had always been by myself, not one of a group, like other girls. I was *that kind*. I glanced around—surely there must be someone here I knew, some girl with whom I had graduated from the 'grades' only a few months before.

At last I found one.

"Can I stay with you?" I asked timidly. "Will you help me?"

She nodded her head. How grateful I felt. Some day I would do something for her to pay her back for her great kindness.

I began to see others of my class, girls and boys with whom I had graduated. They looked at me curiously. Yes, they knew.

I waited patiently. I who had always rushed forward was learning now to wait patiently. I could not move any more until another moved, showing me the way.

I would never understand. To which room did I go for this subject? There were so many rooms. The building was entirely strange to me. Dumbly I followed the leader, the girl I had approached the first day and who was rapidly beginning to consider me a nuisance. But I clung to her. I would not let go, no matter how much exasperation there was in her face sometimes at what she considered my stupidity. My stupidity was really inability to comprehend, for how could I do so when the gnome stole the words? Someone must help me. That was all I knew. I made mistakes. I lost the girl—or perhaps she had managed to lose me—and blundered into strange classrooms. The instructor, annoyed, told me I was in the wrong room.

"I am deaf, I am deaf," I repeated over and over again. I said something, words which had no relation to her words. The class roared with laughter. Didn't the teacher understand I couldn't hear?

"I am deaf, I am deaf," I repeated over and over again.

Finally some intelligence penetrated to the teacher's head and she wrote down her words. This was what I had been waiting for all the time, and I escaped. The cruelty and the curiosity of those who were of my own age, laughing at me. . . . Damn them! Damn them!

After a few weeks I began to understand the routine. I knew where the various rooms were. I knew the names of the teachers. I knew where I was to go for a certain lesson. It seemed incredible to me that I had finally arranged everything in my mind.

Every morning all the classes were herded into one big room to listen to prayers or music. I would sit dumbly with the others, patiently wondering what it was all about. Every act contrived to make me realize my difference from everybody else. But I persisted. Every morning I came to school.

I sat dumbly in my chair in the various classrooms, silent except for a repeated snuffling. I was unconscious of the noise I was making, and that I was annoying teachers and pupils. I saw repulsion and hostility on their faces, but I continued to snuffle.

"Use your handkerchief," a girl says.

I stare at her blankly and continue to snuffle.

How I envied the girls who had friends to walk with. I walked alone, avoided. I had no friends. I was out of it, completely out of it. Why did I continue to come to school, anyway?

My class marks went down, down, down. I who had always been first, or among the first, in my class. The teachers talked, talked, talked, explaining the how and the why and the wherefore. I heard nothing, of course. Should I go up and ask the teachers to write it down especially for me? I was too timid. I had received too many rebukes to think I would ever receive kindness. Besides, I felt that the teachers had no time for me. I felt too that they resented my presence. I was the discordant note in the class. With me in the class, there was not the smoothness there should have been. I demanded special attention.

I was out of place. Vaguely I sensed that I should be receiving special instruction—perhaps in a different kind of school. I did not belong here. I doubted the fairness to the teachers. They wanted and could teach only physically normal children. But I knew the uselessness of talking to my father and mother about special instruction. They were ignorant. They thought that now I was deaf I was good for nothing any more. I could see my father's sneer. They were too busy with the houses, anyway, to give time to my problem.

For them I was deaf—useless. I could not do anything any more. There was nothing for me to do now except to stay at home and mop the floors.

Sometimes moods of wild gaiety seized me. Home after school was a nightmare; in school I was almost free. During the few minutes before school officially started, when the teacher had not yet come into the room, the place was a bedlam and I was the ring-leader. The blackboards were chalked up everywhere with the pupils' 'talk to me.' This meant reprimands, for it was against the rules to write on the blackboards. But reprimands meant nothing to me.

I paid no attention to the rules and regulations of the school. There was always that inner torment and bewilderment that kept me restless, always restless. I had not adjusted myself to the new world, the new reality. It seemed impossible to adjust myself. I would never learn how to carry the gnome about with me. He was the awkward baggage over which I was always tripping. I forever tried to hide him, but to do this I must hide myself. And no one saw, no one understood—me. No one bothered to take time to help. I struggled alone, and this bewilderment rendered me now sullen, now wildly gay, and always restless.

From school I went home, to the taunt, "you aren't good for anything; you can't do anything."

I was a wild one. I roamed the streets at night like the haunted animal that I was. I roamed the corridors of the school. What was it that I was running away from, or trying to get away from? Those words, "you can't do anything, you aren't good for anything." . . .

A few months after I entered high-school, the social activities began. There was to be a dance and the freshman class was invited to it.

I had never been to a dance or a party. This would be my first party. I had no thought of remaining away. Like a fool, I still believed I was like everybody else.

For weeks I thought about the dance. I could not dance, I had no proper dress, but, nevertheless, I was going. The night of the dance came and I was ready to go. I was still in my school dress. But—where were my hat and coat? I knew suddenly. *They* had taken them.

I would go even without my hat and coat, even though it was winter. But *they* stole up. From my corner near the piano where I was held captive, I kicked and fought.

Damn you . . . damn you. Finally they got my shoes off and I was left sobbing on the piano top. A little later I crept off to bed, my hiding place.

I never forgot my first dance. Years later the thought came that they had perhaps done this for my own good, that I would most surely have made a fool of myself, but even so my hatred and resentment did not diminish.

Most of the time I acted as I pleased, spurred on by that restlessness and bewilderment. In school, I could not sit still in my seat as the others did. I was tormented by questions. What was I doing here anyway? I was an object of curiosity, a freak, when I walked through the halls, in the classroom. I was a stranger to the boys and girls I had grown up with, in school at least, even if our association had not extended out of the school. A few months ago we had all graduated from the grades; a few months ago we had been equals, more or less. Now I was suddenly a stranger to them. They shunned me. I was an unknown, a not wholly sane or correct quantity. And they could not see that it was just this attitude on their part that was making me more and more an unknown quantity, even to myself. Bewilderment was completely engulfing me. Who was I? What was I? If only there were someone to whom I could talk, who would see beneath the wildness which my bewilderment was pushing me to. Such a person might help me stand up. I was trying to stand up, trying alone, but each time I fell down again. The gnome was stronger than I. He was pushing me into my mother's arms, trying to make my mother's neurotic imagination mine. He was trying to make me fear the world to such an extent that I would finally seek a hiding place and never come out of it. Was he succeeding? Was he? He had my mother, the people, on his side. Could I, single-handed, hold out against them all? Should I stop fighting and let myself become really deaf?

If only there were someone. . . .

There was one teacher whose dry, crusty tongue we all feared. She was an anomaly in that she had not been ground into mediocrity like the other teachers. We called her horse-face behind her back.

She was about forty, with the coarse-pored pink nose of a drunkard. Her eyes were steel-gray and hard, hard as her jaw-line and her mouth. She was more a man than a woman—as I had heretofore known women.

She introduced the cult of masculinity into the school. She called the boys by their last name, and the girls too. She was trying to instill in us some of her own hard independence and individuality. But most of us after eight or more years of school and teachers who had tried to make us as one collective pupil instead of thirty individuals resented her appeal and disliked her. We were comfortable in our mediocrity, and did not want her sharp prick-points. A few boys had acted up, more from pleasure at being called Jones rather than Charles.

We sensed that the other teachers were against her. They were on our side. They, too, disliked her hard, salty freshness, the toughness of her mind, and, most of all, her courage. They had none left.

She tried to come near me.

"Can I be excused from getting up in front of the class and reading my paper?" I asked her. I feared that most of all. Getting up in front and letting them look their fill at me. Their eyes ate me up.

"No," she answered.

And I—I hated her for it. I did not see that she was trying to make me appear like the others, in my own eyes if not in theirs; that she was trying to treat me, unlike the other teachers, as a full member of the class. I, who wanted nothing more than to be treated like the others, shrank when given the opportunity. I had not the courage to follow her lead. I wanted to hide, after all. I wanted to follow the line of least resistance, after all. In moments by myself I had dreamed of getting up before the class, confidently. But there was always the gnome holding me back.

Skulking in the cloakroom, watching the boys and girls talking together, and myself being out of it, absolutely out of it. One girl in particular I envied. What did it matter that in class she was stupid? She had light brown hair and a creamy skin. All the boys vied with each other to talk to her. In the cloakroom I would take a long time to hang up my coat and hat so that I might be near this laughter and this talk even if I could never participate in it. I saw the boys reach clumsily for her hand, their sincerity making up for their clumsiness. She might have been a Francis all over again, but a heavier Francis, being wholly of this world. No, she was not Francis. Francis had been of another world a world without sensuality.

I would have given anything to be looked at as she was looked at.

There was only one girl who seemed to treat me as an equal. I never spoke to her. I never came nearer to her than to pass her in the hallway, going to and fro from the classrooms. But every time I passed her she smiled at me. I sensed the wonder of her smile. I responded to it as a person who has lived in a land of gloomy dark days responds to a beautiful day. Something in me, something not shy or tormented, or growing out of that very shyness and torment and inferiority, that something grew an inch when she smiled. I would never come near to her, never talk to her, she was so much above me; yet when she smiled at me it was as if further intercourse were unnecessary. She had said all she had to say to me with her smile. Was there pity in that smile? My eyes, sharp, searched but did not find any pity. I wanted pity even less than I wanted curiosity; I preferred curiosity if I must have one of the two. It was a friendly little smile, I thought, coming from a nature spontaneous and friendly because sure that no word could be uttered against her, no hand raised against her. She was a superior being. I who had had words uttered against me, who had always lived in an atmosphere of suspicion and distrust, who had touched and been touched by things that she would never want to touch and that would never touch her, I who had a dark knowledge, I loved her. To me it was more than the mere friendly little smile that it was. For the moment it established the illusion of equality between us. She raised me by her smile. Even the gnome was no longer.

When the smile faded, the illusion faded; but while the illusion lasted, it was enough.

Sometimes instead of the regular teacher, we had a strange one. The old one, knowing that I could not hear, knew how to handle me—that is, she left me strictly alone. The new teacher of course did not know I was deaf.

The roll-call, the roll-call. I waited in agony for it to begin. Smoothly the strange teacher called the names, and those she called answered. When my name was called, I would not answer. The regular teacher would look up and find me with her eyes and be answered that way, but the strange teacher, ignorant, would repeat my name several times, until someone told her I could not hear. The pupils never failed to find this curious and amusing— being there and yet absent since I did not answer to my name.

I hated their laughter. Day after day I let myself in for these things, these blunders, awkwardnesses. I wondered why continued. Was it not best after all to go home and hide?

At home I lived as if there was no one except myself in the house. I went about with my eyes to the ground. But they still had the upper hand. My mother, trying to draw me into her net of evilness, would have my sister write down something particularly cruel and nasty about my walking on the streets by myself. I would shy away, refusing to read it, but my father forced me to with his blows. That was their method of getting their thoughts across to me.

This did not help me to stand up.

I sat in the rocking chair in the dark front room. I rocked back and forth as I looked out of the window. I wanted to go out on my usual nightly expedition of walking on the streets, head down, talking to myself, making up conversations wherein mercifully I was both questioner and answerer. In this land alone I could pretend that I was not deaf. In this land alone I made no blunders, aroused no laughter. In this land alone the gnome could not play his pranks on me, stealing words meant for me and leaving me helpless.

I would be denied this land tonight. I could talk to myself here, but I would be interrupted, looked at strangely, called crazy. I had been called it so often that I was familiar with the outline of the word on their lips. That I talked to myself because I was terribly lonely they did not understand. I did not bother to analyze it myself.

I loved the streets. As my legs walked, up the lighted street and down the dark streets, I ceased to be conscious of my surroundings. There was pleasure in the quick movement of my legs. The movement, if I walked well, supplied a beat, a measure, and unconsciously my self-conversations would keep time to it. I would come to a halt by a corner, and the two busy people in my brain halted also.

There was a woman in the town who had a beautiful walk. She had the delicate narrow hips of a man, and a man's slender yet compact body, and when she walked it was a joy to watch. I all but followed her on the street, as I had followed the band, and for the same reason.

Now and then in my walks I would come to a stop and begin again, this time trying to walk with the lithe movements of that woman. For perhaps half an hour I would succeed in creating the rhythm and sustaining it, but then my body slumped.

I sat in the rocking chair and thought of what I was missing. Down the dark tree-lined streets. Up and down. Looking no one in the face if it were possible, although they sometimes forced themselves on me, as children who knew I was deaf and therefore a freak. It was these children whom I dreaded most of all, who could make me shrink the most. Their eyes, filled with a terrible fundamental curiosity, laid me bare, bare, bare. They made a nothing of me. This was the reason why I preferred the night to the day. There were fewer children at night. I was not afraid of grown-ups— "men," as my mother was always hinting. What did I care about men? What men could or might do to me would never equal the breakage or personal loss a child could create in me by one look.

I sat and rocked, plotting to find a way out. But it was winter and useless. They had my hat and coat. If it were only summer! Then let them see if they could detain me. I dreamed of the summer when I would be free, free. But it was winter now. Why did they see into my walking the streets what they saw? Because they could see nothing else, my mind said. Because they thought of nothing else.

I rocked and rocked, talking softly to myself. Suddenly the room was flooded with light. My father came toward me and pulled a kitten, only a few weeks old, from under one of the rockers. I had crushed it to death. I had not known it was there, had not heard its tiny cries. I had kept on rocking, rocking, rocking, crushing its bones.

I always tried to reach home before the school near our house let out. I knew what I would have to undergo if I got caught by the children. All children were my natural enemies.

I knew that these children, all children, would strip me if they could. Only fear of the grown-ups kept them from doing it. A nightmare that kept returning to me was one in which I was lost in a land of children and they were doing with me what their eyes said they would do with me if they ever got me where there were no grown-ups and no fear of punishment. I knew children for what they really were. I knew their instinct for cruelty, their sadism. Grown-ups! What did grown-ups know about children? They had forgotten, or did not care to remember, their own childhood. The instincts of that time made such a far-from-charming picture that they did not care to remember. It was safer to substitute a more conventional picture.

To children, I was a strange toy. They wanted to touch me, feel of me, and . . .

In the holidays I feared to walk on the streets during the day because of the children let loose. They were there on the streets, a pack of wolves, and I was the single sheep. No sheep in a land of wolves was ever more haunted than I. Small boys, in the winter, ran me into corners and pelted me with snow-balls and tried to lift my dress. The girls, more dirtily subtle, not quite so cleanly daring as the boys, were also more cruel. Their eyes . . . I hid at home during the holidays.

The clothes I wore to school. I had no clothes like the other girls in school. I never received anything at home, and after a while I cried at them that I wouldn't ever take anything from them.

Damn Jew . . . damn dirty Jew. . . .

When one side of my middy blouse got dirty I turned it over and wore it on the other side. That it was on the wrong side was obvious, but I went my way, indifferent.

It could not last much longer, my remaining at school. I alternated between sullenness and gaiety. I paid no attention to discipline. My bewilderment was interpreted as defiance.

It could not last much longer. The wonder of it was that it had lasted as long as it did, long enough for me to receive and leave impressions. I was learning nothing. I was present and yet absent. My very presence was an upset. Why did I come anyway, since I learned nothing? I did not know. I simply came. It might have been to get away from home. In spite of their words, "you can't do anything, you aren't good for anything," I was determined to continue with my education. But I was not getting one. I heard nothing. I had no contacts. Yet I continued to come.

One morning at a class held by a man teacher I burst out laughing. I had glimpsed a hole in the man's pants. I wondered how his wife had overlooked the hole. And the women teachers, had they too overlooked the hole? Probably. Only I, hearing nothing, wholly living through my eyes which let nothing escape, had seen it.

That little hole. Before I knew it, I had burst out laughing. The whole class looked at me. I continued to laugh. I could not stop the giggles.

A little later, I was handed a piece of paper. It read:

"Go home. Stay home."

That marked the end of my school days.

PART THREE

Stand Up! Stand Up!

I walked down the street, choosing the longest way home. Go home, stay home.

How I was to explain at home I did not know. What should I say?

"I got expelled," I said, as I walked in. I went upstairs without waiting for them to say anything.

Now I began a life in which there was no time. School, which had marked time for me for almost ten years, was over and done with. I did not protest over the unfairness of it. I was growing used to the idea that no one would ever see the real me. Only the gnome, and what the gnome had done to me.

I had not yet even adjusted reality and the dream in their proper places. Had such a thing happened? Or had I merely dreamed it? Was it only a picture met on that journey down into the darkness? There was one picture which especially haunted me. An ugly little deformed man placed beneath the counter of the little market where we had been young and happy together. Had there been such a man? Night after night I struggled to clear my mind of the ugly deformed man.

How often the little market had occurred through my dreams. The little market, not the big market. In that journey down into the darkness I had met pictures which I had supposed forgotten or left forever behind in the streets of my former lives, when I had moved to other streets and other lives. But I had neither

forgotten nor left behind. The journey down into the darkness
had broken the crust of my subconscious where all my sup-
posedly lost or forgotten or left-behind things were. And now
a wild mix-up went on in my brain. In addition, I was deaf. I
was imprisoned in a tower of silence. I had no contacts with the
world of the people which might have righted me. No people,
no reality, entered my brain; or rather, not the right people, not
the right reality. Reality and the people were merely a continuation of the jumble in my brain. My mother, my father, my sisters,
curiosity, the people, eyes, eyes, eyes. The eyes of children, the
eyes of the people.

Under those eyes I could not stand up. If only in this reality, however a makeshift one, I could come upon someone or
something. I would then steady myself upon that someone or
something, as a child just learning to walk steadies himself on a
chair at the moment when the world shows signs of tottering at
his feet and he knows that he will be precipitated on the reeling
world unless there is something to take hold of. For a chair! A
chair! I was a child. No one could be more timid and bewildered
by the reeling world than I. I must learn things all over again.
Unless I could soon find a symbolical chair I would never be able
to stand up.

I moved through the house. Having me always there irritated
them into "doing something" for me, if only to ease their consciences. My mother took me to the city to see an ear doctor.

On the train I was among strange people. How I loved them!
They did not know! They accepted me as an equal. They did not
know. If they knew, their eyes would not be so free and clear as
they looked at me—or, rather, did not look at me. If they knew,
I would see reflected in their eyes that curiosity that stripped me
bare, that left me nothing.

I sat in my seat and basked in their clear glances, in their total
indifference to my existence. They did not know; therefore the
gnome was out of sight. Ha, ha, I laughed at him.

But I had not counted on my mother. Not even on a train could she keep silent, stifle her curiosity, mind her own business. It was not long before she had entered into conversation with those around her. *She was telling them.* They *knew*, and their eyes were no longer indifferent, beautifully indifferent. Clearly in their eyes I saw my secret. I saw the gnome. I saw their pity and all their obscene curiosity wallowing in their eyes. Unholy liquid from the darker depths of their beings. I cursed my mother in my heart. Why couldn't she let me alone? Why did she always give away my secret, expose me to the world? Why did she talk about me always and point to me as if, as if. . . .

I sat in my seat rigidly, cursing her, cursing everybody. My mother revelled in their pity, their curiosity. It was she who received for me the pity and curiosity that I did not want. Leave me alone. Can't you leave me alone? That's all I want.

I sat in my seat, rigid, to be stared at by men and women, of all classes, yet united by that curiosity. I was a picture, curious, exaggerated, obscene, macabre. I could see the sensation the picture gave them. They were safe, so they could stare. The people. They loved to stare, always standing some inches away from the picture, of course. The people.

It satisfied my mother's conscience that she was taking me to the doctor in the city. There was satisfaction in the expense that she was putting herself to.

After a while I refused to go any longer. The doctor was a liar. What were doctors compared with Kings? I did not believe his words. In three months, in three months, he always said. He was a charlatan. I refused to go. The money spent had a great deal to do with my refusal to go any more. I was always made conscious of the money spent on me.

"Keep your dirty money," I cried. "I don't want it."

But my mother would not let me alone. She took me to a still greater city where a woman said things to my mother. If only I had known what she said. If only she had talked to me. But

she talked only to my mother. Her eyes, however, now and then
turned to me. They seemed to understand. I did not know then
that she, too, had a gnome. If I had known, I would have breathed
to her:

"You can stand up. I am trying to. Please help me."

But I did not know. I merely knew that I was thirteen years old,
that I was in a great city which terrified and yet exhilarated me. I
merely knew that I was being dragged from one place to another
where 'deaf people' might be helped.

I sat, silent, and sullen, while my mother talked.

I did not know that the woman with the understanding eyes
had told my mother that she would help me. But I must be left
in the big city, where I could be educated, where I could learn
lip-reading.

If I had known what the woman had said to my mother, I,
having my knowledge of her, would have laughed and said:

"You're a fool. You can't make my mother do anything. Leave
me in the big city? She isn't unselfish enough to do that. She
wants me under her eyes every minute. She wants to lock me up,
stifle me. She hates me because I won't let myself be locked up,
because I kick and scream and tell her I wish she was dead when
she tries to lock me up. If that isn't enough, lady, my mother is a
Jew. Do you know anything about Jews? Lady, it is deadening just
to live with them. They have a dreadful inertia, a fatalism, which
prevents them from doing anything. The family tree of the Jew is
full of rotten branches. Only the Jews won't admit they are rotten
branches. They make poetry out of the rottenness. They call
the rottenness lamentation, or resignation, or irony. Rottenness
made into poetry, poetry made from rottenness. Poetry that
imposes defeat on the soul even before the body has made an
effort. Run from that poetry, lady; run, run! But thank you, kind
lady, thank you, thank you, even if you can't make her do anything. Someday, when I am older, when I am no longer thirteen,
then we shall see."

As I would have predicted, it never came to anything. They could not be stirred. Only *I* would find my own salvation, my way up, up and out.

My mother and I returned home. I would never again go to the doctor, to anybody. I would not give my mother her satisfaction. But one day, a time would come. . . .

I watched my sisters go to school. I had never before realized how much school meant, the mere routine of it, something to do, something sure.

"You can't do anything, you can't do anything," rang in my brain.

I begged or stole the money necessary to go to the movies. I had gone to the movies ever since I could remember, and now, after I became deaf, I returned to the movies again, considering it not only a pleasure, but as an escape from home, my father's sneer, my mother's neuroticism, the taunts of my sisters, the thousand and one hells that made up my home. After I became deaf, this necessity to escape was more evident than before.

At the movies I knew forgetfulness. For four hours—I always stayed for the second show—I was in another world. I did not hear the piano, but I did not mind that after awhile.

No matter how far back among the grown-ups I hid, I was marked-copy during the intermissions for the children. That was the only drawback to the movies.

But the movies palled. Besides, I could not get money to go as often as I wanted to go.

There was the library. There had always been the library as far back as I could remember. I had had a library card ever since I had been able to persuade my father to sign, which he had done only after I had assured him that it did not cost him anything, or involve him in anything. My father and mother had the fear of the immigrant in a new land of signing anything. Unacquainted with the written language, they feared that they might be giving away their very lives if they 'signed anything.' I had always had this suspicion to combat in them.

But now I was afraid to go into the library. I owed the librarian back dues, and I thought that I would not be allowed to set foot in the library. Night after night, when the library was open in the evenings, I hung about its big windows. It was the promised land to me. If only I could enter! If only I could enter! I had not been in there since the gnome came. I had had no straight desire or impulse of any kind until this desire to return to the library became stronger and stronger. Everything else faded. The library! The library!

I owed the library about three dollars. Finally I got the money from my mother and went in and boldly paid my dues. I received a brand new card.

I was truly master of all I surveyed. But there was still another obstacle—the librarian. Dare I approach her with books to be registered? Suppose—suppose she asked me 'something'? I would not, because I could not, answer. She was always talking. She knew that I could not hear, yet she, like others of the people, persisted in talking to me as if I could hear, and when, inevitably, I floundered and blindly struck out with some inane, haphazard remark, she laughed and the others in the vicinity laughed. She did not seem to understand. When I asked her—as I asked others of the people—to write it down, she looked annoyed. That was why when someone with intelligence and quickness did understand immediately and 'wrote it down,' I felt as if the greatest favor in the world were being done me. I was humbly grateful, and said to myself, "Perhaps *she* would understand."

But when I looked into such a person's eyes again, I was afraid. I was afraid to ask the great favor of understanding. That girl in school with the wonderful smile, I had thought that she might understand. But to approach her, to ask her to listen to me, even if I could have put it into words—no, that was impossible. I would never have had the courage. And suppose I was wrong about her;

suppose that look of annoyance, of vexation, of unintelligence, which I knew so well and which killed a little more of my soul every time I saw it on a face, suppose that look came into her face? I could not risk it.

To save the people as well as myself embarrassment, all I asked of them was that they should not talk to me. I went out of my way to avoid them so that I might save them.

Dare I approach the librarian? Desperate, I finally decided on a plan. I would take the books out without first stopping at the desk to register them, and when I brought them back I would not leave them at the desk but put them back in their places on the shelves. This plan worked until there appeared a librarian, short and plain, but with a smile almost as wonderful as that girl's had been. Timidly I took my books to her. She registered them without a word. My heaven was a place where no words were spoken. A place where smiles were enough to say, 'hello friend,' 'good-morning,' 'good-bye.'

My heaven was a place where no words were spoken; yet, what were the people saying? What were the people saying? I walked with my head down, but I raised it now and then to devour the sight of the people with my eyes. I devoured their fish mouths. What words were issuing from the fish mouths? Mouths opened and shut; lips came together unexpectedly; were projected unexpectedly. I devoured the sight. The fish mouths of the people fascinated me. I put words into their mouths and this gave me a slight satisfaction. But only a slight one. I was hungry, terribly hungry, for more. I hated the people, but it was really the envy of a man who knocks at gates that are forever closed to him, and I knew it.

What were the people saying? Oh, what were the people saying? What was this fish mouth and that fish mouth saying? Because I could not hear, I had no conception of the true reality. I magnified the importance of their words. I thought their words must be wonderful, marvellous things. Oh, fish mouth, fish mouth, oh, what are you saying?

Sometimes I could not stand it any longer. Then I would hurry home with a tale.

"Ma, Miss Williams said thus and so. . . ." I would tell a long story.

"How do you know?" asked my mother.

"Oh, I saw it on her mouth," I said vaguely, irritated by the question.

"You're a liar," said my mother, and I would have to slink out of the room.

Oh, what were the people saying? What were the people saying? Fish mouth, fish mouth, often unbeautiful, often unlovely, but what are you saying?

If I had only known! I would have gone out into the world and heard and heard and heard for that time when I heard no more. But I had not known. And now there was nothing to do except to gape at every fish mouth I passed.

Restlessly I roamed the streets.

Crossing the street was an adventure. My mother, who always feared that I would be killed crossing the street, would have locked me up in the house and never let me out. But I had other ideas. My deafness had not made me physically timid, however timid I might be about accosting people. Nor had it softened me into letting others who knew better, who were, in short, authority, have their way with me. I would go out. I would cross the streets.

Once, a policeman had taken me by the arm and crossed to the other side of the street with me. I raged at him. It was fear alone that kept me from kicking him, as I kicked at my father and mother when they had me in a corner. Cunningly, I realized I could not do that to a policeman. I was learning that in this world one must be cunning or one would be 'sent away.'

As I crossed the street with the policeman, I imagined that the whole world had stopped to watch me. I imagined that all eyes were on me. I raged silently at the policeman. I didn't want his help, I didn't want it. He too was trying to make me really deaf.

My mother with her habit of secreting my hat and coat and even my shoes to prevent me from going out, the policeman, did they imagine that because I could not hear, I also could not use my mind? Did they imagine that I had no mind? They seemed to think just that thing.

I hated that winter. I hated all winters, but this one in particular, the first winter of my deafness. My hat and my coat were my jailers. My mother would get hold of them, and I was a prisoner. When spring came . . . when summer came . . . when I could go out in the clothes that I wore. . . .

As soon as it became warm enough to go out without my hat and coat, I went into the country. So had I gone, years ago, to get away from the stores and the houses. So now I went to get away from the stores and the houses and the people. Always the people.

I took a notebook and a pencil with me. In the conversations that I held with myself, I sometimes spoke a phrase that haunted me, that would not go away. I took its words apart and arranged and rearranged them, until the phrase was, I thought, perfect. I was not content, then, to throw away this phrase, into a passing stream, or leave it behind me under a tree where I had sat. I wrote it down in my notebook, and returned to the phrase again and again to admire its particular flavor, follow with my eyes the particular rhythm, as I had followed years ago the movement of my mother's hand across the white expanse of sheet and pillowcase, waiting for the rhythm that came and took me away from the market to another world.

If ever such a phrase came, I wanted a notebook with me so that I might write it down. Sometimes weeks and months went by without such a phrase coming, but nevertheless I wanted the notebook with me. One could never tell when such a phrase would make its appearance. Suppose something came and there was nothing on which to write it? I knew from experience that I had to put down these somethings immediately or they would be gone from me, never to be recaptured.

I began the cycle of menstruation.
"Do men have it?" I asked.
"No," my mother told a sister to write.
"Clara and Lillian?" I persisted.
"All girls," said my mother. "All women."

I could not believe it. Why had I not heard anything about it before? I who had thought I had known everything. My eyes were suddenly opened a little wider than they had been. Life was a dark room; more knowledge meant more light to see into the dark places.

My curiosity grew. What was—it? I knew even less than the average girl. My mother, her words, her early net of ugliness, had awakened in me a hatred for all sexual subjects. Nevertheless, I wanted to know. I went to my mother and began to ask her questions. But she could not look at these things as I looked at them, with an impersonal curiosity. She could not answer clean questions cleanly. It was a thing not to be talked of or discussed openly. It was a thing only to be suggested—as insults, as things vile and ugly. She considered my questions nasty.

She almost silenced me, but my curiosity was stronger than my distaste. Was it only as she said? Or was there another side? Could it be approached from another angle? The books I read were sometimes about love, but I read them without believing. I knew too much about life as it was lived in the houses to believe the books.

There was no one to answer my questions since my mother refused. I could not go to girls. I disliked the talk of girls anyway. I had fought shy of their sex talk when I could hear. It was dirty, nasty, the way they talked. Their talk was merely a continuation of my mother's.

One of the rooms upstairs in our house was rented to a Mr. Mays. Mr. Mays was over sixty when I first met him. Drink and women were his two passions; to acquire them he worked eight hours a day in the mills. On Saturday afternoons and Sundays he sat on the porch and watched the world go by.

Sex interested him more than anything else. Sex made him succumb to every travelling salesman with a line of suit samples; the suit to be sold on the installment plan.

He had been a railway conductor, a school-teacher, a telegraph operator, and there still remained about him all these professions. He would turn from an inspection of a woman to argue with me the finer points of a word and its correct—as against provincial—pronunciation. He taught me how to use the dictionary so that I could find the word I was looking for in a minute. He told me stories of his life. He told me about the women he had known. He was even more ingenuous and naive than I was, although neither of us knew that we were ingenuous or naive.

He was the only person I knew, except perhaps the lawyer, who still considered me the same as I had been before the gnome came. More imaginative and adaptable than most of those around me, he bridged the chasm from talking to 'writing it down' without effort.

I would see him coming down the street, medium height, stout, paunchy body, the red nose of the confirmed drunkard, leonine white head, blue eyes surprisingly clear. He had no illusions. The pretenses of the world to the 'finer things of life' made him laugh. There was one thing, and one thing only in the world, and that thing was sex.

When he had first rented a room in our house, he came home drunk every night. My mother, with her instinct for concerning herself with the lives of others, remonstrated with him. Mr. Mays, always polite to a woman, promised to reform. He reformed to the extent of keeping his debauches for Saturday nights. On week days, instead of drinking, he sat on the porch and commented on the passing women.

I always knew Mr. Mays would be ready for a talk. What community of ideas could there be between a fourteen-year-old girl and a sixty-year-old man? My mother and father, seeing only one thing in life, like Mr. Mays, but not being as clean about it as he was, forbade, when Mr. Mays moved to a room in one of the houses, that I go to see him. I, for my part, could see no reason for remaining away. What if Mr. Mays did live alone? I was unconscious of conventions. What had his living alone to do with me? I was going over to see him whether or not the neighbors 'talked.' We liked each other. I could say whatever was in my head to him, ask him whatever was on my mind, and he generally had an answer that was as clever as it was cynical. He was better than most books. His attempts to touch me, place his arm around me, I regarded rightly as being of no importance. What mattered was the sense of companionship he gave me. I guessed that he was as lonely as I was in spite of all the memories he had to keep him company. He was as much an anomaly in a small town as I.

My father's blows meant nothing to me. They failed to keep me away from Mr. Mays.

"If you don't want me to go there, why don't you tell him to move?" I sneered at my father. But that was more than either my father or mother would do. Mr. Mays was treated very well. After all, he paid five dollars a week. It was only I who was beaten, accused, insulted.

My mother's deep repugnance to privacy extended to her family. She would never allow me to have anything to myself. She was jealous of any contact I made outside of the house, believing that I belonged to her. She was jealous of my friendship with the lawyer, with Mr. Mays. She was jealous of any letters I received and opened them herself. She could not read, but my sisters were always willing to read them to her. Her curiosity, her lack of complete satisfaction in her own emotional life, prompted her to pry into the lives of others, I saw. I would look at my mother and father as people sometimes, and wonder how they got on together. Were they happy in each other? I doubted it. There had never been any privacy for either parents or children; we had always been cooped closely together, in the two rooms over the market, in this little house, and before the gnome came I had heard low, sometimes angry, talk between my father and mother when they had believed us children to be safely asleep.

The market had been an outlet for repressed emotions to my mother, but the market was gone; and now the houses were beginning to function without her. She turned to her children. My father, I perceived, had in some way failed her.

Now with some leisure for her children, she wanted their attention, but they had grown beyond her. They had learned to do without her during the years of the market, and the early years of the houses. To get attention, she must pretend. She gained attention by crying. I, with my knowledge gained through reading and exploration into all kinds of books, understood that she was neurotic, neurasthenic. My greater understanding should have given me compassion with her moods but it did not. I had too much against her.

The market had laid its hand on my mother. The years when in her bold young womanhood she had lifted sides and forequarters of beef from their hooks as confidently as my father and even more so, when she had got up before dawn to steal down through the dark, dirty, liquor-smelling public hallway to the market and to return only at midnight when the market was closed, when she had passed back and forth from the warmth of the back room to the chill of the market, those years of over-exertion were beginning to tell on her now. She was often in the hospital with the rupture that had come from lifting the sides and forequarters of beef. The rupture went, reappeared, went, reappeared, always reappeared. She must have known that, at thirty-five, the death sentence had been passed on her, and would be executed in only a few years, four or five at the most.

She was lonely without the market. She had no women friends, no real friends at all. She never spoke to the other Jewish women of the town. She despised them. She preferred the Americans to the Jews, anyway. "I would rather have one American than ten Jews," she would say.

She wanted sympathy, but she could not get it. She wanted life, she, half dead, spending a living death with the rupture as a constant companion.

"Who is that letter from," she would ask sharply as I came in with a letter—a rare occurrence since she always managed to get my letters first.

"None of your business," I taunted her.

My mother had been nagging me all morning. We were alone in the house as we so often were now that I was no longer at school. She was hysterical. More and more she was losing control of herself, of her temper, at the least contradiction. Her eyes and lips worked with the words I could not hear. But I had no need of hearing. I understood well enough.

I formed countless plans for running away. She could not seem to leave me alone. It was as if she deliberately went after me, goaded by something I did not understand.

"You——, you——," I said, goaded beyond control. "You——"

There it was—out. The word I had picked up somewhere, that I knew meant terrible, unspeakable, things.

"You——" I called her it again. I had called my mother that word. Her eyes and mouth stopped working; the froth about her lips suddenly looked foolish. I started blubbering, terrified. Not at the blows I would get from my father—I was used to them and to his insane rages. I was terrified at my own audacity. There it was—out. It had popped itself into my head and I had used it, caught at it, as the only available weapon to stop her. I had burned the last bridge.

"Let me alone, let me alone." She could not keep her hands off me. My refusal to mop the floor was only an excuse for her to break loose from any last self-control. I was a thing on which to spend her hysteria, her instability. My father was out, my sisters at school. I was the only one handy. I could not hit her back. I could only cower and formulate plans for running away.

"I wish you were dead, I wish you were dead."

"God made you deaf because you were a bad girl," someone said. "Because you said you wished your mother was dead."

To get away I went to Mr. Mays. It was a night on which the library was closed or I would have gone there.

When I returned home, my mother and father were waiting for me. My mother started her usual flow of obscenity. Suddenly I had a suspicion.

"You went up there, didn't you? You peeped through the windows."

I knew from the expression on her face that I was right. I laughed suddenly.

"Ha, ha. Isn't it too bad you didn't see what you wanted to see. Ha, ha. Isn't it too bad you didn't see what you wanted to see. Ha, ha."

I jeered at her over and over again, hating her. I had never known until then just how much I hated her. To stoop to as low as that, to stoop to peep through windows. I knew her suddenly. I knew her by that action. She had given herself away completely. She had given away all the hell of her life by that action. She had shown me her mind and its sick depths.

Where is the proud figure of yesterday? Where is the figure in its apron and dust-cap talking to the salesmen in the market? Where is it? Where are you, poor mother? Your racked body is driving you almost insane. You go about with your hand pressed to that part of your body where the rupture is. It grows larger and larger. It subsides, and you have a moment of peace; but then it comes again and grows larger and larger. You are hungry for pity. You say, feel, feel, feel. Rupture, beautiful souvenir of the market days. Everything seems to go wrong. You do not know what to do, so you sit down by the stove and burst into tears. If you only had someone to talk to! But you have no one. A husband and children are not enough, you have always been reaching out for something more. You are not stupid enough, as the other women of the town are, to be content.

"I'll run away. I'll run away."

"You can't do anything. You aren't good for anything any more." They hurl the phrases at me.

One morning, when my mother comes toward me again, something in me snaps. I walk out of the house. I walk to the end of the street. I come to the end of the houses. I am out in the country. I walk on. After awhile I grow tired. I am dusty and thirsty and hungry. I come to a new town. I ask a child if I can have a drink of water. I walk on. I pass a town pump, another town pump. It is all a dream. I do not know that I am walking in a circle. I grow tired. I think longingly of home, even of my mother.

I am too tired to go on. I stay overnight at a farm house. I confess everything to the woman, and she telephones my mother.

Nevertheless, even this poor imitation of a runaway has an effect. Evidently I can still do something. My mother tries to control herself.

It is Friday night. Friday night in a Jewish household. The atmosphere of candles and candlesticks pervades the house, even to the farthest room upstairs.

My mother has a shawl over her head. She is saying something over the candles. Her hands form a canopy over the candles as she prays. My mother's mouth is not entirely a fish mouth to me because I can remember her voice, and therefore, in my way, I hear her. All other mouths are fish mouths, my father's, my sisters', the people's. To the last, I heard my mother. So, I hear her as she prays over the candlesticks, a shawl over her head. I snicker a little as

I have learned to do—for am I not a good American? America has taught me to be a good American, to snicker at anything unusual, 'foreign.' But on Friday nights my snicker is silenced. My Americanism is far away. I am in a Jewish household. I breathe Jewish air. I remember uneasily that I am a Jew.

I sit down at the table. Only on Friday nights do we have such a meal. It is such a big meal that afterward my father and mother lie down to digest it, and we children escape—to the streets, to the movies.

On Friday nights after the big meal has been eaten, the dishes washed, my father and mother out of sight, the children at the movies, there is peace in the house and I partake of this peace. I love Friday night's peace, as I love the peace of the American's Sunday. I sit alone in the kitchen, my hands on the white tablecloth, not wholly white, for there are wine spots at my father's place, and my sisters and I have bad table manners. I sit alone and read. I like the kitchen when it is like this. The very light seems less hard. Perhaps it is my father who makes the light seem so hard. I am afraid of him. I cannot bear to be in the same room with him alone. Instantly I rise and leave the room. Why do I do this? I cannot explain exactly. I only feel. My skin shrinks, and the soul within the skin also shrinks. Perhaps my skin is remembering the beatings my father has given it. Certainly it is fear. I do not mind being alone with my mother, but not with father.

I sit at the table reading, my elbows on the cloth. I savor the aloneness of the room, the soft light, the peaceful air.

Winter came again. Books palled, the movies palled. One night, when the library was closed, and I could get no money for the movies, and my hat and coat had been hidden as usual, I got out my notebooks filled with sentences and phrases. I began a poem. That is, I thought up new sentences and they rhymed. I continued, interested. I forgot the hell downstairs.

Every night, almost, I came back to my poems.

My own mouth was a fish mouth for I could not hear my own voice, no more than I could hear the voices of the people. Having lost control of my voice, although not my voice itself, it ran now high, now low.

My voice was a wind. I played games with it. I could not hear my wind, but I could feel it. Some days I had but to put my hand on my throat and I could feel the wind very clearly. When I talked I could feel through my fingers the melancholy sound the wind made. A monotonous, melancholy swinging sound, always the same sound, in the same key. Had my voice only one refrain now, I wondered? Even so, I loved it. I talked, and as I talked, I would forget that I was talking and exactly what it was that I was saying, and listen to the wind, the monotonous wind, in my throat. Sometimes it was more the death-rattle of the wind than the swinging wind itself; again, the sound might be a series of little water-chuckles. Listening through my fingers, I would laugh at the sound, it was so happy.

"Vibration," the people said with their usual lack of imagination. As in everything else, I preferred my own interpretation.

I insisted to myself that I could still hear. I heard in my mind the sounds of streams as I passed them. I knew the sound the river made, that river that I had known always, the river by the marble house. In my mind the river washed with a low intimate sound. I had no need to hear as the people heard. True intimacy needs no ears. I knew the sound of birds; I heard them as they hopped about. I knew the sound of words also. It was words that I most intensely heard. I had not always the river and the birds—they appeared far away at times. I did not always want river and birds, but I always wanted words, and I always had them. I would have been terribly lonely without them. With them always in my mind, I could not be truly lonely. I played with them; I set them to music; I achieved endless variations with them. They were never weary, as other things could sometimes be weary.

Yes, I said to myself, I can hear. Only the people defied me. Only the people. They remained fish mouths. But for the people I would not be deaf.

They said: head noises. But again I preferred my own interpretation. It was my brain working. And what a noise it made! The brain must be a crazy thing indeed! A thing immeasurably more active than the body. And I, alone of all others, had been allowed to hear this activity, this inward working.

There were different noises. It was not a machine, well oiled, going on always in the same smooth, regular way. No, it was not a machine. It was more a human being, a strange unusual, human being.

Sometimes there was a great clatter, as if a million and one dishes had suddenly been dropped on the floor by the perverse human being who was my brain. Again, he might take it into his head to be a bird—but a marvellous bird!—and sing with inhuman sweetness. I never knew what he would do next.

Walking up the alley to the houses. Walking up the alley. Sometimes I forgot to continually turn around and see that no car was coming from behind me. At such times it was only instinct that saved me.

It was humiliating when I saw the people watching. They were laughing at me.

I was suspicious, ever on the defensive. They were all my enemies. What they had said—was it true? Could I believe them? Could I believe the things they told me? It was terrible, my reliance on them, on what they said. I knew my mother's propensity for making up horrors to scare me into obedience. Before the gnome came, I could laugh at her. I could find out for myself. But now—now I was at her mercy. She could fill my soul with all kinds of bogey-men.

The knowledge I was given was perverted knowledge. My mother, neurotic, was doing her best to make me neurotic. Her scenes—I shrank from them as from obscene things, as I shrank from her attempts to enter my life, as I had shrunk from her attempts to save me by locking me up in a cage.

Every day I must be on the defensive. I could trust no one. Was it true? Had the 'authorities' said that I was not to be allowed on the street, but remain always in the house? Or had my mother made it up? I felt again that I was being stifled, as if the wind in my throat was being choked off. It brought the same feeling as when my sisters said:

"You can't do anything, you can't do anything. . . ."

I cursed my mother, my father, my sisters, the authorities. Some day, some day, I would pay them back.

When I shut myself up in my room to write my poems, there were always intruders. My mother sent my sisters up. What was I doing, what was I writing? They were suspicious. What glee there was when a poem that I had sent to the magazines came back. What glee! What laughter!

Quite as much as I hated my mother, I hated my father. Only my hatred for her was an articulate hatred, while my hatred for my father, inarticulate, reached a depth of intensity which I carried around with me night and day. I did not mind his blows, his insane rages, when I got used to them. Nor did I mind his silent sneering at my 'refinement,' my ways that were different or tried to be different, my contempt and detestation for the thousand and one intimacies that the others committed. Most of all there were his sneers at my writing.

One day I penetrated my father. His hatred of me was really envy. Long ago he too had written poems, had tried to be 'gentle,' and he had failed. He had not had the strength to hold out against my mother who was a materialist. If he had been me, he would have told my mother and the children to go to hell, and gone his way writing and living as he wished. But he had not had the strength to hold out against her as I was holding out.

But I had the strength, possibly inherited from my mother. And now he was trying to kill all the longings I had inherited from him; he was trying to break my will as his had been broken. But he could not. For I had her in me as well as him. I had her endurance that would persist, that would not admit failure.

I dared not walk on that side of the street. I wanted to go over and look in the store windows on that side, but I dared not.

No one else saw them, only myself. The long line of people standing on that side of the street. If I went over, their eyes would turn on me. They would strip me with their eyes. I dared not walk on that side of the street. I kept my eyes away from it when I must walk past it on the safe side of the street. All the same, I knew that their eyes were following me, following me. I could feel their eyes boring into my back. Can't you see them? Can't you see them? Only I seemed to see them. But they were more real to me than the everyday people I saw on the street.

I knew that it was a hallucination, but I could not rid myself of it. Like the habits I had had in childhood, the wriggling of the nose, the twitching of the lips, the jerk-jerk-jerk of the shoulders, only time would rid me of it. Meanwhile I suffered.

"Your dress is sticking in," I said bitterly, contemptuously, to my mother when she arose from a chair.

More than anything else I hated that 'sticking in.' The dresses of 'ladies' did not stick in when they arose from sitting down. To me, that was the sign of a lady. To be like the ladies, to arise from one's seat and know that one's dress in back was smooth, was not sticking in. To forget entirely the back of one's dress; never to carry the knowledge of it around with one, to be free of giving that surreptitious movement to see if everything was all right.

"Your dress is sticking in," I said to my mother, hating her, ashamed of her.

My own dress—was it sticking in? Was it sticking in? It became an obsession with me. Was it sticking in? My hand went back and gave that surreptitious movement of smoothing down, smoothing down. My hand continued to go back, go back, go back, and smooth it down, smooth it down, smooth it down. It became a habit. On the street, my hand aimlessly went back and smoothed down, smoothed down, smoothed down. If there had been anyone left who doubted my craziness, his doubts went as he saw me on the street, smoothing down, smoothing down, smoothing down. The bums on the street imitated the movement to my face.

The people on that other side of the street, the people who appeared to be unseen save by myself, were they watching me? Was my dress sticking in? The invisible people can be more exacting, more critical, than the visible people. No one knew this better than myself. My hand nervously, again and again and yet again made that movement of smoothing down, smoothing down, smoothing down. Oh, save me from the invisible people! I cried. I am afraid of them, I am terribly afraid of them. In my world there seemed to exist only invisible people, and they were closing in on me.

When I was fourteen or fifteen I went to the factories and applied for work. Anything to get away from home. I tendered the forelady or foreman a piece of paper on which was written that I was deaf, and that I would like to have a job. In this way, I did most of my talking. Because I could not hear my voice, I did not trust it. I might have been dumb as well as deaf, for all I used my voice.

I wanted a job, not only to get away from home, but I wanted to show them that they were wrong.

"You can't do anything, you can't do anything," I was taunted.

I would show them.

But my jobs, when I managed to get them, never seemed to last for long. I could not make myself like the others in the factory. Why, some had been in the factory for a quarter of a century. How could they do it? To have no other life except the life of the factory. To come, day after day, after day, after day, to come here, to sit down at a machine, to be released from the machine only when it was dark. Meanwhile, the world, the marvellous world, was going by. What of the world, and the marvels in it? Did they never think of these things? I sat down at my machine in the factory, the second day, hating it. I could not make a straight line anyway. Fear entered my heart, set my soul quivering, so that no amount of 'sh-sh, dears' could stop it. Was it true? Were they right? Was I not good for anything any more? As I had been expelled from school, so was I being expelled from the factories? I could not seem to understand routine, doing the same thing over and over and over again. God! How I hated the factories and the machines and the foreladies and the foremen! Why was there not a revolution, a war, but a different war? No people should be killed; a war in which all factories were dynamited, so that the people might file out, free.

Crazy! Crazy! It rang in my head all the time. They said I was crazy. Was I? Were they right? I had peculiarities, had always had them, for I had my own way of doing things, and that way was not the way of the people. Now I had still further developed peculiarities. Or so they said. In reality, I knew that I was only being natural; in a way that they would never be natural.

Now, more than ever, I was not of the people. I went my own way, and that was the secret way of a gnome. It was as if I had taken on myself the personality of the gnome and was doing things *his* way, gnome's way.

Were they right? There were so many on their side, and only I on my side. The gnome was drawing me down. I was going through life like a gnome, in a secret gnome's way that was not like the way of the people.

"You can't do anything, you can't do anything . . . you're crazy, you're crazy. . . ." Were they right? Were they right?

Yet I was only trying to stand up. If there were only someone to help me, someone who would understand and take my hand and help me to stand upright. Stand up! Stand up!

Crazy . . . crazy . . . crazy . . . it rang through my brain. Then I thought: I must not let the people get me, I must not let the people get me. If I did not take care, they would most surely have me crazy. My mother with her perverted words, instilling fear into my soul. Were they after me? Everybody was after me, according to her. Would they put me away? Was I crazy? What did she mean? What did her words mean?

"Go to hell," I said to my mother. "Go to hell," I said to the authorities. It was all the satisfaction I could get. I would go my way, the gnome's way. For it seemed to me that I had become him. There were no longer two of us, the gnome and myself. There was one: the gnome, and the gnome was myself. If I addressed the gnome, I also addressed myself. It had always been so, but it had taken a long time to learn, and after learning, to admit it for the final thing it would ever be.

The people . . . the sober sane people who said I was crazy. . . . The plumbers, the carpenters, the grocers, the druggists, the butchers, the tailors, the clothing store keepers, these were the sober sane people. Deep within me, the gnome and I laughed and laughed and laughed as we watched them. This laughter within me, it seemed to be the only thing that had escaped, the only thing that the people had not been able to touch. My laughter was happy. Within me, somewhere, when I laughed, life was joyous.

George lived in one of the flats at the houses. Like Mr. Mays, like almost everybody else who lived in the houses, he was a habitual drunkard. He lived with a woman who might or might not have been his wife. I liked to go to his flat on Sundays to read the Sunday papers. George was kind. He was kinder than the good people. He belonged to the simple people who followed the band, who followed simply like children the beautiful music.

George, like Mr. Mays, did not mind writing it down. He made of the rite something as simple as himself. I always felt more at home among the simple people. Such people were more to be found among the poor, among the oppressed, among the uneducated.

My mother, to stop me from going to George's, said he was no good, that he was a drunkard. But what had that to do with me, I thought? He had never touched me. He let me alone. Sitting on the bed, I read the papers and was happy. There were other people in the room, drinking, smoking, playing cards. They let me alone. I paid no attention to them and they paid no attention to me. I was aware of them only when I raised my eyes from the papers, which was seldom. It was a typical Sunday atmosphere in the flat of a factory employee. Yet my parents objected to my going there. I had been threatened with a whipping if I went. I continued to go every Sunday. I would not give up the close warm smoky atmosphere of George's flat, the friendliness of George and his wife. It was another way of escape from my home.

My parents could not believe my innocence. One Sunday afternoon returning from George's I was whipped. My father beat me, all but killing me. My mother, after seeing that I had received enough, interfered. This time I did not thank her for it. I had got hold of a bottle of milk and longed to smash it on my father's head. If my mother had not interfered I would have smashed my father's head in with the bottle. Ever afterward when I thought of that time, I trembled.

Sometimes I wondered why I did not complain to the authorities. There was one woman who might have befriended me. My father hated her; years before she had hauled him into court for almost beating his horse to death. Why did I not go to her? Because my mother had said that all the authorities were against me. Would they believe me? Would they see my side of it? Would they believe me, sitting silent and sullen, except for a flame, now and then, of passion? *They* would do all the talking, taking advantage of my deafness as they had taken advantage of it from the beginning, scaring me with their perverted knowledge. No! I could not ask for help. Here, as in other ways, I must struggle up alone.

They were trying to close all avenues of escape for me. I was to be shut up in the house, like an animal not to be let loose, because it was too wild, too crazy. These attempts to shut me up only served to make me wilder, more crazy.

My father's mother came to live with us. She was almost seventy, and had just come from the old country. She could not speak English. She went about as she had gone about in the old country, in peasant clothes with a shawl on her head. I was always ashamed of her, but as I saw what she was being subjected to from my sisters with no interference from my parents, I stood up for her, defending her in a half shamed way. She, like I, was a prisoner in this house, at the mercy of the jailers. I, the younger one, tried to ward off the blows of the jailers, from her as well as from myself.

'Honor thy father and mother,' my mother and father said. Was my father honoring his mother? He allowed his children to make fun of her so that she must complain to the neighbors.

Yet there was something in my father that struggled. Was he, like me, ashamed and disgusted when my mother, knowing no restraint, made her filthy suggestions about me, stinging him into beating me? Did he envy me my youth, my ability to run away from all this if I but had the nerve some day? He hated me because he could not run away from all this. Sometimes, watching my father, I saw things, no more than a gesture perhaps, which, nevertheless, made me stop and think, for it was from nothing more than such gestures that I pieced together the people. When he beat me, was he not working off his hatred, his weariness, his discouragement, his disillusionment, his dissatisfaction? Somewhere, inside, his spirit struggled. He had been trapped, trapped, by my mother, trapped in a town where there was no man fit for him to associate with.

The books he used to read? There was no time now to read his books. First it was the market, and then the houses. His books were stored on the top pantry shelf. My mother had put them there. His blows were harder, remembering. My mother did not like to see him reading when there was 'so much to do.' She considered reading a waste of time. I could be allowed to read, for, after all, I was deaf. I was not good for much else.

My mother did not accept my constant reading without a struggle. It was only after it became obvious that I was not much good for anything else that she gave me up. She took away my books and bought me a pair of knitting needles and some yarn. But I had not the patience or the inclination to knit. I was not clever like my sister, who kneaded bread every Saturday night while my father and mother joined in a chorus of praise. I was also a failure as a floor-mopper, a dish-washer, a sewer, a bed-maker, an ironer. All these things my sister could do brilliantly. I was an ignoramus. I was good only for books and 'writing poems.'

On my walks down the dark streets I often passed the same man and woman walking together, arm in arm. I never saw them by day, or even by night on the lighted streets of the town. Only on the dark streets. As they walked, close together, I felt in them the dark color of the outcasts. Why did they walk like this, unlike other people? Why did they walk with their heads down, afraid to meet my eyes, or, if our eyes did accidentally meet, why did they turn away, afraid, from the curiosity in my eyes? Was I one of the people to them? There was about the girl both fear and defiance as she clung to the man.

So girls walked who had just returned from the reformatory, afraid and ashamed before the people, cowed by their curiosity. Had she just returned? Or did she belong to that dark row of houses on the Extension? Had this man taken her out of that life and made her his wife, but they could not walk under the light because the people knew?

I met and passed them again and again, feeling a sympathy for them, understanding their fear and defiance, for did I not know fear and defiance myself?

I wove a story about these two; gave them a romance which they probably did not possess. The man's face was nothing, and the woman's face was stupid except for that glimmer of defiance to which I responded.

Every evening they gathered there, on the same corner, a few young men and women. The women were street-women, and the men were bums, loafers, my mother said.

I went past them on my walks up and down the streets. Their open carefreeness and laughter were strange in a place where everybody was the people. I would have joined them, but I had not the courage. I was deaf—for that reason I must walk alone. I could not approach anyone, or find a friend. My deafness was a wall that kept me from everybody.

Although I could not join them, I could watch them. The men seemed to have no jobs. They hung around the corner all day. The women did not join them until the evening. They probably worked in the factory all day, and this was their way of having a good time. Because they did it openly, they were outcasts.

The men were bums, loafers, because they did not join the other men in the community and become respectable citizens, accept responsibilities. They preferred to spend their time on the corner, waiting for their women, whiling away the time with talk or silences.

But the people got them after all. One of the girls showed up one day with a big belly. One of the men married her. I saw them on the streets afterward, walking together, no longer happy and carefree, hating each other, faces turned from each other, walking mutely. They had had to marry. Here were two free things, two more free things caught. They had had to marry. As if marriage was the way out, the solution to the problem. As if marriage was the answer to everything. Keep the surface free and smooth, by all means. Never mind the hell that goes on underneath.

Many of the brightest, prettiest girls of the town were caught this way. While they worked in the factories they wore marvellous clothes, made possible by the installment-plan system. These factory girls dressed better than any of the other girls in town. They had more style, being "foreigners," for the most part French and Polish. A ten-dollar dress looked better on them than a dress imported from New York looked on the daughters of the wealthier parents of the town.

They were wonderful to look at, in their silk dresses, their legs in the thinnest of silk stockings, their feet trim in patent leather pumps. Their faces were as carefully dressed as their bodies, lips and cheeks painted, eyebrows plucked to the thinnest of lines.

On Sundays I would sit on the porch and watch them pass. Did they care what the people said about them, their painted faces, their lovely slim bodies? They did not appear to. They guessed rightly that it was merely envy of their youth and joyousness.

But a few years later they married and the streets saw them no more. Respectability had got them. Once a year, perhaps, when there was going to be a parade and the whole town turned out, one might see them. Then one saw with a shock that this was *she*, with a baby, and another one on the way. She looked tired and wore old clothes. Was she the bright happy girl I had seen only a few years ago? The people had got her, and now she was indistinguishable from them.

A smaller sister would not put on the heavy underwear my mother made us wear for winter. I watched while she struggled in my mother's arms, trying to keep her leg out of the underwear.

"I won't put them on," she said, over and over again. "I won't! I won't!"

"Don't, then!" I said, understanding, for I, too had hated the heavy winter underwear. "Don't, then!" I repeated in all the arrogance of my fifteen years, and in the fact that a year ago I had flatly refused to wear winter underwear.

My mother flung me a glance of hatred. I was a bad influence in the house with my open flouting of parental authority, which incited the other children to rebellion.

I loved the dictionary. But the one put into my hands was abridged, for the use of children. I would come across a word which contained wonderful possibilities for enlightening me on that subject which had begun to bother me. I would look up the word in the dictionary, only to find the meaning cryptically hidden in another word, also a stranger to me. Words were strangers who might prove to be flat or interesting. I looked up the strange word, and the same thing happened—its meaning was hidden again in a still stranger word. The dictionary was like a grown-up speaking to children, a grown-up who never spoke honestly or simply, but hid himself in evasions.

I was not easily defeated. There was a big dictionary in the library. I took the strange words and in the big dictionary traced them to their simple common source. But not wholly to their source. The big dictionary was a grown-up who was only apparently more frank and honest than the grown-up of the abridged dictionary. The big dictionary was for the use of grown-ups, grown-ups who did not face things honestly and simply, who answered each other with the same evasions that they answered children. Their honesty was only apparent. They still retained their inhibitions.

My mother had told me not to be nasty, not to speak of such things—although five minutes later she was inconsistent enough to hurl all sorts of filthy phrases at me; nevertheless, I still wanted to know. Since neither my mother nor the dictionary were of help, I must try elsewhere.

No one except myself ever seemed to patronize anything except the fiction rows in the library. I sniffed hungrily at the shelves marked 'Biography', 'Biology', 'Poetry', 'Literature', 'History'. I took books out and put them back in the wrong places. This aroused the antagonism of the librarian who, if it had not been for me, would never have bothered much with those shelves. She was always asking me to tell her what it was that I wanted, but since I did not know myself, how could I?

Under 'Biology' I came across what I was looking for. Here it was—prosy, flat facts. In the books I learned that *it* was called the sexual act, which seemed to me much less imaginative and picturesque than my mother's name for it. As I read on, I learned that babies were the only reason for the sexual act being in existence. I was not interested in babies. This was not so different from the way my mother talked, except that she took one extreme—that it was dirty and they took the other—that it was merely a thing for the reproduction of the species.

I continued to read, but I failed to share their enthusiasm for babies. I also did not believe that people came together because they wanted a baby. I had seen life at first-hand as it was lived in the houses. Babies were just incidents—what seemed to matter was the relationship between the man and the woman. The man and woman looked happy when they 'got along well together'; when they did not get along well together they looked miserable, they spoke sharp words to each other, they often fought; the man looked at other women, and the woman looked at other men. Yes, there was more to the sexual act than these books were willing to tell me.

Sex continued to trouble me. My mind was alive to whatever it might be. I did not look upon it as the girls around me did, *letting themselves go*, losing themselves in it, eager to lose themselves in it. I did not want that. That was evil, unclean. That was where the evilness in it lay. My mind stood off, clear and cold. I had seen what it meant if a woman let herself go. I had seen what it had done to my mother. Look at her. It was not the children it had brought into being, nor the gross body—body that had once been slender and proud—*but what it had done to her mind*. It should never do that to me. I would sooner let it alone entirely.

See what it had done to her. That was all she could see now. She could not see beyond it. She could see no action in any other light; it colored all her interpretations. All married women were the same. And girls—they were eager for the same thing. Why didn't the women who knew tell the girls of the mouse-traps they were about to put their heads into? Why, instead, did they urge their daughters into the mouse-traps?

And the girls—why couldn't they see for themselves? Why didn't they look at their mothers and fathers and see as I saw? Everybody seemed to see without seeing.

I did my thinking on the streets, walking with my head down, so that I might escape their eyes, although all the time I was busily thinking about them. I did not look openly. I stole odd glances, and when I had achieved a glance, I stole away with it and worried over what I had seen. When I had picked the glance clean, I returned for another glance. I walked on the streets, talking to myself, silently, my lips moving. The two people in my head were very busy.

PART FOUR

POETRY

I had been writing ever since I could remember; ever since that time when, catching my mother in a momentary good humor in the market, I had read my stories to her while she leaned back against the cash register.

Then for a few years the desire to write left me; what expression of self I wanted was satisfactorily achieved through the physical avenue—school, playgrounds, skating, climbing, jumping. Then the gnome came. I was shut up within myself. But I could not remain enclosed within these walls. I would choke. A door must be opened or I would become really deaf.

The movies had failed, books had failed. I wanted something else. I must have something else. My poetry became the door that led me out of my deafness. First, perhaps, I wrote for forgetfulness, to forget the gnome, to forget that I was deaf, to forget the people and their fish mouths. I did not ask for more than this. Then I began to write as I had begun to read, first blindly and devouringly, then with a glimmer of fastidiousness and self-criticism.

I wrote and forgot almost immediately what it was that I had written. My parents sneered at my writing. One more craziness on my part. But I kept on writing.

One day I read in a paper an interview with a poet. His life, as he told it to the interviewer, was so like mine that I began to think. I had imagined myself to be the only one in antagonistic surroundings. Evidently there were others. Yet this man had been able to rise above them, above his home and parents, and had made something of himself. But how could I compare myself with him, I wondered in despair. I was deaf, deaf, deaf. He was not. He had no gnome on his back, doubly bearing him down. He had no gnome to set him apart. I, if I would rise, must balance myself upright with the gnome always on my back. Only in that way could I rise above the gnome. This man had had parents who did not understand his aspirations toward a something, a crystallization of all the restlessness in his soul into something fine and beautiful. I studied the man's face trying to find in it some resemblance to my own, for I wanted to find some basis for comparison. What he could do, I could do. He had risen—could I, in spite of the gnome? It was the old cry in my soul. If only I could stand up! If only I could stand up!

My poems, my poems. Many nights I had taken them to bed with me, feeling each one to be a friend. Could my poems be the way to our standing up, gnome and I? But there could be nothing in the poems. I sent them to the magazines, and they were returned. I was laughed at when the long envelopes returned.

For a week, two weeks, I went about with the clipping of the interview with the poet. Again and again I read the lines; again and again I studied the man's face. His word and his face were courageous. He must be a beautiful person, as I had always known poets must be. Poets were the beautiful people of the world. Poets were not the people.

I read Shelley. One day I came upon the facts of his life. For a week I could not touch Shelley. Could it be true? I felt a revulsion toward the very name of Shelley.

Then it came to me. What a fool I was, what a narrow fool I was. What did I know? What right had I to judge? What I had read was *their* side—the people's side. How did I know but what Shelley might have had something to say for himself, if only he had been given the chance? His life was mine. My life was his over again.

All anybody ever saw was the people's side, for the whole world was inhabited for the most part by the people. Everything and anything a poet did was beautiful and right. The people—damn the people. Who were they? What were they? Judges without imagination, horribly without imagination. My Shelley, my dear, dear Shelley, I whispered, begging pardon for my week of neglect.

This man was as beautiful as Shelley, as kind as Shelley. Could I ask this man to understand me? Could I dare ask him to come and be my friend? I studied the man's face, and came to a resolution.

I would send him my poems. He would tell me if I were worth saving, or if I should let go the small grasp on reality I had managed to get in the three years that had passed since the gnome came. Was I worth helping to stand up? I would send him my poems and ask them to say for me what could not say for myself.

But how was I to reach him? Where should I send my poems? There was no address in the interview. Then I decided to send the poems to him in care of the paper in which interview had appeared. Should I write a letter with the poems? Suppose they did not say what I wanted them to say? Suppose they were still too young and inarticulate to say what I desired to say through them?

I would write that I liked his poems, although I had never read any of them, had never heard his name before. I was still asleep to contemporary poets. Shelley existed, and Keats existed. I read all the books under 'Poetry' in the library, and when I came upon a rhythm that could attract the attention of my own particular rhythm, I continued to read. What I was searching for—and for the most part unconsciously—was a rhythm that could release my own rhythm, awaken the music in my head as my mother had awakened it ironing the white expanse of sheet and pillow-case.

That I had not found him among the books under 'Poetry,' I blamed the library. The library was incomplete. Therefore I was not really lying when I said I had read his poems. It was not my fault that I had not read his poetry.

I sent him my poems and the letter. One sentence in the letter must have been articulate with my misery. I did not, however, tell him about the gnome. It seemed unfair not to tell him, but I could not bring myself to write the words. I wanted his picture of me to be the picture I had of myself, and that was a picture that did not include the gnome.

He replied. He said he would like to see some more of 'my work.' My work! How wonderful that phrase sounded. He would help me, he said. He was interested, and would like me to continue sending my poems to him. He would correct them. There was not much in them as yet, he said, but he could see something large struggling through. He would help me. He would write to me.

I could not keep that first letter to myself. I must wave it before my father, mother, and sisters.

From the beginning I battled with myself back and forth. Should I tell him about the gnome? But I could not. If I told him, that obscene something would immediately enter his mind and soul—even if against his will—and he would hold me different from himself. I would tell him after a while perhaps, when he had come to know me well through my letters. I would then tell him about the gnome, and he would realize that the gnome had made no difference, as the people seemed to think the gnome had made a difference. I would then tell him, and he would understand. I did not doubt his understanding, but I could not tell him now. I was a coward. I was still the child with the gnome on her back who whimpered and crept off into the darkness and hid, for although the darkness might be replete with other gnomes and fantastic creatures, the people were not there. And what the child feared most was the people. The people with their fish mouths.

How I worked on my poems to make them good so that he might pick out a line here and there for approval. It was a long time before I wrote a whole poem that won his praise.

In my letters I poured out my soul, asking for advice, telling him about the hell of my life, everything—everything except the gnome. That I could not tell.

I did not tear up the letters from him but hid them away in what I thought was a safe place. One day I came upon my sister reading them all to my mother.

Damn you . . . damn you. . . .

After that I carried them around with me by day, and at night I slept with them under my pillow.

They did not understand. They saw ugly, possibly evil, things in his writing to me.

"Leave him alone. He's too good for you. He's clean and decent. Keep your hands off him. . . ." I cried at them.

I knew they would keep his letters from me if they could. Therefore, early every morning I got up and waited patiently half-dressed, in the bitter winter cold for the mail-man to come around.

They were against my receiving letters from him. It was another attempt on their part to frustrate a way of escape. I adopted a new attitude toward my parents because of what the poet said. I was doing them the honor of considering them ogres, he said; I should look upon them, instead, as blind fools. Do not give them the satisfaction of your tears, of seeing that they have hurt you.

I went about the house with a closed face, remote. I was wrapped up in him and his letters. They kept me safe from any contact with them. This attitude, if anything, aggravated my parents even more than my open rebellion against their authority, even more than my curses. Abuse and curses they could understand, for it was their own language, but the more subtle attitude that the poet advised was beyond their comprehension. They could not get at me when I went about silent and unseeing. There was envy too, envy that I so obviously cared more for him and his letters than for themselves. They hated him. They hated him for what he was doing to me, the new person he was making me into.

I went about conscious of him every moment of the day as though he were some secret glory that I carried about with me in my mind and soul. I no longer cared about their laughter. I forgot the people and their fish mouths. I forgot the gnome. I went about with eyes that saw nothing. I was in love. But a love that desired nothing more than his letters. I had no desire to see him.

Then one day there was no letter. He wrote every week, but this week no letter had come. It was true that one morning I had overslept so that I had not met the mail-man, but when I had accused them of taking the letter, they denied there had been any. Like an ever credulous fool I believed them.

Another week went by. Still no letter. Was he sick? Frantically I wrote to him. There was no answer. What had I done? Had I hurt him? Was that why he did not write?

A month went by, two months. Still I wrote to him, even if there was no reply. I had long lost hope of an answer, but still I wrote.

One day I happened to meet the mail-man on his noon round. There was a letter from him. Half crying, half laughing, like a crazy person, I ran upstairs to my room to read it. When I finished it I began to cry again.

There had been letters from him, many letters. My father intercepted them. I had not got them because they had all come on that noon round and I had not thought to bother about that round of the mail-man. All his letters before had come in the morning.

My father had written him a letter, a threatening letter. The poet was to stop writing to me. I blushed with shame as I thought what my father's letter must have been like. All the vileness of expression that he and my mother were capable of had probably been in that letter. My father was a bully, my mother too. Their only method was abuse heaped on abuse. That he should have been touched by them and their filth. I could not bear the thought. I had endured the insults meant for him gladly. That they should have found their way to him and touched him. He whom I had made into an ethereal being. He to be touched by their rottenness.

I ran downstairs to where my father was. I accused him with the hardest, bitterest words I could find. I lowered myself to his level that I might attack him better.

"Damn you, damn you, you damned dirty Jew. . . ."

But he only sneered. I knew that sneer. Could one's words ever reach deeply enough to hurt a person with that sneer?

I wrote to the poet that I had at last received his letter. We began our correspondence again. I dared them to take his letters. To ensure my always getting them, I seldom left the house. If I went out, I was always back before the mail-man came around.

My depression lifted. I could write again. Once more I felt like something other than an under-dog.

Spring came. A whole poem now, instead of a line, received commendation from him. Even I could see the improvement. There were images that were fresh and new.

Look around you, look around you, he said. I made poems out of everyday things—everyday things, yet I had not seen them until he told me to look for them.

He opened my eyes not only to the things around me but to the contemporary world of books. I read Ezra Pound as I read Shelley, and I loved him as I loved Shelley. There were others, many others. How curiously blind I had been!

One day an expected letter from him did not come. Another day went by and still another. His letter failed to come. Had they taken his letter?

They had not taken any letters. I was forced to believe them for I met the mail-man every time he came around. Frantically I wrote to him. There was no reply.

He of his own accord was not writing to me. He was deliberately not writing to me.

I never stopped waiting for him to write, but he never did.

For a year or more he had patiently helped me with his letters, helped me to find the way out, helped me to stand up. I was afraid now; with him gone would I fall down again? Dare I try to continue to stand up? For he had not accomplished all. He had only shown me how I *might* stand up. It was up to me to make the actual attempt. No one except myself could do that. And I had stood up— while he had been there for me to hold on to. Now that he was gone, was I doomed to fall down again? No, I owed it to him to keep on trying to stand up even if he no longer cared to watch over me. A fifteen-year-old child reasoning into the night.

PART FIVE

THE HUMAN BEING

I was alone again now, one against the people. I had attempted to detach one from among them, and had failed to keep him. Not for me were such things. The only one from whom I might expect understanding was myself.

Yet I must have someone, someone who, if he could not help me, would at least look at my poems and say they were good.

For a long time I had not gone to see the lawyer, although when we met on the street we smiled at each other as we had always done.

At home they were talking about him, laughing at him, jeering at his drunkenness. I stood up for him, as I stood up for anyone who had incurred the displeasure of the people for being different, for violating the ordinances of the people. In my heart I united with them against the people. It might be the lawyer, it might be the boys and girls on the corner, or it might be the man and woman I passed on the dark streets. I was with them, and against the people.

I went to the lawyer's office, even if it meant a whipping when I returned home.

The lawyer, as I had found out long ago, had limitations. I watched his face as he read my poems. I did not agree with his corrections. But I continued to go to his office, falling again under the spell of the lawyer and the office. There was a peace in both of them that I could appreciate.

At this time I lived only in my poems. I put the poet out of my mind, but my poems must go on. After I had written one, an exhilaration seized me. I walked among the people without seeing them. The poem might be no good, but I never criticized. I did see, however, that I did not commit the faults the poet had warned me against. But what I loved was the emotion, the flight the creation of the poem produced in me. If I could identify this flight with my rhythm, then I made of my brain itself a poem that kept me above the people—as my mother's hand moving over the white expanse of sheet and pillow-case had taken me above the market and the market-smell.

I took the lawyer not only my poems, but my thoughts. Again, I saw that he could not help me. I saw, too, that he would rather not help me. He did not wish to be involved. He, after all, was in some ways of the people. He was too far gone in the ways of the people.

But like only one or two others, he did not mind writing it down, and for this I was humbly grateful. When anyone took the trouble to talk to me—that is, to write to me—I felt, for the moment anyway, that I was admitted to that other world, the world of the gay, carefree people. For the moment the fish mouths ceased to be fish mouths. I ceased to be held prisoner in my tower of silence. The chasm between sound and silence had been bridged—at least in my mind. The feeling of unreality dropped away; I was not so far, far off after all.

I realized that I must not let go my grasp on this new world that the poet had opened my eyes to. I read books and magazines. I cut out pictures from newspapers. In so far as I knew how, I continued my education.

Then, too, when I wrote a poem, I founded a new reality. At such times I was no longer in my tower of silence, a prisoner. I flew out of its windows. Yet this reality was not the reality I longed for— the world of the people. Yet, it was more real than the reality of the people. In my reality I touched rock bottom. I felt the shock. In the world of the people I felt no shock. I wandered through it like a ghost unable to establish the fact of reality. In my reality everything was sure. Tightly I hung on to this sure world, for I needed sureness to help me stand up. The poet had unconsciously opened up this new reality to me, not knowing that I had not the other reality. If I let go of this new reality I would become really deaf. The old fear never ceased to haunt me. If I once let go, *they* would get me. Not only the people, but the other things I was afraid of, strange creatures with the various faces of silence, the invisible people who lived with me in my tower.

I needed my poems more than ever. Things had gone from bad to worse at home. I never went downstairs without becoming aware of it. I nursed vague thoughts of running away. Could I do it?

Sometimes the reality that was myself faced me. Here I was, almost seventeen, deaf, terribly shy, sullen, afraid of the people, afraid. But I turned from this picture of myself as I was. By turning from it, I could forget it. I was not *really* deaf, anyway. They had not succeeded in making me really deaf. My individuality was intact. It was almost four years since I had become deaf. Was it possible, I would think, trying to remember a time before the gnome.

When people came to the house, I always scuttled off like a scared rat to my room. But sometimes I was caught. Then I knew they were talking of me. I knew it by their glances. Damn their pity, damn their curiosity. I began to think. Somewhere—in New York—there were people who were different from these people; there were people who were not the people. New York . . . my mind returned to the two words often.

To be able to go to the store alone on Saturday nights and buy the groceries. To be able to go to the stores. It was felt impossible that I could do anything, least of all be allowed to go to the stores alone. To go to the store, to speak my wants to the man behind the counter. But they would not let me do it. One of the many things that they would not let me do after I became deaf, and one perhaps that I minded most of all. It helped to establish my feeling of infe-riority. Couldn't I do anything? Was I good for nothing? Had I no place in the world of the people? I hated them, but I could not deny their importance. They ruled the world in which I lived.

To be able to go to the stores and buy groceries, shoes, curtain rods. I was, at best, allowed to go with my sisters, who considered me a nuisance.

There was always with me the idea of getting out. A fifteen I had begun to look over the help-wanted and furnished-room columns of the New York Sunday papers. In spite of what the people said, *I* knew that I was not deaf. I knew that I was good for something. That I was not prepared to earn my living, that I had the added colossal handicap of deafness, that I might have to take the lowest, most menial jobs, these things did not occur to me. I knew that I was not deaf. That was all I saw, and I was supremely confident. If only I could get to New York. That was the first step.

My mother was definitely neurasthenic. I said as much.

"She is not," my sister said, not understanding the word, but considering it derogatory to my mother.

That should have warned me that they did not want the truth, that the last thing they wanted was the truth, but my brain was pitiless.

My mother's only passion left was eating.

"She eats too much," I said.

"She does not," my sister said, hating me.

Again and again my mother went to the hospital, and again and again the rupture returned. My mother was going to die.

She might have been better dead already. She lived a living death. She was tired, tired. Her body was tired, her spirit was tired. She could find forgetfulness only in eating, and she ate ravenously. Her hand was always over her heart, when it was not clutching the spot where the rupture was.

I was not sympathetic as everybody else was. I was suspicious. I would not let her come near me, nor would I go to her. I went

around the house, sullen, cold, self-sufficient. There was a plan
maturing in my brain.

My mother rose at dawn and started the fire in the stove. It was
she who carried in the piles of wood, the pails of coal. I was filled
with a sullen hatred for my father when I saw her do these things.
I was a child again, and I watched as I had watched when she lifted
sides and forequarters of beef from their hooks while my father
read the Jewish newspaper.

My mother was a sick woman, yet had she anyone to help her
as my father had someone to help him with the furnaces at the
houses? I realized again that my father would be nothing without my mother, as the market would have been nothing without
her personality, as the houses would be nothing without her, but
become rotten with mortgages and debts.

My mother collected the rents and rented the rooms. She kept
the books where she entered the names of the tenants in Yiddish, as
she had entered the names of her customers in the market Ledger.
My mother walking up the alley at night, a flashlight and the huge
bunch of keys in her hand, while a prospective tenant followed her.
And my father—what did he do? He barely turned his head from
his glass of tea. Why didn't he walk up the alley in the snow and
bitter cold? Why did she have to get up from her chair? What did
my father do that I should see my mother rise from her chair to
give it to my father; see her hurry to wait on him, bid us children
attend to his wants. Why should he have the best part of the meat?
I was a child again railing at fate.

Why should my father go to the synagogue on the holidays,
go out and visit the Jews? Why should he go visiting when she
never did?

Why had my mother no friends among the Jewish women? Did
she disdain them, and their small women's world? She who was
so much more clever than they! Yet did they look down upon her
because she had no fine clothes, only aprons and the dust-caps

that she had brought from the market? As a child, when I had seen a silk dress on a Jewish woman, I had wanted to tear it from her back. Why had my mother no silk dresses? Why must I feel ashamed of her?

I had come to realize that my mother was always alone. She had no friends. Had she need of none? Other women had time for rest; my mother worked. Always it had been work. First the market, and then the houses. And now nature was taking its due. Why had not my father the rupture instead of my mother? My mother was closed in a trap.

Had it been only work to her? I remembered the long days in the cold market when my mother had scrubbed the blocks, had sawed and chopped bones. There had been pride in her work. That had kept it from being all work. She had felt pride in being able to lift a side, a forequarter, of beef, lift it from the hooks and fling it down on the block. She had taken pride in the clean saw-dust on the floor. She had seen every day that the meat-chopper was clean. She had washed it herself every day.

No, it had not been all work. The market was the world, and she had been in the thick of it, fighting battles and loving the fight.

The houses then, were not all work, either. The houses, like the market, were a world. There were people there. While she mopped the floors and changed the bed linen, the doors of the many rooms had been open and she had talked with the tenants, finding out about them, rummaging among their lives. Her bald curiosity about others, her directness, even while I had not liked it, had yet fascinated me, and I had followed at her heels when she went to the houses, refusing to be shooed away, as I had refused to be shooed away from the market.

Because of the market we had had no privacy; because of the houses we still had none. How could we have privacy when the tenants were always coming to our little house to ask for my mother? My mother must get up immediately from her dinner and hasten to the houses to settle a quarrel. A husband, drunk, was striking his wife. My mother must pacify him. No matter how drunk he might be, he always listened to my mother. The sting of her words—no one could sting like my mother—reached beneath the drink and took effect.

Up the alley to the houses, up the alley to the houses. What would the houses become without my mother? What would my father become without my mother? Up the alley to the houses, up the alley to the houses with the bunch of keys and the flashlight in her red, swollen hand. New people in the town saw the sign on our house and came in and enquired for rooms. They came first of all to our house. How far, to what other towns, did my mother's influence reach?

Now my mother went to bed at five o'clock in the afternoon, because of her 'heart.' It was agony for her to walk. Why was she tired and old at thirty-eight? Where was my mother of the market and of the houses in this tired, neurotic old woman who could barely drag herself around?

After my mother went to bed, life revolved around that bed. All the business of the houses was transacted from it. She could not go to the tenants any more, so they came to her and sat around the bed and told her their troubles. Since she could not go for the rents, they brought them to her. My father and sisters came to the bed—only I held out. I could not go. I was suspicious of this illness. Was she dramatizing herself again?

They forgot her hardness, but my memory was not so convenient. She had hardness. I could not forgive. Forgive—what? If I had tried to put it into words I would have failed. It was a series of broken promises, betrayals, resentments, suspicions, which had accumulated and which had erected a wall between us. I knew that she wanted me. I knew that she asked for me, followed me in my silence with her eyes. But I could not go. Let them think what they wished; let them think me cold, hard.

How to get out? How to get out? I read the New York Sunday papers for the price of rooms. I had some money in the bank, about thirty dollars. It cost ten dollars to get to New York. There would be twenty dollars left. It seemed an endless sum to me. I would immediately get a job, of course, but my dreams for the present did not venture farther than getting to New York.

How to get to New York?

My mother went to the hospital again. As I had not gone to her bed when she lay in the house, so I would not go to the hospital. I knew that she asked for me constantly, but I would not go. It was rather that I *could* not go.

At home I was considered a traitor. They hated me as much as I hated them. Every mouthful I ate was watched and commented on.

Now was the time to get out if ever I was to get out. While my mother was at the hospital. While she was at home, even if chained to her bed most of the time, she was an enemy I had to respect. With her away, however, it would be easy. My father was nothing. Why should I wait for any more disintegration in her, until her actual death, which might be months away? She was dead already. If this—this disintegration of a fighting spirit—was not death, what was it? The actual death would be meaningless. This was death. This neuroticism, this crying of the tired nerves, this bed on which she lay. I who had a picture of my mother as she was, not so long ago, before the market and the houses had worn her out, knew that this was not my mother. This was death.

I must get out. I could not stand the house and the town any longer. Things had come to a climax. My mother was dead—what more was there to keep me here? New York and what it meant beckoned to me. It seemed to me that I had been waiting for my mother's death a long time. Now I could go.

New York. I could go to school there. There must be schools where I could learn lip-reading. I had heard about lip-reading. It seemed that one could hear by reading the lips. By day I would work, and at night I would go to the lip-reading school. At night, also, I would write my poems and read, continue my education. It all seemed beautifully simple. In New York I would at least have a chance. In New York something would happen. I withdrew the thirty dollars from the bank.

One night I packed my clothes. Then I thought of something. Suppose they tried to bring me back? I lacked only one month of my eighteenth birthday, but I did not doubt that they could bring me back. My father would tell them that I was crazy, and I would be 'put away' perhaps. I had been threatened with it often enough.

When I finished my packing, I went out and sought the policeman.

"I am going away," I told him. "I can't stand it any more there."

I did not say anything more. He knew everything about our family as he knew everything about every other family.

"Wait," he wrote down on a piece of paper. "Wait until tomorrow. I'll come over and talk to your father."

But something told me not to wait, to get out before the policeman came to the house, before the law came to the house. For this law and justice—how could it understand? How could it see beneath to my problem? All the law would see was my wildness. It would not analyze the state of mind and soul that had produced it. It would not see to the bewilderment and frustration which were at the bottom of everything. No! I must not wait. I had been foolish even to go to the policeman. I had merely done it as an alibi. If I told the policeman, it would not be constituted as running away. I did not know what penalties lay in wait for those who ran away.

In the morning I dressed carefully. My packing had been done quickly: what I had been able to get into one suitcase. The rest I left behind.

How to get out without being seen? But my precaution was unnecessary. I walked out of the house without being molested. Only my sisters were there. But this was too easy. Perhaps they would phone the station and tell the agent not to sell me a ticket. I knew my father. He would let me go so far and then spring the trap. I knew his idea of a joke. He was the same age, spiritually and intellectually, as that time when he had wrapped up a pair of old shoes and given them to me as a birthday present.

I decided not to take the train from our town. As a precaution, I took the trolley car to the junction and caught the train from there.

On the train I felt terror. Suppose I should meet someone I knew? There were other terrors. It was the first train journey I had ever taken by myself. Where did I change? Where did I make connections? Dared I ask the conductor to write it down? Almost, I longed for my home where I came in contact with nobody, went nowhere. But I must go out into the world. I must not let them make me really deaf. If I stayed at home what kind of future had I before me? It seemed to me that if I stayed there it was inevitable that I become really deaf, really crazy. I would become one of those relatives whom people hide. I must go out into the world. I must master the unknown. I must master the conductor who was the first person I encountered in the unknown world.

On the train. Were the people looking at me? I remembered that other train ride with my mother. Why did my mother keep returning to me? I could not seem to get away from her. I could not get away from her even after her death.

I sat still in my seat, enjoying the fact that I was absolutely alone. There was no notoriety. There was no one to give me away.

But there were the disadvantages to being alone. The conductor whom I had almost forgotten brought me back to the fact that I was deaf. Where had he said to change? He had said something, for I had seen his lips move as he took my ticket and tore off a third. I was in an agony. Connections, change, any contact with the world of the people served to make me think of that phrase:

"You can't do anything . . . you aren't good for anything. . . ."

The conductor was almost at the end of the car. I was panic-stricken. Suppose the next station was the one at which I changed? Suppose, ignorant of that important fact, I kept on going? Suppose. . . . I could not stand the suspense any longer. I arose and ran after the conductor.

It was so I gave myself away—gave away the secret of the gnome. I found I must *tell* in order to get what I wanted.

Curious glances followed me as I ran after the conductor. I never could do anything like other people. Where others walked, I ran. Where others spoke quietly, I spoke loudly. For at the roots, everything was uneasy, suspicious, bewildered.

I must run after the conductor, and curious glances must follow me as they always did.

"Where did you say I was to change?" I asked the conductor.

The conductor said something. It had been my thought that perhaps I might be able to lip-read his words. I had done so some-times at home, although I had hated the sight of their mouths tor-tured all out of shape. It was the way they spoke to a deaf person. It was another giving away of my secret. But it was more than that. I hated the sight for itself. It was ugly, ugly, ugly. Stick your lips, your dirty lips, back in, I had wanted to scream at them. I shrank from the ugliness of the sight. There was not only ugliness in it, but obscenity.

Now I watched the lips of the conductor. But his lips were immovable as he talked. Not a movement escaped to the eye. And all I had was my eye.

I screwed up my face anxiously and asked him to repeat, thinking that if I saw the words again, I must understand, and in the end I would not have to tell him my secret after all.

The conductor's face became annoyed. He thought this was a new kind of stupidity. Then I guessed that he thought I was hard of hearing for his mouth came close to my ear and he shouted. People were looking. I was hot with shame. Why had I let myself in for this? Better to have gone on and on and on. I said some-thing to the conductor and stumbled back to my seat. I who had thought that the instant I was away from *them* I would become a new person . . . here I was again what I had been, a child, become sullen, feeling every hand against her, walking with head down to escape the looks of the people.

I was in my seat again. I sat still for five minutes. But I could not stay in my seat, I had to know. I had to know. And to know I would have to admit to the conductor that I was deaf. I must take pencil and paper to him and confess that I was deaf, that which I tried to hide not only from others, but from myself. It was as if, by not admitting his existence to myself, I might eventually revoke the image of the gnome. It was my last attempt to rid myself of him. I was still the child who went to the forest and sat under a tree all day.

I must go back and admit that I was deaf, for only in that way would I receive the knowledge I wanted.

Nothing had ever been so hard to do before, unless it was that time I had gone to the high-school on the first day of school, alone.

I went to the conductor and handed him a paper on which I had written that I was deaf, and would he please write down the names of the stations where I was to change? As usual, I wrote down my own words, for I had grown more and more shy of my voice, or rather, I had grown less and less to trust myself, and my voice had partaken of this general distrust.

It was not as terrible as I thought it would be. After one incurious glance at me, the conductor wrote down the names of the stations. His apparent lack of curiosity made me think. Were there other deaf people in the world? Was this the reason the conductor did not appear as astonished as I had expected him to be when I told him I was deaf? Had the conductor met deaf people before, and had they prepared him for this meeting with me?

I believed that I was the only deaf person in the world. I knew nothing of the world except what I had learned before my deafness, and what I had learned afterward with my eyes and through reading. I was abysmally ignorant about many things.

I had met one other of my kind, but I shrank from even thinking of him. I guessed that he was really deaf. The people had

succeeded in having their way with him. Yes, the people had succeeded in making *him* really deaf. I shrank from the sight. The
people, having made him really deaf, now let it be shown to everybody what they had done. Everybody could see that he was deaf. I
hated his gestures, the exaggeration of his lips. The people spoke to
him that way, and had trained him to speak that way back to them.
Damn the people! Why did he move his lips like that! Couldn't he
have told the people to go to hell when they had dared lay their
hands on him? I had told them to go to hell. I would never stop
telling them to go to hell. Were my lips moving like that? I ran
fearfully to the mirror and watched my lips move as I talked aloud.
No, my lips did not move as his did. My lips moved, small, pre-
cise, delicate, as they had always done. I had always liked my lips
without putting the liking into words, except to think how unlike
'Jewish' lips they were.

When the people talked to me they moved their lips at me as he
moved his lips. He had moved his lips back, in emulation. He had
been taught by them, taught the way they believed a deaf person
should be taught. But I—I wanted none of their teachings. I preferred to go untaught. I preferred my hiding in the darkness. I
learned that he had been sent away to an institution for the deaf
where he had been educated, taught a trade, taught to work like
others—which meant that he worked in the mills, would always
work in the mills. God, what a life.

An institution for the deaf. It sounded terrible. One was consigned
to such a place by the people, and one emerged from it, branded, as
the boy had been branded. I wanted nothing to do with such a place.
But there must be some place in New York where the people were
human—in New York, I was sure, the people would be human—and
to this place I would go and be taught lip-reading. But—I wanted to
pass unnoticed. I did not want to move my lips as the boy did. It was
ugly, ugly, ugly. It was the ugliest brand in the world. It was a brand
that went to the person's soul. I could see the brand in his eyes, and
I turned from it whenever I saw him on the street.

In New York . . . in New York. . . . I looked down at the slip of paper with the names of the stations where I was to change, and I was happy. I would not think of the boy any more. I would not think of the people. I would remember only that I was going to New York.

I was looking out of the window being happy when another disturbing thought came. I had the names of the places where I was to change, but how would I know when those particular cities arrived? The conductor called out the names, but I would not be able to hear them. I felt despair again. There were so many difficulties in my way, difficulties that I must surmount before I could move. Before I could move, it was as if I must first get a mountain out of my way. I thought of home and the practically hidden existence that I lived there. No, I could not return. I must go on. I must prevail somehow. This was my chance. If I returned home *they* might get me, put me away. Perhaps put me in one of those institutions for the deaf as the only way to get rid of me. I had run away. It was the best proof of my wildness. It seemed to be a terrible thing for a girl to run away. They did not stop to ask themselves what she was running away from; investigate the place from which she was running away. The place might be a nightmare, but that was nothing. The girl must pay; the bullying father, the neurotic nagging mother, were allowed to go free.

I looked down at the names on the piece of paper. If I went back to the conductor and asked him to tell me when the train arrived at these stations, a look of impatience and exasperation would come to his face. I had annoyed him three or four times now. Oh, I knew that look! Nevertheless, meek as any lamb now, the fight taken out of me, I went back to him.

The train was drawing nearer and nearer to New York. I clutched my pocketbook with its twenty dollars. I huddled the suitcase closer to me. I felt wild with the gaiety that sometimes welled up in me. It was raining, but for once the rain did not

depress me. It would not cause me to think any more: now I will
have to be cooped up in the house. I would never again have to
think such a thing.

The train entered the station. Would this long tunnel never
end? It seemed longer than all the rest of the journey. Finally, the
train stopped, and after a short walk through what was left of the
tunnel, I emerged into a yellow glare. I had lived over this moment
so many times in my thoughts that there was no hesitancy. It was
true that I had no idea of what the station would be like, having
never seen it before, but that did not make me any less sure of my
movements. I knew I must find a room. It would be awkward to
carry a suitcase in the rain, so I checked it. I who had never been
allowed to do anything by myself before—it was amazing the sureness with which I did everything.

I asked my way to the subway. By following the waves of many
hands, I came to it. Luckily it was the West-Side subway, the one
I wanted.

My destination was Greenwich Village, of course. When I
thought of New York, I thought of Greenwich Village. There I
would begin a new life. There I would meet people—who were not
the people.

I had reasoned out from my study of the Sunday papers that
Greenwich Village must be below Fourteenth Street. I would take
the subway and get off at Fourteenth Street. Then I would inquire,
and by following more waves of hands I would get to the place I
wanted. There I would look around for a room. It was all very clear
in my mind.

When I got out at Fourteenth Street, it was still raining. The sad
rain of a fall twilight. I looked at the stores, at the great buildings.
Everything seemed of an iron-gray color. At any other time the
iron-gray would have entered into me and lowered my spirits. But
now it did not.

By following the successive waves of hands, I came to the Village.
I saw the Park, deserted now because of the rain. I kept on walking.

It was a strange city about which I knew nothing except what I had learned by reading the New York papers. But I did not feel lost or terrified. I felt as if I had come home at last.

I walked up and down streets. I felt an impatience with my city for that interval which must pass before all these streets became familiar to me. It grew darker as I walked. Moreover, the rain had changed from a fine drizzle into something firm and inevitable. It made me think of the room I must get. I would soon be drenched to the skin. I was getting tired, too. A reaction would set in. The elation would go, and I would begin to feel depressed. Fear, the fear I knew so well, would enter into me. I would feel like a haunted animal again.

I wanted to ask a policeman for the direction to a certain street I had in mind. I had seen it often in the furnished-room columns. There were always rooms for rent on that street. But I was afraid to ask the policeman. He might find something strange in my appearance. He might. . . . No, I would find it alone.

However, I could not find it. But in going up a street I saw a brownstone house with a card in its window. I decided to go there.

The woman who answered the bell looked at me suspiciously when I asked for a room. She said something. I braced myself. The time had come.

"I am deaf," I said.

She stared, and I said again patiently, pointing to my ear, "I am deaf."

She seemed to understand then, and let me come in out of the rain.

"I'd like to rent a room," I said.

She said something.

"Will you please write it down?" I asked.

All the time she seemed to be scrutinizing me sharply. At last she said,

"You're by yourself? You're not letting out?" She wrote down the words.

"Yes, I'm by myself," I said. I did not understand what she meant by the rest of the sentence. I added that my suitcase was at the station. She continued to scrutinize me sharply as I talked. I thought it was because she had never met a deaf person before. Or was I a strange looking creature, wet to the skin as I was?

Finally she appeared satisfied and took me upstairs and showed me a room. It was six dollars. I paid her the money. The sight of the money made her relax.

At last I was by myself. The room was small, but prettily furnished. There was a table on which I could write.

I dreamed of staying here all my life, in this room. I would get a job. The job might not pay much, but I would keep on with this room.

I was in New York at last.

I had no plans. After a while, when my money was gone, I would get a job. That was as far as my thoughts went. Now I lived, exploring the Village on the sunny September days. Never had any place seemed so beautiful. I spent my nickels indiscriminately with the apple man on the corner. I liked to buy an apple at his stand every time I passed the corner, and I would pass it often on my way to and from the Park. I changed dollar after dollar into nickels and dimes and spent them.

I sat in the Park and wondered at the people. There were some I should have liked to know. Dare I approach them? No, I dared not. Nevertheless I cast longing glances at them, and thought of the time when I should know them.

I spent the September days as freely as I spent my money.

This life came to an end when I found I had little money left. Certainly I could not afford a six-dollar room. I found a room in an entirely different neighborhood, but still in the Village.

Nothing could disguise the meanness and dinginess of the new neighborhood. It was a side street, a long row of houses with signs in the windows. The sun never penetrated into that side street, but passed over the tops of the houses to other streets, more inviting.

My room had no windows. I hated it immediately, but I took it because it was only three dollars a week, and because I hated room hunting, or rather feared the ordeal with the various landladies.

Then began my job-hunting. I arose at dawn, but I found that even that hour was not early enough. There were always people ahead of me waiting in line, a long line of the unskilled like myself.

"I am deaf," I said to the employers of New York, and as I said it, I saw a door behind their eyes which had been half-open, shut irrevocably.

From office to office, from factory to factory, I went with my cry, "I am deaf, I am deaf," begging for work. They looked up and saw my deafness. They failed to look further, to me. They made no attempt to see me.

Was New York no different, then? Were the people everywhere the same? I saw in their eyes the old, old, story.

You can't do anything, you can't do anything. You aren't good for anything. . . . In some the words were softened by a look of pity. In others, the words were accompanied by curious glances.

"Yet I am I," I wanted to scream at them. "Can't you see? I am a human being like you. Why do you look at me as though I were not? I do not want your pity or your curiosity. All that I want is work so that I can live. See, I can do something. I have my hands and my brain. I can write and I can spell. I can typewrite. I can run a machine fairly well. If only you will give me a chance. I will take any work you will give me. I will dip chocolates at lower wages than you usually give. I will wash dishes, scrub floors. I am not afraid of work. Only give it to me." But after they heard my words, I am deaf, they seemed to lose interest in me. They no longer believed in me. They looked past me to the one behind me in the long line. They were impatient. I was taking up their time. Next!

My money was giving out. I was growing desperate. The heels of my shoes were run over. I walked the streets, receiving curious glances.

I ate in the automat restaurants. I changed my dime for two nickels. A nickel in the slot for coffee, the other nickel bought two rolls. But coffee and rolls were not enough. I was always hungry, always hungry. I would walk past the hundreds of little windows locked fast—but nickels, ready nickels, could open them—and stare hungrily at the plates of cake, sandwiches, the brown deep dishes which contained chicken pie. When I thought no one was looking, I walked among the tables and stole pieces of cake left over on plates. I saw others doing the same thing. Like members of a secret brotherhood, we espied each other by the furtive glances we gave at the scraps left over on dishes. We exchanged glances of hate when someone else stole a piece of cake, a dish still half full of pudding, that we had had our eyes on. We watched in each other's eyes the agony of a decision. Was anyone watching or not? Was the bloated-faced manager watching? Would it be safe to grab?

I was one of the under-dogs of a great city. I knew them by the hopeless sullenness of their faces. Had my face such a look? We met and passed each other silently, furtively, on the streets, in the green morning hours when we began our job-hunt, praying that there might not be too long a line formed ahead of us.

My self-confidence was going. Where were my dreams and poems? I wrote nothing. My spare time was spent in battling with fear, a fear that made my blood run cold. Where was the school for lip-reading? I had heard vaguely of a lip-reading school. Where was it? I hunted through the telephone book, but only half-heartedly. I could find nothing. Everything I did was half-hearted. Fear was taking my strength away from me, as much as the insufficient food I had. Fear was paralyzing me.

I grew to fear everybody. When I still had some money during those September days, I had loved to walk on the streets at all hours, had loved the silence and darkness of streets, had passed without fear the shadowy men in doorways; but now I was afraid. Before, these shadowy men had been afraid to follow me on the streets, but now they sensed the demoralization that was going on in me, the slow crumbling of defenses due to fear and hunger, and they dared to approach. They even dared to grab at my dress as I passed them. How did they have this knowledge of what was going on in me? How did they sense it? By what secret, telepathic sense did they know that I was afraid, that I had not the defense forces that had protected me from them before?

I was afraid. I was afraid of every shadow. I was afraid of every man, woman, and child on the street. They were all my enemies. They all had their hands against me. They did not want me.

Another and still another day went by. There was very little money left. Not even on Sunday did I cease my job-hunting. Walking along the streets one Sunday, I noticed a sign in the window of a restaurant.

Dishwasher Wanted

I went in the restaurant. At the cash register was a man to whom I blurted out the old cry, "I am deaf," and then hurrying on as if to keep from him the chance to make that shake of the head that meant "Sorry we haven't anything," I said, "You need a dishwasher, I'd like the job. I'm willing to work for less." That was what I always said, "I'm willing to work for less," as if to bribe them.

The man hesitated. Finally he motioned me to come into the back room where the cooking was done, and pointed to the dishes stacked up.

That was the way I got my first job.

It was heart- and back-breaking work. In a few hours my arms were red to the elbows from the contact with the dishwater into which I must put chunks of lye soap. My hands were soon blistered from the half-hourly dipping into the pot of lye soap under the sink.

Dishes, dishes, dishes. What time was it? I looked around for a clock. There was a Big Ben hanging from a nail. I was hungry. It was after the noon hour, and the dirty dishes came through the little opening more slowly.

I kept on washing. Nobody appeared to notice me. There were three cooks in white aprons and caps dishing out soup and meat. Sweat poured down their faces. There was an incessant smell of food.

Waiters came in and out.

I had always wanted to know what went on in the kitchens of restaurants, and now I knew.

It was two o'clock. Scarcely any dishes came. Only a coffee cup now and then. But I continued to stand over the sink, washing. When the interim between coffee cups became longer and longer, I decided to wash the three or four dozen egg glasses which had been left over from breakfast, filled with water, and left to stand for later washing.

The man to whom I had taken my plea for a job came in. I saw by the deference paid to him that he was the boss. He was a dark Italian with bulbous lips and a short stout body.

He said something to one of the cooks and the cook put some meat and vegetables on a plate. The boss brought the plate to me, and motioned me to sit on a barrel and eat it. I could have cried at his kindness. I got on the barrel and ate the meat and vegetables. Pretty soon the cooks, too, ate their dinner. They sat down on tubs and talked among themselves as they ate. They paid no attention to me.

The waiters came and went, but now less hurriedly, less as if their lives depended on hurry, hurry, hurry. One of them I noticed particularly. He was so dark that I decided he had Negro blood. Even I in my ignorance knew that here was a *waiter*, and that he was out of place in a small chop house on Sixth Avenue. He carried his tall, magnificent body superbly, disdainfully.

Now that the rush was over, the waiters were noticing me. They glanced at me as I sat on the barrel. Even the cooks had time for a look at me. This place was run entirely by men. Why had the boss hired me, a girl? Probably because he was desperately in need of a dishwasher, or it might have been the plea in my eyes, or it might have been the offer of lower wages. Whatever it was, whatever motive was behind it, I did not cease to be grateful.

I finished my dinner and went back to the sink. While I had been eating, a sizable stack of coffee cups had accumulated.

As I leaned over the sink that was as big as a tub I felt a pinch on my arm. I turned around and saw that it was the cook who had dished out the plate of meat and vegetables for me.

I frowned and turned back to the coffee cups. He saw my frown and his face became malicious. So I didn't like him, eh?

Ten minutes later I felt another pinch. This time it was one of the waiters. I backed away, saying nothing.

Three o'clock . . . four o'clock . . . I continued to wash dishes. They were coming in faster now. My arms felt numb. My back would break soon. I prayed that my mind would become numb too. But it would not. It persisted in a dull, endless whine like a toothache.

"Oh, shut-up, shut-up," I said to it wearily. "Shut up, damn you, shut up."

I was tired, tired. Never in my life had I felt so tired. How long would this keep up? Dishes, dishes; big plates, little plates, medium-sized plates, side dishes. But thank God there were no more plates with egg stains and no more glasses with egg clinging to the sides and bottom. Thank God that people ate eggs only once a day.

I kept stealing glances at Big Ben. One glance at him and my courage came back, straightening my shoulders, quieting the toothache in my head. It would not be long before the day was over for me. Surely they did not mean me to work until midnight? I had been working since nine o'clock in the morning and it was now almost five. How long had I to work, anyway? The boss came and went but I was afraid to ask him any question. I washed dishes as if my life depended on it. I drained out the sink and let fresh water pour in. I added more lye soap.

Five o'clock. A cook—I could hardly tell them apart—drew a sack of potatoes up to a low stool and handed me a knife. I peeled

potatoes until half past five. Then I went back to the dishes. I spoke
to no one, and no one spoke to me.

It was the dinner hour. The dishes came, came, came. Oh, God,
would I never be able to keep up with them? Would I ever overtake
them? The waiter who had pinched my arm was all professional-
ism now, and darted a glance of hatred at me because he had to
wait until I washed a coffee cup for him.

At last I managed to get some order out of the pile. I felt more
like the masters of the dishes instead of their slave.

Time went by. I was so busy that I forgot to give my usual
glances at Big Ben. When I did, I was surprised to find that it was
half past eight.

At nine o'clock, a queer old man, no taller than a boy, came in.
He was the night dishwasher. He nodded to me, and I nodded
back, staring. He looked hardly human.

I was to come tomorrow at nine in the morning, the boss wrote
down in a surprisingly beautiful handwriting. The hours were
from nine in the morning until nine at night. The pay was fourteen
dollars a week.

I left the restaurant and walked to my windowless room. I lay
down on the bed, without undressing, and promptly fell asleep.
I was tired, dead tired, but in spite of it, the wild gaiety in me
that would persist, cried, "I've got a job, I've got a job. I *can* do
something." Then another thought came: would I keep the job?
And again fear of the people overcame me. But finally there was
no more thinking and no more fear and I knew that I was dead
asleep.

The next morning when I arrived at the restaurant, I found an
old man at the sink, not the same old man who had taken my place
the night before. My heart turned cold with fear. Was I no longer
to have a job here? What had happened? Were there to be two
dishwashers? But I said nothing. The boss had said nothing to me
when I came in. Since the old man was washing dishes, I found the
towel and began to dry them.

There sprang up a hatred between myself and the old man in the days that followed. He was old, almost seventy-five, bald and toothless. He chewed his gums. He tottered on his feet. It was useless to tell myself to remember the maxim I had learned in school: be kind to the old. It was worse than useless. I could not be kind to him, and he could not be kind to me. It was dog eat dog.

Silently we struggled for supremacy beneath the unending round of dishwashing. Who should wash? Who should wipe? Each of us preferred to wash rather than to wipe, in spite of the can of lye soap under the sink which blistered our fingers, in spite of the greasy water which reddened our arms to the elbows.

It was dog eat dog, for both of us could not stay, we sensed.

It was dog eat dog all through the restaurant. The waiters spied on each other, reporting weaknesses and carelessnesses to the boss. There was one waiter especially whom we all combined to hate. He had constituted himself chief spy. He was angling for the job of manager.

It had been war from the first hour between the old man and me. Not only who should wipe and who should wash. I had suggested alternate turns, but when my turn came, he would forget, he would refuse to give me my chance at the sink.

Who should sweep the kitchen? It was really the cooks' business, but they, calculating the strength of the old man and me and believing they would meet with no resistance, had thrown the job on to us. Neither the old man nor I dared complain. We were the under-dogs and we knew it. But under-dogs may and do quarrel among themselves. So, silently and insidiously, we threw the broom back and forth.

Who should peel the potatoes and the other vegetables? This job too belonged to the cooks, but it was given to us. Which one should do it?

"It's your turn," I said to the old man, hating him. "I peeled the potatoes yesterday."

But he only continued to chew his gums, his blurred eyes filling with hatred. Sometimes, when there were two kinds of vegetables to be peeled at once, and he had to take one, I looked at him with a malicious triumph. We hated each other.

He spied on me and I spied on him. He could not seem to wash coffee cups clean, and I, gloating, showed them to the waiter who was angling for the job of manager. On the other hand I could not completely rid spoons of their egg stains, and the old man would take them to the waiter with the same kind of gloating on his face.

I was learning very effectively how cheap and mean and petty human nature can be. To what depths of meanness even a so-called nice person would stoop to pay off a score. I hated it. Where was my despisal of all that was cheap and mean and petty? But I could not help myself. To hold my own, I must retort with like methods. They would take advantage of any lack of defense on my part.

My greatest weakness was Big Ben. I loved to look at him. I loved the relief I felt when the little hand, at last, after years, so it seemed, painfully climbed to noon and began its downward slide to nine o'clock. How I loved it!

My glances at Big Ben were arousing comment. The cooks often caught me looking at him, especially the cook who nourished a dislike for me ever since I had frowned at his pinch of my arm, and refused to meet him outside. He had tried to curry favor with me by heaping my plate over-full with vegetables and meat. He had even bribed one of the waiters to bring me some of the French pastry that reposed in the restaurant itself in ornate baskets, and which did not find its way into the kitchen. But none of these things would make me meet him outside. So he hated me.

He watched for my glances at Big Ben and intercepted them as if to say, "Ha! Another one. Just wait till I tell the boss. Just wait, my girl."

One morning I arrived at work to find Big Ben gone. When, out of habit, I raised my eyes to the beloved white face with the black hands and saw the nail on which Big Ben hung, empty. . . .

The cook was watching me. At the look on my face, he burst into a roar of laughter. It made me think of the time when I had received a pair of old shoes for my birthday, and my father bursting into laughter at the expression on my face.

When Big Ben went out of my life, something else went also. My courage went. Big Ben had distracted my thoughts from the old man, the cooks, the waiters, the dishes, the egg glasses, the spy system, the backache, the toothache in my brain. But now there was no Big Ben. I had never realized how much I owed Big Ben until now that he was gone.

I had another terror. The cellar. There the vegetables were kept. There also were the lockers. Each waiter and cook and dishwasher had a locker with a key to it. There we went in the morning to take off our street clothes and put on the clothes we kept to wear in the restaurant.

Like the others, I had my locker, but I dreaded going down. I was afraid of finding myself alone there with a waiter or a cook. What might not happen in that place that was always dark, even by day? At first I had refrained from wearing my coat so that I need not go down and hang it up in the locker, but the days were growing colder. When I was in the cellar I would glance repeatedly toward the stairs. Was one of them coming down? Had the cook followed me? I was afraid of them all.

Yet even after the long day of nine to nine I could throw off the atmosphere of the kitchen. I could throw off the cooks, the waiters, the old dishwasher, the dishes, the egg glasses, as easily as I threw off my shoes. I could throw off the twelve hours I spent in the kitchen the minute I stepped outside the restaurant.

At nine I threw off the dirty apron that I wore and went down the cellar to get my coat. Then up the cellar stairs, through the kitchen, with scarcely a glance at the cooks, and through, finally, the long restaurant room. I glanced curiously at the people in the restaurant as I walked through. The men were so many black-clothed figures, but the women were exotic, strange. I did not remember seeing such women on the streets.

My co-dishwasher left the restaurant the same time I did. I would see him standing in front of the restaurant, uncertain just where to go or just what to do now, and if I had not hated him so much I would have felt sorry for him, it was so obvious that he was lonely.

At nine o'clock my mood of wild gaiety returned. The toothache in my head ceased instantly. It was as if I had not been standing over a sink for twelve hours, dipping my hand in the pot of lye soap under the sink, letting out the water when it became too greasy, letting more pour in, watching the purity of the new water become greasy and rancid like the old.

I walked away from the restaurant to my windowless room. I ran, not walked. For I had a poem there, waiting for me, written in God knows what spare time.

I was going to take the new poem and the other poems to the poet.

The idea of finding the poet, finding him not for myself, but for my poems, had always been in the back of my mind. I did not want him for myself any more, but for my poems. For my poems I was hard. He did not want to see me. He had said so, or as good as said so, by not answering my letters. But he must still see my poems. He must see what I had done during the two years that had gone by since he had stopped answering my letters. Had I succeeded in standing up by myself? Or had I fallen down? It seemed to me that only he could answer these questions. My poems would be the answer.

He must see my poems.

I had gone to the address of two years ago to see if he was still there. He was. His name was on a letter box in the hall. Tonight I was going to see him. I had thought it all out during those centuries I had spent over the sink listening to the toothache in my brain.

Up the stairs to my windowless little room, down again, this time with my book of poems, then the walk of ten blocks to the house where he lived.

I rang the bell. Would he be in?

He came to the door. This was he, then. I told him my name. I never thought he might have forgotten all about me.

"I want you to see my poems," I said to him. "I am in New York now, working. Will you see my poems? I do not want to intrude myself on you. It's just my poems."

He motioned me to come in and led me to his room.

Rapidly he went through my poems. "This is good," he wrote. "This is not good." I was depressed. For two years I had worked constantly thinking of the reward—when he should look over my poems again. Always I had thought of that. It spurred me on.

"I guess they are no good," I said. I wanted to cry.

"They are good. Keep on."

He asked me what I was doing.

"Washing dishes in a restaurant," I said. I told him of the life I was living.

He shook his head as he listened. "Go home. Go back. You cannot do such work, live such a life, and continue to write."

"But I can," I said eagerly.

"Go home. You are straining against impossible odds. Go home and write. When you can make a living from your writing, then come back. I will write to you. I will criticize your work as I did before."

I had said nothing to him of the past, of the letters that I had written to him in vain. I had said simply, "Will you read my poems?" Now I wondered: would he write to me? Perhaps he would, perhaps he would not. And I did not care. No, I did not care. I searched myself minutely: I did not care whether or not he wrote to me.

I wondered that he did not see what was behind this gesture of coming to New York. Did he not see that it was another gesture of defiance against the people? Against the people and their horrible words: you can't do anything, you aren't good for anything. Could he not see all this, and understand that the dishes, the pot of lye soap, the cooks, the waiters, the cellar, were as nothing beside this gesture of defiance against the people?

Did not even he understand? If he did not, then certainly no one would. Did he not see that my going back meant an admission of the correctness of their words: you can't do anything, you aren't good for anything. . . . Did he not see? But he did not. All he saw was what I had told him of my difficulties in New York, the failures to get work, the crumbling in me. These things were nothing. Really, they were nothing. All that mattered was my gesture of defiance against the people.

"I can't go back," I said, in a last attempt to make him understand. "I'm not afraid of washing dishes. I can wash dishes and still write." I could say that now while the toothache in my brain was still.

He shook his head.

"Listen to me, I know. If you don't go back, if you don't do as I tell you, I won't see you any more. I won't look at your poems any more. You can't come here any more. Go home. If not for your own sake, then for the sake of your poetry."

How to tell him that it was for the sake of my poetry that I had run away, for the sake of my poetry and my soul? Things had gone so far that they could go no farther. The walls were closing in. If I went back, I would become really deaf. How to tell him this? My condition might be half a reality, half the outgrowth of an imagination turned in too much upon itself. What did that matter? The condition existed. It had existed all my life, but I had never felt as I had felt the last six years since I had become deaf. I had at least had freedom before. My imagination had been able to roam. There had been no walls. There had been no one trying to make me really deaf. Really deaf! Really deaf! That was it.

I understood that he was being kind, that he was thinking of me. Perhaps he was right. Was I an ignorant fool? Even so, even if

I did not know what lay ahead of me, what deaths I might not die, even so I would go toward them. I preferred the unknown to old, too well-known deaths that could set my soul quivering. I could not stand more such deaths.

How did he know that my poetry would not survive? My poetry was as hard as I. We had both grown hard thinking of the people.

"Good-bye," I said to the poet. "And thank you."

I had been working at the dishwashing job a month when I was fired. It had ever been a tussle between my co-dishwasher and me and my co-dishwasher remained, chiefly because he had accepted lower wages. I would have been glad to accept the lower wages. Anything to stay. But it was not offered to me. Perhaps they did not want a girl in the kitchen.

I had some money saved up. I decided that I would not hunt for another job right away. I would live on this money until it was almost gone, then only would I look for another job. I wanted freedom. I wanted once more to walk on the streets at any hour I wished. I almost welcomed being fired.

In the morning I would start from my little windowless room in the bright fall sunshine and walk up Fifth Avenue or Broadway to the big library. I loved the sunshine. People were looking at me, at my down-at-heel shoes, my dress that was three years old and rumpled, for coming in from my dishwashing job I had often been too tired to take it off and had fallen asleep in it. And my hair was wild, however much I combed it. Perhaps my face was wild too.

Oblivious to their nudges I walked up Fifth Avenue in the noonday crowd, glorying in my freedom, in the sunshine. I did this every day during my freedom.

I had spoken to no one since I had come to New York, to no one except to those from whom I had tried to wrest employment, the boss of the restaurant, my co-dishwasher, the cooks and the waiters when necessary, my landlady, and finally the poet. I had had no chance to feel lonely while I was dishwashing. I was too tired most of the time to have any clear thoughts. Before that there had been the fear which had consumed mind and soul. Now, with some money, I did not feel so much afraid, and there was no dish-washing to make me tired. I was free, and I began to feel lonely. Loneliness sent me out on the streets in the evening. The library and my poems were not enough. The old craving came to detach someone from the people and make him my own. Not necessarily a man. Merely someone who would understand. After all, had I not come to New York to find these things: companionship and understanding? However much I was forced down into being an under-dog, I must not lose sight of that.

I went back to the poet. He had told me that he would not help me any more and that he did not wish to see me any more, but nevertheless I went back and rang the bell. I was lonely, ter-ribly lonely, surely he would understand that and not grudge me a few words? Surely he might introduce me to some people? Surely there were people who would be willing to seek *me* under the deafness?

I rang his bell. He came to the door. Seeing that it was I, he made an impatient gesture and closed the door again.

I went down the steps. At the last one I sat down and put my arms around my knees. I was not hurt. I was not angry. I was used to being not wanted. That *he* did not want me, well, had he not said as much two years ago when he had failed to answer my letters?

Familiar as I was with not being wanted, I was still lonely. I sat on the bottom step and watched the people, the cars, going by. There were happy groups of people on the other doorsteps. I longed to know them. I would have known them but for the gnome. But for him I would have gone over to them and said, "Please let me be with you. I am so lonesome." I could not go because the gnome stayed every act of my body. I must think. I must stop and think: remember you have the gnome. The gnome atrophied everything. Impulses were born and died still born. The gnome chained me down.

In a minute I would cry. I wanted someone to speak to me. I wanted to see a human voice say something to me, even if I could not have heard the voice. I was not lonely for the human voice, or perhaps I was, without being aware of it. Perhaps it was the human voice that I missed; perhaps it was the human voice that was the missing link between myself in my tower of silence and the reality I wanted so much. Nevertheless, I had my own voices that took the place of the people's voices. I had the long conversations in my head, the music at bedtime, poetry, the poetry of others, as well as my own poetry. It seemed to me that I had sound enough. What I did not have was a human being like myself. There were millions who composed the people and I knew not one of them. I wanted someone to talk to.

I arose from the bottom step and walked away. After a while I came to a restaurant—a cafeteria—and I remembered that I had eaten nothing since noon. Suppose I went in and bought some coffee and rolls? I never went in any restaurant except the automat because I was afraid, afraid that I would be asked something, and thus rendered helpless. But it was many blocks away to the nearest automat.

I peered through the window of the cafeteria. The people took their checks from the cashier without a word, and the cashier did not appear to say anything to them. I decided that no questions would be asked of me and went in and took my check.

PART SIX

The Cafeteria

I walked to the counter and asked for coffee and rolls. It must have been a strange order for that time of night, for the counter man looked at me strangely. I felt the troubled uneasiness of old and wished that I had not entered. But it was too late to go to the automat on Fourteenth Street. I was afraid of Fourteenth Street at night—Fourteenth Street with its prowlers who dared to clutch my arm.

I walked to a chair with my coffee and rolls and the check which had been punched at ten cents. Only then did I look around me, and then my heart began to sing. The loneliness left me. Surely these were my people. The people I had wanted to know. These were the poets, the writers, the artists—my own kind. By chance I had stumbled on their meeting place.

How wild they looked, but no wilder than I looked. It was as if I recognized my own by this wildness, this wildness that was akin to my own wildness. Their hair was not smooth and composed, their eyes were not smooth and composed. I recognized them.

How to get to know these people? I constantly had before me the knowledge of my deafness and it killed every free, spontaneous impulse to action. The gnome, during the six years he had had possession of me, had indeed permeated my whole being. Not even in my dreams—the dreams of sleep—was I free of him. Not even in my dreams dared I accost people. Even in my dreams I had come to do only those things which were possible for me to do awake, within the area of the walls the gnome had built. It was

159

impossible to go over the walls even in my dreams. I could not talk to another person in my dreams. Invariably the picture became blurred, I stirred uneasily and sometimes woke up. So, little by little, I had come to accept the gnome's possession of me. And as it was in my dreams, so it was in reality: I avoided people so that I might not constantly be reminded of the walls, be made aware of my deficiency, my un-wholeness.

These people: would they want to know me if they found out I was deaf? I lived in fear that the countermen in the cafeteria might address me when I was not looking. They would find out my deafness immediately. Too, there was the fact of my voice. I had not used it much for six years, partly from distrust of it because I could not hear it myself, partly because no one had talked much to me: I had lived alone by myself most of the time. The counterman would say to me when I gave an order, "What did you say?" My voice was rusty from disuse. It hardly came out of my throat. I must swallow a few times, water my throat with saliva, so that my voice might come out more freely.

I lived in continual fear of that comedy which must be going on behind my back. A remark addressed to me, and I not observing as well as not hearing—if I had observed it, I would have smiled meaninglessly, stupidly. But suppose I had failed to notice anything? Then they would repeat and repeat their words and when I still failed to turn around they would whisper among themselves, tap their ears knowingly. Oh, I could construct the picture well without having actually seen it, although I knew that it had been enacted, for sometimes I would look up and catch the last reel of the picture in their eyes, or there might be about their hands and face the motions of the last act. The curtain had not yet been drawn down. Or the fault was perhaps mine. I should not have looked around and seen what was to be seen.

The people at the tables—my people—seeing this little comedy enacted by the countermen . . . would they want to know me afterward? It seemed impossible that they should want to know me.

I returned to the cafeteria the next night at the same hour of nine. This time I had fortified myself with my poems. But there was no one in the cafeteria. Only some people who were not my kind. That phrase, my kind, warmed me, made me feel less lonely.

Had they gone somewhere else? Where had they gone? I felt hopeless and alone again. I waited, there was nothing else for me to do. I was tired of walking on the streets, seeing faces that were all closed to me. I waited in my seat, the empty coffee cup beside me. I waited. Ten, eleven, twelve o'clock. Then they came. I recognized them instantly, their laughing carelessness, their complete naturalness, their boisterousness. Nine o'clock—what was nine o'clock to them? Time did not exist for them. The hours around midnight were their hours. They only came in when the timid people scurried off to bed.

I had waited for them and now I saw them, although they were oblivious of me. Would there ever come a day when they saw me?

I propped my book of poems against the napkin-holder and pretended to be absorbed in it. But I was really watching them all the time, hungrily.

It was an ordinary cafeteria, like any of the thousand other cafeterias in the city. There were the too ornate windows, the cashier hunched on top of the show-case filled with cigars and cigarettes. There were the rows of imitation marble-topped tables, each with its napkin-holder and condiments and sauces. There were the counters with their signs, "Salads," "Sandwiches," "Hot Dishes," "Beverages." There were the electric-light clusters hanging from the ceiling, so many lights that not a corner of the room escaped, not even the space under the tables. There were the three or four tables down front with their tags of "For Service Only," and where only the privileged ones sat—that is, the uptown sightseers who came to peer and stare. It was just an ordinary cafeteria, but the people frequenting it around midnight—curiously by day it was what it was: an ordinary cafeteria, frequented by ordinary people, factory and shop employees, taxi-drivers, laborers—transformed or rather hid its ordinariness with their carelessness, their youth, their dreams. It became an extraordinary place, taking on the quality of these people. At midnight and the hours around midnight, the shine of the brass was less hard; it had almost the softness of gold. Even the countermen relaxed.

The owner of the place was a Jew of forty, gross, with highly manicured nails. He had a soul which wavered between ordinary money greed, and a desire for color. He was always threatening to put the twelve-o'clock crowd out because they ate too little and stayed too long. He had a fondness for big white signs with black lettering which read, "No Loitering." When the white became brown from fly specks and smoke grease, he substituted new white signs, although they had no effect on the crowd. And he himself made no move to kick them out of their seats beyond threats, gross little threats like himself. In his brown suit—he always wore brown suits—covering his short, fat body, in his diamond-ringed fingers, his manicured nails, his fat hanging cheeks, his oily, almost strange smile, he sat and observed the twelve o'clock crowd. He had a ringside seat, a seat at one of the reserved tables. There he sat by himself, or someone might join him, and he would play with his manicured diamonded fingers, watching the people with his oily, almost strange, smile.

He realized his power. He meant life or starvation to many of them. One day he might relax, but the next day he would shake his head, smiling his smile. No, no more credit. He would shake his head on its fat baby neck.

He could be hard, but he could also be all obsequiousness. When a group of uptowners came in and the waiter could not bring the glasses of water fast enough, he himself went running, gross in his gross brown suit to bring the glasses of water.

But most of the time he sat in his ringside seat, or stood by the cashier and watched the crowd. People came, uptowners, to watch these freaks with their wild hair and wild faces. The fame of the cafeteria had spread. Perhaps that was why he did not insist on the no-loitering sign. People came to stare and paid good money for admission. He let the freaks stay. He muttered threats when they would buy only a cup of coffee and stay from midnight to dawn, but he let them stay.

The Jew had a wife who was as much a part of the cafeteria as he was. They took turns in being on hand. She had none of his love of color. If he was hard, she was harder. They fought an endless battle over the cafeteria. Neither trusted the other. She wanted the twelve-o'clock crowd kicked out. She distrusted their color, their unordinariness. In the end, there was more money to be made out of the ordinary people. This popularity with the uptowners would be merely a transient thing; the crazy people would go elsewhere, and the uptowners would follow them. The crazy people never stayed long in any one place. Now it was this cafeteria that they frequented, now that tearoom. They were not permanent as the taxi-drivers, the various habitués of the underworld, silent people who came from nowhere but were expensively dressed and ate and bought freely, were permanent. She and her husband were constantly at war. She made a bid for the taxi-driving crowd. She installed a five-cent gambling machine in the back of the cafeteria.

The cashier was the henchman of these two. He was more than a cashier. He was as much of a personality as the owner. He could be fawning or snarling, depending on whether the person before him had money or owed a bill which he could not pay. He had curiously cold, disillusioned eyes. He would stare out of them at the twelve-o'clock crowd, unmoving, but when a chair was knocked out of place, he would run snarling to adjust it.

This was the cafeteria and the three who stood over the twelve-o'clock crowd.

I, too, stood over them at first, but I did not want to continue standing over them. How was I to get to know these people? I wanted to know them all, the long-haired men and the short-haired girls who flitted, light as birds, from table to table.

These people appeared superlatively beautiful to me, almost magical. And how hungry I was to know them!

I returned night after night with my book of poems, and that other cheap notebook in which a new poem was forming. I began to receive glances, speculative glances. They watched me curiously as I drank my coffee and ate my rolls.

How to seek admission to them? One night a girl approached me, one of the girls I had seen flitting from table to table, laughing, always laughing. Her face was dark and small. Her body was small, and I imagined that its skin must have the same lovely dusky quality of her face.

She said something to me. I shook my head shyly.

"I am deaf," I said. "Will you write it down?" It was a plea for her to stay.

She sat down beside me and I gave her the pencil I always carried around with me in case somebody would want to talk to me. I handed her the cheap notebook.

"What's your name?" the girl wrote.

I told her.

"What do you do?"

"I'm a poet," I said. This was the first time I had ever dared to say the thought aloud.

"Won't you come and meet my friends?" she wrote again.

For a second I hung back. I was the child again with a fear of the people, a child who wanted to creep into the darkness and hide. Then I braced myself. I must make this effort.

"Yes," I said.

We went to another table and I was introduced.

The cheap little notebook was soon filled with words, words, words. They replenished me as food replenishes a hungry man. Words, words, words, I was hungry for them.

These people were wonderful, I thought, because they could talk my talk, or rather the talk that went on in my head. They could use words which I had come upon only in books. I, too, had used

THE CAFETERIA   165

these words—in my head. But they used these words easily, as if
they were their everyday words, as if they were their living language. What did they talk about? I could not remember afterward
unless I consulted the cheap notebook and read their words over
again. I did not do this. I did not really want to know what they
said. All I cared about was the spell.

I was drunk with the cafeteria and the people in it. I lived impatiently through the day until midnight came when I could go back
to the cafeteria and be among them—my people.

They did not seem to mind my deafness. They wrote in my
cheap notebook and perhaps when someone else had the notebook and they wished to say something to me and could not wait,
they used the napkins as paper. After I began to frequent the cafeteria, the napkins decreased with almost incredible rapidity in
their holders. The Jew must have cursed me silently in his heart.
Perhaps he muttered his threats, but no one paid any attention to
him. The napkins continued to diminish in their holders.

I was drugging myself with the cafeteria. I forgot to write new
poems, I seldom went to the library. I forgot the world outside,
until I was almost down to my last dollar again.

Again I began my round of job-hunting. I arose at dawn and
walked through the streets with my newspaper list of jobs. I had
marked a cross before only the lowest, most menial jobs, the 'leavings' as I said to myself. I knew the futility of going to offices by
now. What did it matter that I had intelligence? All the employers
saw was my deafness. Through the streets I walked to the places
where might be found the leavings. Dishes to be washed, floors
to be scrubbed, the meaner factory jobs. These things were all
that I was good for, I had found. Would it not have been better
to have allowed them to make me really deaf? Then I should not
care so much, or feel so much. Nothing would have mattered then.
I should have become a ward of the state, perhaps. But I had not
wanted that. I was still a human being and I wanted to live and

be recognized as a human being. But the people did not appear to want me as a human being, they refused me employment now, as they had refused me the understanding I had wanted to help me stand up. No, I did not want their condescension, their pity, their charity. To hell with condescension, their pity, their charity. I wanted to be classed as a human being, and they would not class me as such. If I let go, their charity would take care of me—if I would let go. But I would not let go. To be still in possession of a hard, cold mind that saw things clearly, myself clearest of all, was a nuisance. It would have been better to let them make me really deaf. What good was it doing me now to have held on to my intelligence? To have remained human being? The rest of the human beings would not admit I was one; they would not give me work so that I might live. If I had let myself become really deaf, my troubles would have been over.

With the newspaper under my arm I went up dirty elevators, one after the other, that took me to mean factory lofts, or I entered restaurant after restaurant, but when they heard my cry, "I am deaf," they made those gestures that instantly made me into something not quite human. Why did they make those gestures? Why could they not write it down, damn them! Was their time so beautifully precious? They were impatient. A look of impatience and vexation came into their face at the very idea of my coming here and applying for a job. I seemed to think that I was human! That look was as effective as those words, "You can't do anything; you aren't good for anything." Like those words, it set my soul quivering.

How far away the cafeteria seemed as I walked from place to place, looking for a job. What would they say if they saw me doing this? What did they know of life with their romantic dreams? What did they know of hell? They were given the consideration that human beings were given, at least. If they only knew how much that was.

I walked on. I threw away the newspaper. The jobs listed there were not for me. The jobs advertised there, even the leavings, were for human beings, not for such as me. I must get work some other way. I walked on. I turned my face downtown again, and began to look for the sign "Dishwasher" or "Dishwasher Wanted" in the windows of cafeterias and restaurants. But there were no such signs. When I did not want a job, the windows were full of dishwasher signs, but when I did want a job, there were no signs.

I continued my walk. Suddenly I saw other signs hanging from the outside of buildings on narrow streets between Fifth and Sixth Avenues. Signs not too regularly lettered and painted on shoebox cardboard. Strange signs advertising strange work—or rather work that was strange to me. A sign read: "Pinker Wanted." What was a pinker? Another sign read: "Examiner on Ladies' Dresses." "Expert Buttonhole Maker," read a third sign. "High class Sewer," read another. I stopped before the sign that read "Examiner on Ladies' Dresses." Surely it did not require ears to examine ladies' dresses?

I drew my notebook from under my arm and tore out a page. On the page I wrote, "I am deaf. I would like to have the job of examiner." I wrote, on the old principle of not trusting my voice to carry my message.

Then, paper in hand, I climbed the three flights of stairs to the third floor where, the shoe-box cardboard said, the examiner on ladies' dresses was wanted. I opened the only door on the third floor timidly. I saw two men in a long room which contained only a table.

One of the men looked up. I went toward him with my paper in hand and held it out to him. He read it and then stared at me. Then he made that gesture toward his mouth meant—I had grown wise interpreting gestures—could I talk?

I nodded and said I could talk. Perhaps if I had gone in with full poise and confidence, and spoken my request, instead of tendering the piece of paper—but I would not have been the person I was if I had done that.

He hesitated, looking me over from head to foot.

Finally—it may have been the plea in my eyes—he led me to a rack where some dresses hung. He took up a pair of scissors and showed me how one examined dresses. I watched him cut off the tiny, almost invisible threads that clung to sleeves, the neck, the hem.

He gave me the scissors. It was not as easy as I had supposed. Too, my fingers were clumsy. But I must have satisfied him sufficiently, for he gave me the job.

It was a sweat-shop, I saw, when I had a chance to look around. What I had seen was only two-thirds of the loft. In the other third, half-heartedly partitioned off with a curtain were some women seated before machines pushed against the wall. There were two big windows, unwashed. The floor was strewn with buttons and scraps of cloth.

As I had learned something from the restaurant, so I learned something from this place. The women were Jewish and came to work in fine coats and dresses. In the shop they took off their fine clothes and put on old aprons. There was one big woman who did not seem to mind that her apron was cut so low that the upper part of her breasts showed plainly. There was another woman, small and wiry, who had more force in her body than the rest of the women put together. She might have been a Communist. She might have been one of the new women under the Soviet régime. There was another woman who sewed buttons without raising her eyes once, unlike the other women who sewed and talked at the same time. Unlike the others also, she had no fine clothes. When the cold weather came in earnest, when the snow began to fall, she came to work with her feet wrapped in rags. When she sat down at her low chair by the trays of buttons and snaps, she carefully unwrapped the rags and laid them by her chair. Was she alive? I would wonder. Had she intelligence? I would see her and wonder what she was as we waited downstairs in the bleak winter morning, huddled close to the door, waiting for the boss to come. Like me she was over-early. Was she, like me, driven by the fear of being late? Or perhaps she did not mind getting up early, and did not know the fear of falling asleep again for 'five minutes'—and waking up around noon. Perhaps she scorned sleep. The faces of workers at dawn are haggard with the need of more sleep, but her face was clear at seven in the morning, with the clearness and unshadowedness that mine would not attain until several hours had gone by. I would stand and search for her eyes, as we waited. It was a difficult feat, for she wore blue glasses. But I saw her eyes once, during the lunch hour when she sat eating her rye-bread sandwiches. Yes, she was both alive and intelligent. I wondered about her often, and would have liked to come nearer.

The man whom I had seen with the boss when I had first come in asking for a job was the tailor. He could be insolent with the boss. He emulated the boss in the matter of a big black cigar always stuck in his mouth. He was a tailor who knew his worth as a designer of dresses for the six- and eleven-dollar Fourteenth Street trade. I liked him least of all. He had a smooth face that was too smooth, and lips that were also too smooth, too sensuous.

The presser was a Hungarian who looked out of place among these people, Jews from the boss to the pimpled boy who carted away the finished dresses. He was big and raw-boned. He hung his watch on a nail beside his ironing board, and every time I went near him to get more dresses to examine, I glanced at the watch, as I had glanced at the Big Ben in the restaurant, and with the same idea in my mind of getting courage to keep on till the place closed.

I felt better with a job once more. If only I could count on a job all the time, then I would not know misery any more. I did not care that the jobs I managed to get robbed me of all my energy, left neither time nor inclination for writing, or the dream of learning lipreading. What I was now afraid of was being cast into the streets again, to look for another job. I had known hunger, and worse still, terror. I had walked through the streets while rain and snow and terror had poured down on me. What was to become of me? There was no thought of turning back. I had forgotten home, but what lay ahead of me? The unknown racked me with fear.

Now that I had a job, I returned once more to the cafeteria with my poems and the cheap notebook under my arm. My life really centered about the cafeteria. I never went there before midnight, and I never stayed more than an hour, but I received from it what I needed to keep me going.

I did not see it as a cafeteria. I did not see the cafeteria at all. The place was an illusion, even the people who frequented the cafeteria were for the most part illusions. But even if had stopped to think this over, I would not have cared, I would not have discontinued my midnight visits. For I had need of this illusion, I had need to think the people super-creatures, after the too-reality of my life by day in restaurant or sweat-shop.

With my poems under my arm, my little black book of poems under my arm always, as if to say, "Look, I have these to make you forget that I am deaf. Look, these are what I bring as my right of admission," I went through the swinging door and took my check at the counter and then I paused a second to look around. This was my stage. I loved this moment's pause when the people at the tables looked up at my entrance.

I pulled out a chair, and leaving my black book of poems and the cheap notebook on top the marble table in front of it, I went to get my rolls and coffee.

I wanted to go to their table and sit down beside them. But I was too shy. I waited for one of them to come to me. I did not think much of myself. My poems were another part me—the best part—but there was still myself, a lame being to be reckoned with. Who would want me? I had not escaped from the people. They had branded me very well. I was timid, inferior, always on the defensive. Why did I say that I had escaped? This deafness had not occurred through any fault of my own, yet their laughter, their curiosity as though I were a freak, had forced me to be ashamed of it, had forced me into my attempts, foolish and pitiable, to hide it. I could not turn around without seeing what they had done to me. They had forced me into a cage in which, after a time I had voluntarily enclosed myself, as the only way to escape them.

I was trying, now, to be free of this cage. When I entered the cafeteria I left my cage outside on the sidewalk, as one leaves one's rubbers and umbrella on a rainy day. And I believed that these people in the cafeteria understood all this; I believed that they reached out their hands to help me.

I sat down to my coffee and rolls. Would someone come talk to me? That was the awful thought that could spoil my contentment. Suppose no one came and opened the notebook and talked to me? I did not want to be isolated as I first had been. I did not want to be stared at. But after a while someone would come and sit down beside me and open the notebook and write. Then I sat back and relaxed. Yes, they considered me one of them.

I took them at their word. They were poets, writers, artists, they said. I believed them as implicitly as I believed that I was a poet. I did not know that all except a very few were poseurs. If anyone had told me that, I would have asked, "What is a poseur?" It was true that I was always willing to show them my poems and I never saw any of theirs—except for one or two—but what of that? I saw them talking, talking, talking. And I marvelled. What were they saying? What were they saying? How I longed to hear! But merely to be in the proximity of this talk, even if I sat silent myself and heard nothing, even if I was always in my tower of silence, was enough to fill the void, and I was happy.

I did not know it, but I was something of a mystery to them. I had nothing to do with them outside of this communal hour. They wondered. They speculated. Why did I buy only rolls and coffee? Was I starving? No, I was not starving. When I was starving I did not come here, I would have told them. When I was starving, I hid in my room when I did not roam the streets looking for a job. It was only when I had a job that I could afford the ten-cent admission fee of my rolls and coffee. When I starved, I remained away. But they wove a story around me: I was starving.

The weeks and the months went by. By day I worked at the sweat-shop examining dresses for infinitesimal threads or helped the button woman sew on buttons. When the ordeal was over, I hurried home and waited impatiently for midnight to come. I passed the time reading, ruining my eyes under the poor light. Waiting, waiting, until midnight, when I could go forth to the communal hour at the cafeteria, sit in the midst of the marvellous talk.

I did not ask myself in these days where I was going. It was enough that my job continued, that sometimes I wrote a poem.

I was living in the windowless room when the news reached me that my mother had died.

"Oh," I said to the teller of the tale. And that was all I said.

I went to work as usual, and at night when I came back I lay down on the bed and wrote a poem which I called 'Broken Faces,' thinking perhaps of the broken face of my mother. I did not feel any emotion at her death, the way I supposed a person should feel when his mother died. I tapped myself for any running emotion, but I was dry, dry, dry. Then I remembered that my mother had died long ago for me. She had been dead a long, long time. The person who had been my mother the last few years was someone else entirely. My mother was a woman whom perhaps I had hated, but whom nevertheless I could appreciate. She could run a market, and she could run the houses. I appreciated that mother, but she had been dead a long time. The neurotic, neurasthenic, broken woman who went about the house with her hand on her rupture or her heart, who must go to bed at twilight, who was no longer gallant—no, that had not been my mother.

Nevertheless, the broken faces in my mind persisted. I got out my notebook and wrote and rewrote. *Broken faces*, I said, *I think death comes to you as a musician who recreates the eternal cadence life sometimes mists to an inertness which can be aroused once more only by death. Remoulded by this aroused cadence, the basic ceremony of each face is not arrested by death.*

The poem finished, at least for this time, I continued to lie on the bed, under the poor light. For once I did not go to the cafeteria. I wanted to go, but I was afraid, suddenly. Afraid to move. I felt that someone was in the room with me, watching me.

I fell into an uneasy sleep. When I awoke, the light was burning. A question tormented me. Had I, or had I not, turned out the light just before I fell asleep. Had someone, had *she* turned on the light?

I had known fear, fear of the people, fear of what would become of me, but the fear I felt in that moment exceeded any of the other kinds of fear.

In the windowless room where everything seemed windowless, I sensed my mother's presence. From which direction did her regard come?

She forced herself on me, as she had so often done. It was impossible to disregard her. To get away from the hallucination that she was watching me from the ceiling, I thought about her. She had sacrificed herself for her husband and children—and what had *she* got out of it? Questions came to me—the old questions and attempts to fathom the relationship between men and women. What was it? Hadn't she ever wanted freedom? Had she wanted to stay? Had she wanted responsibilities? Had she wanted children? I remembered the market, the conversations I had over-heard between my mother and Mis' Levretts. I remembered conversations which had tormented me, which had remained in my mind, and which only now were becoming clear.

My mother had been beautiful once, at nineteen, and only twenty years later she had died looking, at thirty-nine, like fifty.

She had worked all her life, worked like a horse, as they said, carrying her husband and children up with her. She was a pioneer. She had come from the old world in the steerage of a ship. She had borne six children in America. She had started the market—and it had become truly a market-place. The farmers for miles around came to her with their produce, as well as the salesmen from the meat-packing plants. They had asked for my mother, not my father. How proud I had felt!

Then the houses had come to take the place of the market.

She had carried the houses on her back as she had carried the market, being a business man, lying, hard, inexorable; in short, being a business man when it came to the making of money. Being absolutely democratic. "If you've got the money, you're as good as anybody else." An absolute American, my mother. No one had ever been more American than my mother. America could be proud of her. She was one of its pioneers.

Was I wrong in thinking her life wasted? She had lived, there had been no halftones in her existence. But what of her secret rebellions? Of the law that submitted her to her husband? And the law of menstruation? Women who rested during the seven days, she had worked all through them, cleaning the meat blocks, lifting sides and forequarters of beef from the hooks. The cramps had gone through her; she had known the weakness when the sides of the stomach appear to be caving in, but she had continued to work. And the day of menstruation—would the menstruation appear? As she waited, her tone to the children had grown sharper and sharper with dread and fear. And we had hated her because of the tone, not knowing what caused it.

Through the night, afraid to go to the cafeteria, afraid to go to sleep, I thought about my mother, until finally I fell asleep.

I overslept. Through the morning I hurried to work. In my windowless room, I never knew when morning came, except by deduction. I had an alarm clock, but I never set the alarm. Of what use? I would not have heard its clamor. I trained myself to be up at six. But this morning I had overslept.

What could I say to the boss? What could I say? I said something. He merely glanced at his watch and said nothing.

How long would this job last anyway? Employers seemed to like their employees to show an interest in the work. I could not. What was there of interest in the work I did? My lack of interest, my almost hatred, was apparent. I glance at the presser's watch so often that finally he took it from its nail and put it in his pocket. Here was the episode of Big Ben repeated. I seemed to be anti-social. I could not hide, play the hypocrite.

How long could one stand this life? This and the life in the windowless room. My country color, the red in my cheeks, was going. There was no air in the windowless room. I was growing careless about myself. I brushed my teeth only now and then. My hair was dry. I who had loved to wash my skin carefully, regularly, was too tired, too spiritless, now to do it any more. There was no hot water in the house. On Saturdays the landlady grudgingly heated the water, but there were so many wanting the bathroom on Saturdays that I never had a chance to use it until late at night. By that time I didn't feel like taking a bath. Then, too, the bathroom was cold. After the bath I would stand shivering and catch a chill. The one towel a week the landlady allowed was insufficient. Even my room was cold, in spite of the gas heater. I could never dry myself quickly enough. I gave up trying keep myself clean. The demoralization of the spirit that was going on in me showed thus on the outside in carelessness, uncleanliness. Why should I fight against something that was too big for me?

I would leave the little gas heater going all night in spite the danger of asphyxiation. Who cared? It was more important to me that in the morning the room was not freezing cold. I hated cold—the cold of a cold room most of all. I was afraid that if the room was too cold, some morning I would not get up at all. I would not care about my job, about anything. I would stay in bed, cuddling myself in the warmth.

In order to get away from the cold, the loneliness, I went the cafeteria. How many others were there in the cafeteria who came for the same reason?

The days passed. One day when I came to work I was told that I was no longer needed. It was the middle of a particularly bitter winter.

I walked through the streets again, looking for work. After weeks I was taken on in a bookbinding factory. And again it happened. Once a job was found, my spirits lifted. I forgot the terror pursuing me. I returned to the cafeteria at night. Always the cafeteria to return to at night, to let myself be bathed in the beloved illusion.

Why did I hide it from myself? Sometimes they came to my table, and sometimes they did not. The novelty that was myself was wearing off. I sat alone more and more. From the distance that was my peculiar being, I watched the laughter, and the truth came as it always did. Not even here, among my people, could the gnome be vanquished. I would always sit apart, a spectator. Now and then someone, more kind and more thoughtful than the rest, might come and talk to me. But it was so hard to talk to me! Such a bother! Who wanted to be everlastingly writing it down, writing down?

But for the gnome . . . but for the gnome . . . Because of him the laughter and the talk went past and over me. I sat in the midst of plenty, lonely and hungry.

I did not dare to take a seat where they were sitting. For of what use was I? I, a silent person, among all the talk, contributing nothing. My seat would be good for someone who could join in. If I ever took a seat at their table, I would want to apologize for my negative presence.

I never seemed to stay long on a job. It may have been my deafness, or it may have been because of the queer wild being that was myself. The first two weeks of any job was torture to me. I was like an animal who has been caged. For days I would do my work in restaurant, sweat-shop, or factory with a terrible longing to break away. Who was I to be caged? I who wanted to walk on the streets in my crazy, down-at-heel shoes at all hours, loving the sun and the moon and the smell of freedom. Who was I to be caged? I roamed about the factory restlessly. I watched the clock. I went to the toilet every five minutes because when I returned from my meaningless visit to the toilet it was a few minutes nearer to five o'clock. I could not for the life of me be like these others here who did their work obediently, mechanically. I could not. I could not.

But in a few weeks I felt better. I would feel a change stealing over me. It was as if I had got my wild soul in my hand and had succeeded in crushing it to stillness. There was no longer a sign of mad life. I felt in me the required deadness that was necessary to endure the confines of the cage. Then I too, like the others, went about my work, obediently, mechanically.

I might succeed in doing this, but I could not dull myself to the proper colorlessness that the foreman required.

I would laugh, and in the factory there was an invisible sign,

NO LAUGHTER ALLOWED

Laughter, like talk, took up time. I would laugh—at nothing most of the time, and I would make the other workers laugh too. A hole in the stocking of 'the boy' would set me off, and I set off the others around me.

Also I had communistic ideas without knowing that they were communistic. I was ignorant of the many labels that I would have acquired naturally if I had been able to hear.

"Shut up," I was advised by a girl. "Keep them things to yourself. If Jake hears you, he'll kick you out. He'll think you're trying to make trouble."

But I could not shut up. I was in love with my ideas. I had ideas on every subject, my head was a jumble of them; ideas on religion, on love, on work. Some I had picked up in the cafeteria, some I had thought out myself during the long years when I had talked to myself in the darkness. Ideas were live people in my head and I played them against one another.

Especially was I for freedom. Freedom of the individual. Freedom from such awful things as factories and sweat shops. I *knew*. My ideas were not just empty words. Freedom to do as one wished, go where one wished, like the birds. I was a bird myself. That was how I wanted to live, that was how people should live.

I continued to talk. One day, little more than a month after I had been at the factory, I was fired.

Now I was desperate indeed, for I had not had time to save up any money. I had only enough money for a week.

When I came to the cafeteria the night I was fired, I noticed curious looks directed at me. Someone approached me and told me a secret. They were going to give a benefit dance for me. All through the Village lately I had seen signs in the windows, signs that read, "Poet's Benefit Dance." So I was the poet for whom the dance was to be given.

My coffee and rolls, and only coffee and rolls, had started the legend of my starvation. They supposed that I could not afford anything else, which was only half the answer. The other half was that I dreaded asking the counterman anything that would open up a lot of questions.

Everybody sold tickets for the "Poet's Benefit Dance." I wanted to cry to them, "stop, stop, stop," in spite of fact that the money realized would be a real help to me, out of a job as I was, and with only a few dollars between myself and starvation. But I did not want money that way. I did not want money accruing from benefit dances. With all my soul I did not want it. There it was again, this insistence that I was a helpless person, less than human.

I tormented myself with questions. Had it really been disinterested? Had it not been merely the Jew's taking advantage of me, as I had been taken advantage of before, to gain publicity for the cafeteria?

The night of the dance—which took place in the cafeteria—I sat lonely and miserable while the people danced. Reporters from the newspapers approached me. What were they saying? What were they asking me? What were they writing about me? I had had enough of notoriety. I had had enough of it at home.

Nevertheless, with the money from the benefit dance, I had freedom, the freedom I wanted, freedom for the first time.

With my new freedom I went to the cafeteria more than ever. I learned to know the people there thoroughly. If the illusion persisted, it was because the illusion was stronger than any mere reality. I had built that illusion myself, without much aid from reality, and I hung on to it because I had need of it. Most of the people were poseurs, I found. I had learned the pronunciation and the meaning of the word poseur by now. Three or four who came to this place were real. Only three or four. Yet I continued to go to the cafeteria because I had need of it.

We had all one thing in common, whether we were 'real' or whether we were 'poseur.' That thing we had in common set us apart from the rest of mankind. We were child-men and child-women. We would never grow up and bow down to reality. We would ever chase butterflies in our brain. The rest of mankind had no butterfly in their brains.

Sometimes, instead of a butterfly, it was a dark thing, an obsession. It looked like a butterfly, but alas! it had no wings. It was a dark, sick thing that poisoned mind and soul. Then he or she was a sick child-man or child-woman.

To the cafeteria came poets and painters, poseurs, prostitutes, uptown sightseers, men hungry for color and willing to pay for it.

Such words as 'bad woman' and 'fallen woman' did not mean anything here. Many of the men and women lived on their wits. Sheer viciousness was sublimated, or, rather, it became something that did not appear to be viciousness, but something careless and gay. Many of them lived—how they did they live, I wondered? Yet they were all careless and gay. I loved this carelessness and gaiety. It was all new to me.

I learned about the girls whom I had seen flitting from table to table like birds. Girls who lived off their wits, girls who were curiously hard and curiously lovely. Girls who gave themselves to men who came to the Village seeking color and willing to pay for it, and gave themselves again to these men of the cafeteria without a thought of money. Where did these girls come from? Where did they go? They came and they went. Lovely ones went, but even more lovely ones came to take their place.

And I—I was always the looker-on, intensely curious, but without courage to dabble in the pool. I was afraid. If I did not fear pregnancy, then I feared the diseases about which I had heard so much. I envied these people who could let themselves go. I could not let go. Nor was it a question of morality. Morality had never troubled me, as the conventions had never troubled me. Rather it was that I thought beyond the act, reflecting on its consequences, and as always, my mind, hard and cold, said no.

I was self-sufficient. I lived in myself for the most part, yet if I was self-sufficient, I was also lonely. Someone to understand! I cried for someone to understand.

How far had I gone in my search for someone to understand? I was still always by myself. My friendships went no further than the cafeteria tables.

The benefit dance money did more harm than good. It aroused jealousy, a jealousy that amounted sometimes to hatred as they saw me eating while they did not. They crowded around me, but they were not the people I wanted to know. They had fooled me months ago, but now I knew them. They were the hangers-on, the sick child-men. I did not want their flattery. It sickened me. So I had seen them flatter the little prostitute when she had left her protector, each for himself hoping to get the post of new protector.

Over the cafeteria table I came to know a poet who wrote beautiful verse and lived by his wits, lived in a way frowned upon by society. I tried to make these incompatibilities—to me—compatible, but gave it up. The only way was to accept him as he was, and not look too much beneath. Another one I came to know was the little prostitute. Over the cafeteria table I read her philosophy, her values, as she wrote to me when her eye did not wander around for possible customers. Bit by bit I learned of her life in this way. She had been a shop-girl and seduced by her employer. She had lived with him for ten months. Then there had followed other men. Then she had been forced to seek her customers on the street, in cafeterias, in public places. She liked to read good books. She asked me for a list of 'good books.' She was even writing a story of her life. Would I read it?

I would not believe that she was a prostitute. I with my beliefs that prostitutes were not human creatures. Why, she was a child, infinitely weak. She always talked of getting a job next week—but alas! Next week never materialized. Meanwhile she wrote bits of her life to me on paper napkins, with her eye on the door for possible customers. Only in this way did she betray her profession. Her eye was something by itself, hardly human, that went to the door out of habit.

"If you are ever broke," she said, "come and live with me. I've got two rooms. You can have the other one."

"Thank you," I said. No one had ever said such a thing to me before, no one in all the great city.

For the people who came to the cafeteria she had no respect. She held them in the lowest contempt possible, poet and hanger-on alike.

"Taxi-drivers are decenter," she said. "They're *men* anyway."

I would watch her, her upper lip that would quiver like a hare's when she talked. Her mouth was the most expressive thing about her.

"I like you," she said once. "You're the only one here that's decent. Say, kid, you're in the wrong place. Get out—before it gets you, or you won't be able to get out."

But I persisted.

The place had a hold on me. I had need of it. And I had undoubted standing here, if only as a freak who could write poetry. Even if, like any of the people, they held off and I was lonely. Even if I doubted that they accepted me as a person.

I came to get away from loneliness, but even in the midst of many I was lonely. Always that tower of silence, always that tower of silence walling me in, that invisible yet strangely obdurate tower of silence. I might look over it with lonely eyes and always I did, but I could never join in the play with the people outside the tower walls. The least of them, those with rotten eyes, were better off than I.

Once indeed I thought I found somebody. But he was unstable—and I too was unstable. I wanted no one who was so much like me. I wanted someone who would be stable to my instability, someone who would be permanent and unshakable, someone in whom I could believe forever. That would be best for my poetry, something in me whispered. My poetry first. A man who would stand back of me, who would lift me up whenever I fell down. He would have to be extraordinary, such a man. For who would stand me? A creature more than human in some ways, and less than human, a freak, in others. I was a fool. I had better refrain from dreaming. I had better live as these people lived, take whatever life offered. But again I could not. I wanted no contamination, no dirty hands laid on me. I had need of feeling that my body belonged to me and to me alone. I had need of that perfect lightness of spirit-kinship that existed between my body and my mind. I wanted nothing in the outside world to break that perfect relationship.

This is not to say that I loved my body. I seldom paid any attention to it. It was a gross thing, a peasant thing. I looked admiringly at the slim American girls and envied them. No, it was not the physical aspect of my body that concerned me. It was the psychic stream that ran between my body and my mind. My well-being depended on that psychic stream remaining untroubled. It was really another version of the standing-up idea. When I could not stand up, I could not write. I felt helpless, a prisoner in my tower of silence. As those months during which I had washed dishes in the restaurant; the endless walk in the streets looking for work; the evening walks when I had been clutched at by men who sensed my utter demoralization and dared to approach. At those times my psychic stream had been troubled. I had fallen down. I could not stand up.

It was but right that my mind and my body should be so closely interlaced, that they should feel each other so sensitively, for were they not locked together in the tower of silence? They must listen to the within, rather than the without; the sounds they heard came from the within; the disturbances that most keenly affected them were the within disturbances. The world was but a million moving shapes, fish mouths opening and shutting, lips moving busily, contractions of throat and cheek, the swallowing of millions of Adam's apples. This was the world; this was the way the world began and ended. The only thing that could transform the strangely dead and yet strangely living spectacle was my imagination.

When the world was utterly without reality, when my imagination did not suffice to bridge the gap between myself and reality, then it was that despair seized me. I wanted so much to be a part of this world. Could I find no one in this world overfull of people who would unlock the door and let me in? I was tired of this aloofness.

The summer went. I had not thought beyond the summer to the time when the money given to me from the benefit dance would be gone. I would have to find a job again, but I ran from such thoughts. What had I done with the summer? It had gone so fast! I had not written much. When I had washed dishes, when I had examined dresses in the sweat shop, when I had carted away heavy piles of books in the bookbinding factory, I had thought of the time when I would have freedom to write. Well, I had had freedom, and I had written nothing. Instead of working, I had lived. I had whiled away afternoons sitting in the sun in Washington Park; I had read; I had taken long walks; I had been free for the first time in my life. Free and alone, away from parental authority. I had gone out when I wished, I had gone to bed when I had wished.

Most of the time I had spent over the cafeteria tables.

After this week there would be no more money. Now I had to look for a job again. Worse still, it was autumn, and it was becoming cold. If it had been summer, I would not have minded, but I dreaded the cold. I had grown lazy during the summer months. I had forgotten the life that always lay just around the corner for me, and the fact that one day soon I must go back to it.

I began my job-hunting life again. A week went by, two weeks. The old feeling that I was a hopeless under-dog came back. What good did it do me that I was a poet, that I had superior brains? I was unskilled, but most of all I was deaf. The gnome . . . the gnome . . . the gnome. . . . All they saw was the gnome.

I was hungry most of the time, and lost weight. One day I was faced with something new. The day when I began the cycle of menstruation arrived, but the period did not come. I was abysmally ignorant of procreation. I knew only that when a period did not come, one was going to have a baby. Therefore I was going to have a baby. That I had given myself to no man did not quiet me. I would have learned much about sex in the cafeteria, but my ears, closed, had allowed no information to enter my brain. That the period might stay away because of hunger, of great mental worry, of fear, all of which I was undergoing after a time of relaxation, I did not know. I knew nothing. Except that I was sure I was going to have a baby.

What should I do? What should I do? Perhaps it was not a baby. A glimmer of sanity returned to me. But I ran away from it. I was convinced that I was going to have a baby. Perhaps someone had broken into my little windowless room while I had been asleep and chloroformed me and then raped me. Excitedly my imagination ran on, increasing in hallucinations as it so easily did in this windowless room, in this awful house.

In spite of even myself, common sense returned. I would find out. I would go to the clinic where I had gone to have a tooth fixed. I had often seen women big with child there. I would ask them to examine me.

I had not the forethought to tell the woman who made out the applications that I was married. Instead, like a fool, I stumbled out that I thought I was going to have a baby and wanted to be examined.

The woman stared at me a second. Then she wrote down, "I am going to telephone a lady I know. She is lovely. You will like her. I want you to go to see her. She will help you."

Half an hour later I was ringing the door-bell of a small, detached house on a side-street.

I was shown into the presence of a woman who seemed be expecting me. I glanced around in not a little awe. It was a beautiful place in my eyes. The floors were waxed, the woodwork polished. What could this place be?

"Would you like to stay here," the woman wrote down, "if we find that you are going to have a baby?"

I nodded.

But what kind of place was this anyway? Why didn't she say something to explain? Why did she glance at me so impersonally, as if she did not see me at all? Why hadn't the woman at the clinic said something other than that "she is lovely" and "you will like her," putting me on a fictitious level with this woman and this house.

"First you will be examined by our doctor," said the woman.

We went upstairs, up several stories. On every one I caught a glimpse of many rooms. The place seemed to be a boarding school—as I had pictured boarding schools to be from an extensive reading of such tales long ago. There were girls on every floor, in gym bloomers and middies. I did not look too closely at them from shyness. If they were boarding-school girls, they were certainly superior beings, far superior to me.

On the top floor I was taken into a room where there was woman doctor. She beckoned me to undress and then I got on the operating table. Then she explored me as I had seen my mother explore the insides of a chicken with a finger. I was shocked and revolted. She finished her exploring and began to finger my breasts.

I began to be afraid. It was all a hallucination. Sanity returned to me. But this woman, her explorations—could my hallucinations be true then? Had someone—perhaps the ape man in the room next to mine—broken into my room and raped me? Anything could happen in that room where no light penetrated, except a poor electric light, and that house with its dark corridors. How often, too, had I not run from my hallucinations into the light and sanity of the streets and of the cafeteria.

"Am I going to have a baby?" I asked the doctor.

It was really too soon for her to make a diagnosis. Only a day and a half had elapsed since my period had not come as usual. Nevertheless, she said "yes" to my question, which, according to her experience, was the proper thing to say. Why was I here, except for that reason? I was the best one to know whether or not I was pregnant. My presence here presupposed that I had had sexual intercourse with a man, or I would not now fear pregnancy. So she looked at me and from her experience she said "yes," without really looking at me or thinking of me. A long line of girls marched before her, girls who had climbed on the operating table as I had climbed, whom she had poked with her finger and condemned as she had just condemned me. I was just one more girl. Why doubt that I was pregnant? Why look inside the case? She condemned me on circumstantial evidence.

I dressed and she began to ask me questions.

Who was it? she wanted to know. How to tell her of the ape man and my hallucinations—which by her "yes" she had made realities rather than hallucinations. But they sounded crazy. She would certainly think I was lying or insane.

It was, when I stopped to think about it, a highly improbable tale. The product of a terrified and lonely imagination, of a sojourn into too long a silence, a silence which had become morbid, perhaps. Could I tell her of the ape man? But I must tell her something. It could not have been an immaculate conception. Yes, it must have been the ape man. I shuddered, picturing it all. Could I tell her of the ape man? Could I? She might think me crazy. Yet my child must have a father. In my imagination, I picked him up from the streets. I was cold and hungry . . . I had been tempted.

"I don't know," I said. "I don't know who the father is. I picked him up from the streets. I was cold and hungry. . . ."

She nodded, satisfied. It was the old story. I saw that I need not say any more. She did not want to hear more.

"Do you want to stay here?" she asked, repeating what the woman I had first seen, had said.

Why did they say that? Why did they put it in just that way? What kind of place was it anyway? Why didn't they tell me? Why didn't they say something so that I could know what it was that I was doing, what it was that I might be signing away? Nervously I glanced around. It seemed all right. The stairs I had come up had been polished. The floors on all levels had also been polished. There were girls who wore gym bloomers. It was a boarding school. In a second I was eleven again and my favorite heroine was a girl who went to boarding school. If I had not so blindly entered this detached house, if I had stopped a minute and looked up to the second- and third- and fourth-story windows and seen the iron bars at the windows I would have wondered at them, and known that this was not a boarding school, for boarding schools do not have iron bars at the windows. If I had stopped a minute to see what there was to be seen, I would not have so confidently rung the bell of this house. But I had seen nothing. I knew nothing. All I knew was that this woman doctor had condemned me. What was I to do now?

"I'd like to stay here," I said. Stay here—exactly what did it mean?

The doctor—she was a psychiatrist also as I was to learn—took a blank sheet. Then she started to ask me questions. How adroit she was I never appreciated until afterward. I gave her a fictitious name, told her my father and mother were dead. It was half true. But she did not believe me. Adroitly she wormed at me, as a dentist worms at a tooth, as she had wormed her finger into me ten minutes before. She was a past master at what might be called a feminized third degree. So she had wormed the truth out of many shivering girls, that long line of girls who had gone before me. I led her up a blind alley and left her there, so I thought, while I ran out into the street again, free of her. In vain! When I reached the street corner she was there ahead me, waiting for me. Finally, I succumbed, as the girls in the long line ahead of me had succumbed. And like the others, I succumbed more to her smiles, her pretense of equality, of comradeship, her protestations of "I won't tell" (which confidence she betrayed as soon as my back was turned), in short, all the paraphernalia of the social service worker. She had promised "not to tell." I told her and rested easy on her smiles and on her promises.

I was to come the next day and bring all my things.

Now that I had accepted the idea of a baby, I was glad of it. A baby was something of my very own to love. Perhaps that was what I had always needed. A baby would not mind that I was deaf. I continued to dream until I remembered that the ape man—who else?—was the father of the baby. I shuddered. To have something of that thing in me! How often had I not shuddered as I passed the ape man in the hall? He was not human. There could be nothing more degenerate than his face. His body was stooped and bent like that of an ape. He would not have been able to get lodging in any other house except in a house like this, in a street where the sun did not penetrate. How I had feared him. Now to know. . . . My dreams became nightmares. What would it be like? What would it look like? It would look like something horrible. Yet I could not entirely relinquish the dream, and unconsciously, with that gesture that is hereditary, my arm stole around my body and remained there in that protective, all embracing attitude that guards the unborn against possible hurts.

The next day I gathered my things together. A few things, a very few. In the afternoon I walked to the detached house with my suitcase. Again the image of the boarding house came to my mind.

If I had looked up, this last time and opportunity, and seen the iron bars—but I did not look up. Nor did I particularly notice the marked scrutiny directed at me by the people on the street as I waited after ringing the bell. They knew what the house was even if I did not.

As I waited, I felt happy. The cold sun looked friendly. The people in this house were kind, marvellously kind. I had not thought such people existed. Here they had solved my problem with a simple interrogative sentence, "Would you like to stay here?" No more hunger, no more cold, no more worry, no more hunting through the streets for a job, peering into restaurant windows for the sign "Dishwasher Wanted." Yet there was something wrong somewhere. The suspicion that had been inculcated in me through experience, the desire to look behind an apparent kindness to see what might not be hiding, this troubled me. It was too easy. It was too simple, somehow. The people did not do such things. I knew the people well by now. Why hadn't the two women said something? Why had they merely said, "Would you like to stay here?" And the woman at the clinic with her too-cordial equality, "You will like her . . . she is lovely."

But I could not go back to my windowless room now. I had given it up. I had only two dollars in the world. I was truly at the end of my rope.

I waited for someone to answer my ring. At last a girl, dark and quite young, opened the door. Evidently she had been expecting me. I looked around for the woman I had seen before. But the ground floor was empty. All I saw was this dark, unsmiling young woman. She seemed impatient at the way I looked around.

She took my suitcase and put it in a room. Then she led me to another room, still on the ground floor. It was a bathroom—a strange thing to have alongside the other rooms which were offices. She motioned to me to undress. She turned the shower on me, and after that sprayed kerosene onto my hair. I protested that I did not have lice, but she paid no attention to me. Then she gave me an old bathrobe and bedroom slippers which I put on. All this came to have a symbolic meaning for me later. I left myself and my clothes downstairs. I cast off my real self and the clothes of that self in the bathroom, so that when we left the bathroom I was without any defenses.

As we left the bathroom I noticed and thought it curious that as she had unlocked the bathroom door, so she now locked it behind her.

We went upstairs to the top floor and I was shown into a room. I was to stay in that room until the doctor saw me, leaving the room only to go to the bathroom, the dark young woman said. The bathroom on the ground floor? No, there were two bathrooms on this floor, she pointed out to me as we left my room and walked through the empty hall. One bathroom was for the syphilitic girls, to be used only by them; and the other bathroom was for the girls who had no venereal diseases.

After this tour, we went back to my room and the dark young woman went downstairs. I was left alone. As there was no chair, I lay on the bed. I was puzzled. Why had she taken my suitcase and clothes away from me, forbade me to take them upstairs? Why was I in bathrobe and slippers at two in the afternoon? Where were the girls I had seen in their gym costumes as I came up the stairs before? And the two bathrooms? One for the girls who were syphilitic, and the other for girls who had no diseases. The dark woman had left the paper on which she had written her explanations, and I re-read her words. This was a strange boarding school, or perhaps the boarding-school books I had read had told only half the truth.

I began to regret my hurry. Why had I made such haste to come here? Why had I not waited until evening? Why had I not. . . . I lay on the bed, tormented by questions.

The room I was in was small and scrupulously clean. It contained a cot on which I was lying, and a bureau. The window near the head of the cot looked out on a yard. As I looked out of the window, I noticed for the first time the iron bars across the window.

A desire to go out seized me. I wanted to go out! I wanted to go out! Then I remembered what the woman had said . . . I was to stay here until the doctor had examined me. No doubt the doctor would be here in half an hour, and after she had examined me I could put on my clothes and go out again. I would come back later, when it was quite, quite dark.

A long time went by. I tried to obey the woman's order not to leave the room, but my curiosity asserted itself too strongly. Why did no one come? Where were the boarding-school girls? Where were the boarding-school girls who were to come tramping in, welcoming me to the school, to their parties, their games? Jolly girls, jolly boarding-school girls . . . where were they? Perhaps they were out shopping with their chaperon, as they had so often gone shopping in the books. Or they might be at their games, or in class. I wished they would finish whatever it was that they were doing and come to greet me. I was bored alone here.

I got out of bed. Stay in this bed, in this room? It was a distinct challenge, a delightful one. In the boarding-school books, the heroine, or the girl whom I had most admired, had been the kind who had broken rules, had defied rules and regulations, but quite nicely. It had really been only high-spirits. It was understood that she was not really bad.

Now, thinking of that girl, that composite of a hundred heroines of a hundred boarding-school books, I went into the long hall. I peeped in awe and terror into the bathroom where only the syphilitic girls bathed and went to the toilet. What did syphilitic girls leave behind them that non-syphilitic girls must not use the tub or the toilet? I opened the bathroom door a little wider. The tub was shining with cleanliness, the toilet seat and bowl too. I thought of the various rooming houses I had lived in, and thought what a good idea it would be if there were two bathrooms in such houses, one bathroom marked with a card, "Syphilitics Only," and the other with a similar card, except that the lettering should read, "Non-Syphilitics Only."

I continued my soft shuffle down the hall, peeping into the open rooms. They were all like mine. Some, larger, had two beds in them and two bureaus.

I pictured the rooms as they would be when the boarding-school girls came back, laughing, happy girls. I was suddenly timid. Would they accept me? Would they mind the gnome? In book boarding schools, 'queer' girls weren't liked. I remembered how in the books, such girls had been ostracized and shunned. I prayed that they would not consider me queer.

My tour ended, I crept back to my room. My thoughts turned to the baby. I did not see the absurdity of it, that girls who had babies coming, and illegitimate ones at that, were not allowed in boarding schools. I dreamed on about the baby, until a girl appeared in the doorway, and then another girl and still another. It was just like the boarding-school books.

They were not in their gym bloomers as they had been before, but in gingham dresses. I did not lower my eyes to the shoes on their feet or I would have wondered. Girls in boarding schools—or at least the boarding schools of my eleven-year-old dreams—did not wear shoes with holes in them, old broken shoes, cast-off shoes. After all, little more than six years had elapsed since the gnome had come to live with me, and it was as if my deafness coming upon me stealthily, immersed in my boarding-school books, had locked me in with them.

The girls stared at me. It was all true to boarding-school tradition, this coming to the new girl in her room and making her welcome. Later I learned that here, as in the boarding schools of my books, it was customary, when a new girl came, to gather in her room and ask questions about the outside world. Later I was to do it myself. This was really a boarding school, only not of the type that books are written about for eleven-year-olds. And the questions asked here were different from the questions that are asked in the world of book boarding schools.

Some of the girls sat on the bed, the rest gathered around me. I could have loved them for it, that they approached me without fear, approached a freak without fear or obscene curiosity. They were curious, yes, but not with *that* kind of curiosity.

When they learned that I was deaf, a girl ran off to her room and came back with a paper and pencil.

The first question was, "What did you do?" That puzzled me. I had done nothing. What did they mean?

"I'm going to have a baby," I said importantly, as if it was the most natural thing in the world to say that I was going to have a baby to these girls who were no older than myself—many of them seemed younger, only fifteen or sixteen.

They accepted my remark without comment, passively. This passiveness was strange, suddenly. I had not noticed before, but now I did, how strangely passive they all were. How passive their very arms were. It was then, for the first time, that I really looked at them and noticed their eyes. They were dead eyes. What eyes were not dead, were cowed and cringing, worse than the wholly dead eyes, because in them I could still see life, life plainly dying. Only the corners of their lips lifted with the sniffing curiosity which could not reach their eyes, because the door to their eyes was closed and locked forever.

The girls remained in my room a little time, talking among themselves, always with that strange passivity, not like the high-spirited young girls of my boarding-school dreams. Occasionally they would glance at me, and now and then one would write a question such as, "How does it look outside?" This hunger for the outside . . . it puzzled me.

Suddenly they got up. No doubt they had heard footsteps, or a bell. The boarding-school idea lifted its head. How true to book boarding schools! They would be punished in some innocuous way if they were found in my room. Perhaps it was against the rules for them to come into my room until the doctor had examined me, as it was against the rules for me to leave the room, except to go to the non-syphilitic bathroom.

They trooped out (how I hung on, with something like terror this time, to my boarding-school dream) except for one girl, about seventeen, who, from courage, or more probably from indifference to fate, remained seated on my bed. It was she who had asked me the first question, and whose eyes I had first seen—dead eyes, which had made me go in haste to the other pairs of eyes, only to find them also dead or dying. Her eyes seemed to be the most dead, the most indifferent. They had been dead for a long time. There was even a faint yellow of decay about them which made me turn away.

"When will the doctor come to examine me?" I asked her.

"I don't know," she said, in a curiously pretty handwriting.

"Will I be able to go out tomorrow?" I asked.

"You can't go out," she said.

I stared at her. "What do you mean?"

"Don't you know what this place is?"

I opened my mouth to say boarding school, but my words died their foolish death before I could say them. I could only shake my head at her.

"It's a reformatory," she said. She laid the pencil and paper down as if she had written enough, and was tired, not physically, but mentally, tired. Then, having an afterthought, she picked up the pencil and paper again, bit the pencil reflectively several times, stared with her dead eyes at the paper, and then said,

"Nobody can go out."

I leaned over to look at her words, and then, having comprehended them, I looked at her, but her dead eyes were far away. I could not reach them. Then I saw that they had come back from their terrible distance and were fixed on the bureau top where I had laid the three or four handkerchiefs, all that the young woman had allowed me to take upstairs from my suitcase. The girl's dead eyes were fixed on these handkerchiefs.

She arose as if in a trance, the dead eyes made it appear as if everything she did was done in a trance, and going over to the bureau she put her hand on a handkerchief that was embroidered with a red flower. The girl's dead eyes were fixed on the red flower. She took the handkerchief in her hand, and her finger went over the flower back and forth, back and forth.

"Can I have it?" she asked. I did not need the pencil and paper, and the writing down of the words, to understand them. They spoke to me and I heard them.

"Sure," I said.

Without any thanks, or even turn of her head, she took the handkerchief and went out.

PART SEVEN

"Home for Girls"

I was alone again. What had she said? I leaned over to read the words on the paper. Reformatory. So it was to a reformatory that the woman at the clinic had sent me with her "you'll like her," and "she's lovely." She had sent me to the reformatory with a smile. And no one had said anything until the girl with the dead eyes had told me. They had let me stick my head in the trap. No doubt they had sent me to the reformatory so smilingly because that appeared to be the place for me. I deserved it. But for some reason I differed from them. I did not at all believe that I should be in a reformatory just because I was going to have baby, and that baby illegitimate. I did not believe that I belonged in a 'home for girls.' And I—the fool!—had come here by my own accord. That woman at the clinic whom I had observed many times when I had gone to have my teeth fixed, that woman with her flirtatious ways, her hair primping, her mouth always babyishly half open, her buttocks visible beneath her too tight dress, moving up and down as she walked, her too high heels—who was she to send me to the reformatory? What was she? I had a suspicion. But this was the difference between that woman and the dead girls here; they were the under-dogs, they were caught swiftly in the petty traps the law laid for them, while she—she belonged to the upper-dogs and could escape—get away with it. That was the refinement of law and civilization. The under-dogs were within the law, and the upper-dogs were outside it.

I lay on the bed. I wondered what time it was. After a while I grew hungry. I wondered where all the girls had gone. I could feel the unusual quiet; there were no stirrings of air currents that meant the people were somewhere around. I arose from the bed and went into the hall. The rooms were empty. There was no sign of the girls. If anyone saw me, I could say I was going to the toilet. I walked down the hall and back. Just as I reached my room and lay down once more on the bed, a girl came in with a tray.

My dinner consisted of a roll, a half glass of watered milk, and two vegetables. It was true that outside I should have been able to afford only rolls and coffee for my dinner, and my room would not have been as warm as this, but I would have given all this and many times over, to be out in the cold, even without a room and with only two dollars in my pocket. I was not thinking of the stigma of being in a reformatory; I was thinking of the words of the dead girl, "You can't go out. Nobody can go out." There was about them the same hopelessness that had been about those other words: "You can't do anything, you aren't good for anything." They made me feel suffocated. For I must go out. I must have freedom, or I would choke to death. It was like the time when my mother had hidden my hat and coat and shoes to prevent me from going out.

There was another fear—my poems. How would I be able to write my poems here? I wanted the little black book with me. I wanted it even more than I wanted freedom, that minute.

Was I going to have a baby? Sanity and common sense returned to me as I lay on the bed. Wasn't it all a hallucination? Hadn't the windowless room, the weeks of walking the streets looking for a job, the hunger, the worry, the fear—hadn't they turned my brain, made me a little crazy? Yet the doctor had said . . . but then I realized again that I had convinced her myself. I had said . . . I with my story of giving myself for sale on the streets. I had told it so convincingly that I had half believed it myself. Yet I could not have told her about the ape man. I had cunningly told her something she would understand, something without imagination, for she could only accept imaginationless things, like everybody else. The ape man would have been over her head, beyond her understanding. She would have said I was crazy. She might even have 'sent me away.'

I lay in bed. By and by I started to cry softly. I hated the baby. I wanted my poems, my books, the familiar papers I loved to touch, or at least know they were there, on the table, waiting for my touch. Where were they now? They were more real to me than any baby. . . . Where was the doctor? Why didn't she come to examine me?

Night came through the window. The girls came upstairs; they had been having dinner downstairs, on one of the other levels. They trooped stealthily into my room. They talked among themselves, ever with that passiveness. Then they trooped out again. Lights went out at nine o'clock.

Things began to seem unreal. I must have fallen asleep, for I was awakened suddenly by a flashlight in my face. An enormous woman was standing by my bed, holding a flashlight which almost blinded me. I could make her out behind the flashlight, enormous and vague, enormous and terrifying because of that very vagueness.

She held the flashlight on the paper as I read, "If you need anything, call me." I wanted to tell her—for I made out that she was smiling at me and I still had faith in smiles—that I was hungry, but something made me close my mouth on the words. If I said those words, she might stare at me and say, "What do you think this is, a boarding school?"

I found out later that she was a policewoman. She sat up all night at the bottom of the stairs, and every half hour she went through the halls, flashing her light into ever room to see if the girls were in their beds, to see if anyone was attempting to escape in spite of the iron bars and the electric alarms at the windows. She was a great strong woman, equally efficient in preventing escapes and in administering punishment to those girls who were not as yet completely dead and gave too much signs of life.

After the woman left I could not sleep. Everything was strange, strange. How was I to survive this place? It did not seem to me that I could. I might survive, but all my poems would die in me.

The place filled me with horror. All night, almost, I walked back and forth, back and forth, to the toilet and back to my room, the length of the cage. I did not care what the policewoman would think, I did not care about the rules. I walked. I passed the open doors of the girls' rooms, and in the rooms where there were two beds I saw the two beds drawn up closely together, instead of with the width of the room between them as they were by day. The beds were noiselessly pulled apart when it was time for the policewoman to cover her beat, but when she had gone again, I saw almost naked girls pull the beds together once more. I saw suppressed laughter, suppressed whispering, I saw strange distorted faces, unlike the passive faces of the day. I saw strange things as I walked from my room to the toilet, from the toilet to my room.

The next day went by and still the doctor had not come. I kept to my room as usual. But in the evening of that day, while the girls were at their dinner, a girl clothed as I was in bathrobe and slippers, stole into my room. She was about twenty years old. She was a new girl, brought in that afternoon after a night in jail. There was still an abundance of life about her. I liked her. The policemen had raided the 'place' she had been in, she told me. But she was philosophic about it. "When I get out, I'll find another place all right. My husband will find it for me."

"You can't get out," I said, repeating the words the dead girl had used.

"Oh, yes, I will. I'll escape some way. I'm not going to stay here."

I said nothing, having my superior knowledge which the girls had given to me. The windows were electrically wired, as well as having irons across them. And there was the massive policewoman on guard. It was only by a miracle that one could escape from here.

Another day went by and still the doctor had not come to examine me. But before the day was half over, something happened.

The period came. It was not much more than three days late, and it had finally decided to come, persuaded perhaps by the warmth, the rest, the regular if scanty meals.

In the evening of that day the doctor also came.

"See, doctor," I said. But she was suspicious.

"Abortion or miscarriage," she said, looking at me hard.

Now was the time to tell her everything, blurt out that it had all been a hallucination. But her face was unsympathetic. Also—she would not believe me. Suddenly, absolutely, I knew that she would not believe me. She had not the imagination. Nobody, probably, would believe me. They would say I was crazy, or laugh at me. Only a person with imagination would understand what a windowless room, dark walls, a dirty rooming-house with degenerates in most of the rooms could do to one.

Also, would it do any good to tell her? She did not want anything unusual, she did not want to look beneath the surface. My sole problem now was to get out of here. After all, I could get out. No one had committed me here, no police had raided my 'place.' I had come, like a fool, of my own free will. Now I wanted to get out. Why didn't they let me out?

The doctor was mysteriously uncommunicative. Again my blood froze. Surely she would not make me stay here, among these people, among these dead people. Didn't she see the difference between them and me?

The next day I was allowed to dress and leave my room. They gave me a gingham dress like the others wore, and a pair of turned-down shoes. This was to be my first mingling with all the girls in the 'boarding school,' my first penetration into the other floors. I was tired of my cage, of the walk from the toilet to my room, from my room to the toilet.

The rising bell rang at seven. As I would not hear it, I asked the girl to whom I had given the handkerchief to come and wake me.

When we were dressed, we went downstairs to a big room where I saw many other girls who had rooms on the other floors.

The room was big and sunny with a Victrola and a piano. Only the girls were out of place. They sat around with their sullen, cowed faces. Only here and there was there any trace of the rebelliousness that I was feeling.

Now that I was not going to have a baby, I could see how impossible it was that I should have stayed here for nine months. I would have gone crazy.

As I was a new girl, those from the other floors who had not yet seen me crowded around me, eager for news of the outside world.

"Don't say anything," one girl, different from the others, said. She was an intelligent-looking Jewish girl. "A lot of the girls are spies. They report everything."

"How did you get here?" I asked, curious.

"My husband put me here. He said I ran around with fellows. I had a baby, but it died."

"Aren't you sorry?"

"No."

Another girl told me her story. She too had had a baby, and she too was not sorry that it had died.

Except for the intelligent Jewish girl, and one or two others, most of the girls had weak faces. Some of the girls seemed to be subnormal in intelligence. Their eyes were stupidly dead, instead of containing that kind of deadness that tells of intelligence and high spirits clubbed to death. These were the real under-dogs, the submerged tenth, who perhaps had grasped at color in the shape of dance halls, boys. But the system was too much for them. They had not had the wit to circumvent the system. So there were places like this for them. They sat around without hope in their eyes.

I wanted to get out. I wanted to get out. This place filled me with horror. The sunshine streaming in was a mockery.

The intelligent Jewish girl stuck close to me. Perhaps she understood what was going on in my brain. I liked her. There was sullenness and rebelliousness about her, akin to my own defiance.

We started talking about books. She was eager to know what books there were being published in the outside world. There were no books here; only the books, pollyannaish in tone, that nobody read.

As I talked, I watched the girls. There was one girl in particular. I could not take my eyes off her, she was so pretty. Her skin was a lovely pink and white. She was very intimate with another girl, her roommate. She started the Victrola, and she and her friend danced together. I thought I had never seen a body more lovely or more graceful. It was a shock to me when, afterward, I saw her going into the syphilitic bathroom. I was shocked and bewildered. Could it be possible? So lovely, so light and delicate and fresh. I had imagined syphilitic people to be almost black, repulsive, hideous with sores.

The breakfast bell rang. We all trooped downstairs.

The dining room was another large room. There were five tables in it. We stood behind our chairs, waiting, waiting for whom, I wondered?

Then I saw some women come in. There was the woman I had first seen, the woman who, according to the woman at the clinic, was "lovely . . . you'll like her." Then there was the dark young woman who had let me in and given me a bath. The others were, I was to learn, the social service workers.

They had a table of their own, the longest table, the table with the linen and the silver. We had the smaller tables, without linen, and our knives and forks and spoons were not silver.

We sat down after they sat down. As we ate our rolls and drank our dishwater coffee, we watched them sullenly, as they ate their nice food. We smelled the aromatic coffee poured from the silver coffee pot—our coffee was made from the dregs of that, no doubt. We watched them break hot, golden biscuits, while we tore apart cold rolls. We watched the hot biscuits disappear down their throats, then the cereal, then the berries, then—but what had they not to eat? And all the time we tried to eat our rolls and drink our coffee. It was refined cruelty. All this lovely food near us, and yet so far away, not for us. What did they know of hunger? They were older and did not know the hunger that the young know. What would we not have given for those hot golden biscuits, the real coffee. . . . What would have happened if we had rushed up and grabbed that plate of hot biscuits? What would have happened?

We sat in our chairs and ate and watched sullenly. Why did they have to torture us like this? Why couldn't they eat by themselves, so that we need not see them and compare their food with ours? It was too refined cruelty. They laughed and talked as they ate— who wouldn't laugh and talk with such food in one? We for the most part were silent. What was there to talk about? We were dead people.

When would I leave this place? When would I leave this place? I wasn't going to have a baby. It was all a mistake. Why had I come here anyway, even if I was going to have a baby? Hunger and cold were better. I had known both, and I preferred them to this. Anything was better than this place. I wanted to get out. I wanted to get out. I could have screamed. I controlled myself by looking at the girl opposite. Her dead, indifferent eyes calmed me.

After breakfast we trooped upstairs again. This time we had to clean our rooms. A social worker was with us, the one I had seen in the doctor's office when I had first come here. She was a nurse, and as I found out later, an adept at mental torture.

I watched her as she unlocked the door where the brooms were kept. Everything here was under lock and key. Everywhere was suspicion, distrust. I watched her, her painted, haggard face, as I had watched the other social service workers at the breakfast table. They were all young except this nurse. After we were in bed, they could go out, go out to the men and the dances and the parties that were waiting for them, do the things that the girls here had been put in the reformatory for doing. What did the social workers really think of us? What secret laughter was in them as they looked at us? These girls who had got put away for six months or more for being nothing worse than delinquents, most of them, for doing nothing worse than attempting to step out of their environment; these girls who would have their lives ruined ever afterward by parole officers who checked up their least act, who told their employers 'what they were,' with the result that they were fired. No work . . . oh, what was the use! They drifted back to their old habits, and inevitably they were brought back here. What else was there for them to do?

Those other girls, the better educated ones, they were no different from us, but their superiority consisted in being able to get away with it. They had no fear of being caught; they exercised the proper secrecy and caution, they showed composed eyes to the world. The girls here were more simple, more innocent, more direct. They did not know enough, they had not been educated enough, to take the proper precautions. So they were sucked under; so the system got them. They were taken to the courts and put away to be 'reformed' in modern 'homes for girls.' They got caught with babies because they did not know, as the girls with superior education and cunning knew, about birth-control.

But—when would they let me out? When would they let me out? That was what I wanted to know.

I cleaned my room as I was told. The nurse was not satisfied. I cleaned the room again. Still she was not satisfied. I cleaned it again, again, again. "God, I hate you, you bitch," I said silently to the painted face. If only I might throw the broom into her face, as I had thrown, long ago, the shoes into my father's face.

I cleaned the hall. As I cleaned, on my knees, another social service worker went down the hall. She never looked at any of us directly in the face. We were not human beings to her. We had no individuality. She passed us with an averted face, almost.

A girl, also on her knees, cleaning the syphilitic bathroom, reminded me of the ape man. She had the same brutal jaws.

We all worked, cleaning, sweeping, scrubbing. Now I knew why the stairs and the floors shone so. They were cleaned every day by the girls, cleaned and polished again and again until the social service workers were satisfied.

At noon another bell rang. We filed down again to the dining room. Again we went through the same ritual of waiting behind our chairs until the staff was seated.

Then we watched, as we had watched in the morning, as they received once more the aromatic coffee in the shining silver pot. Then followed meat and vegetables, white bread, the beautiful yellow butter. We received our own meager helpings, and the rolls again. There was also a pat of what looked like butter, but wasn't. If only they would not eat in front of us! If only we had not their food constantly before us! We would not have minded so much the meagerness, the coldness, the colorlessness, of our own meals. But to see them! To see that beautiful food! To see in their faces contentment, while we arose from the table still hungry, still unsatisfied.

After lunch, we filed into the big sunny room, and one of the social service workers came with us, to watch over us.

The social service workers were as tormenting a spectacle as the table heaped with beautiful food. There was one girl especially, tall and willowy, marvellously dressed, her hair done in a marvellously unreal coiffure. As she sat with us, she worked at some fine embroidery. We could not take our eyes off her. She was like a being from another world.

We did not go near her, and she made no attempt to come near us. Always there was that distance between us. Always that distance. Yet I learned later that she was here to do research work for a book she was writing. She must have done her research work among the statistics, for she made no effort to come near any of the human beings. We were all human beings, didn't she realize it? Why didn't she look up from her fine embroidery and see the anguish in our eyes? Why didn't she look up? Did she think we were not human beings, just because we were 'bad'? We were all human beings, even those with subnormal intelligence. They were the most human of all, if human meant pitiable. They sat straight in their chairs, their arms passive, their hands patient, looking straight before them. Couldn't she see the terribleness of it all? How could she sit and sew at fine embroidery here? This was not the place for such things. It was almost too much.

In half an hour we were herded into another room. The idea seemed to be to get us in one place and keep us there as long as possible until the time somehow passed until bedtime.

In the new room, without the social worker, some of the girls tried to talk, but most of them sat about, dully apathetic. Everyone here was either dead or dying. I wanted to get out. I could not stand this atmosphere any more. I would go crazy, unless I died first like the others. Although it was against the rules, I wandered out in the hall. I wandered down a flight of stairs, then another flight. Downstairs, in the offices, the social service workers were gathered, talking and laughing and drinking coffee from fragile little china cups. Damn them! Couldn't they see how callous they were? Damn you! Damn you! What right had they to be free, drinking coffee, while the girls upstairs sat around, dead, in their chairs?

The nurse spied me. She grabbed my arm and pulled me upstairs. She hated me because of my habit of wandering around the place, because I was not properly cowed yet and would not stay in my room, like the other girls, because I would have nothing to do with discipline.

"What do you mean walking down those stairs," she said, pulling me into an office and getting pencil and paper. "That's the staff's stairway. You're not supposed to go down it. You're supposed to use the back stairs."

Rules and regulations—they had never meant anything to me. I stared at her sullenly.

"I want to get out of here," I said.

She laughed in her fussy painted way that said, "Oh, you do, do you, my girl! Just try!"

"I want to get out," I said wildly. "I want to get out." I would wash dishes for the rest of my life, anything, anything, was preferable to this.

She gave me a push. "Go upstairs and stay with the other girls or you'll get worse yet."

Go upstairs and be among those girls with their dead eyes. Try to kill time, time that did not exist.

"Can I have a pencil and some paper?" I asked in despair.

"What for?" she asked. I did not know that paper and pencil were given out only at stated times to write letters.

"I want to write a poem," I said. I did not. But having a pencil and some paper with me would make me feel less lonesome.

She stared at me. Probably no one had ever said that before here. Finally she gave me a pencil and a pad of paper.

I went upstairs to the room where the girls were. I sat down and tried to write—anything. But there was too much deadness in the air.

The intelligent Jewish girl looked over my shoulder.

"If you're writing a letter," she said, "it won't do any good to complain. They read all the letters, outgoing and incoming, and censor them."

But I wasn't writing a letter. To whom could I have written?

I could not be still. I wandered up and down the room. The girls looked up at my restlessness, and then looked down again, indifferently.

There was only one way to kill time. Would someone talk to me? Might as well make use of the pencil and the pad of paper. There was one girl, I learned, who had come here again and again, for six-month periods. She could not get along outside. She was beaten. There was nothing to do except come back. There was another girl with a baby on the way. There was another girl who had a baby with her, which she tended indifferently. It was thin and sickly. It was probably not very well fed. I did not think it would live long. I did not think its sixteen-year-old mother would be sorry if it died.

I wandered out in the hall again. I could not stay in that room. I wandered upstairs and stood huddled against the doctor's door, crying. Where was the doctor? I had thought her to be my friend, and now she was keeping me locked up here. I wanted to get out. I wanted to get out. I would go crazy if I did not get out, away from these dead people, this absolute indifference.

I wandered down the staff's stairs again to the offices. I went in one of them and sat down. I did not care if the nurse, if anyone, found me there. I was not going back to that room where dead girls talked listlessly to pass the time.

There was a booklet on the desk in front of me. I was hungry for something to read. I picked it up and turned the pages. It was about the reformatory, or 'Home for Girls' as it was called in the booklet. On the first page it contained the names of the patrons and patronesses of the Home. It went on to ask for money, contributions, gifts. It was evidently the kind of booklet that is sent to people in making requests for money to carry on the good work.

I turned to other pages. Now it told about the girls of the Home. A girl had come, I read in the booklet, to the Home, a girl who had had an unusual supply of dirty language. After three months of the Home, she had been cured of the obscene words and phrases. The booklet did not tell how the Home had effected the cure. I wondered: did these ladies and gentlemen to whom the booklets were sent with a respectful request for funds to carry on the good work, did these ladies and gentlemen know how the cure had been effected? I thought I could have enlightened them: I who knew of the existence of the heavy policewoman. There were other things in employ too, to effect the cure; I did not know exactly what, but I could see the results in the dead eyes of the girls. And was this girl really cured of her predilection for obscene words? It all seemed rather naive, anyway. How about the girl's mind. What went on inside of it? Was it not more black now that there was not the relief of speech? However, she did not speak the words any more. That was all the Home cared about. Surface. Surface. If the surface was smooth, who cared what hell went on beneath?

I turned another page. Many of the 'graduates' of the Home, the booklet said, were now respectable waitresses, stenographers, factory workers. One was even an actress. Some were even married. The Home dwelt long and lingeringly on marriage. To get a girl, especially one who had had a baby, married, was the peak of the Home's achievement. What sort of a hell went on after the marriage, the Home did not concern itself with. Only to get the girl married. Surface. Surface. Let the surface be smooth. Marriage could conceal anything, and usually did. Marriage could hide a past 'mistake.' No wonder the Home was all for it.

I turned another page. The Home was, above all things, modern, I read. The Home stressed particularly the mental health of its girls, as well as the physical. Thus the psychiatrist, rather than the doctor.

Yet what did the psychiatrist do? How much did she mingle with the girls? Now and then she held hours when she poked fingers into the girls. Most of the time she was away. All that was done with the girls was to herd them together, girls who were prostitutes, girls who were syphilitic, girls who were merely delinquent, girls who were . . .

Another page. Environment was mostly to blame, the Home said. I thought: why then were not the homes corrected? Why then were not the poverty, the too closeness, the lack of any humane privacy, the nagging mother, the bullying father—why were not these things corrected? Why were not the nagging mother, the bullying father, put way? Why did the children have to do the suffering? Why were the children put away, beaten mentally and physically, until they were so properly cowed that when they returned to their homes they would be indifferent to the nagging mother, the bullying father? Was it the fault of the children? . . . The surface again. An energetic scratching of the surface. Social adjustment. Meantime, the core was rotten, rotten, rotten.

Another page. Unless the patrons and patronesses sent money, the good work could not go on. What was the money for? Did *we* have any of the things bought with the money? I was hungry. The others were hungry. They arose from the table unsatisfied. The money seemed to go mostly to the upkeep of the staff, to the staff's table, with its biscuits, its aromatic coffee, its plentiful butter and meat and vegetables.

Another page. But then I felt a hand on my shoulder. I turned around and saw the woman I had first seen when I came here. She seemed very angry.

"Don't you know you must not read that?" she asked.

"I didn't know," I said sullenly.

These booklets, I should have known, were not for the girls themselves who would read and laugh cynically. If only I could steal one for the intelligent Jewish girl to read. How we would laugh together. No! These booklets were for the society patrons and patronesses who knew nothing about the real conditions, and who would give money not because they cared, but from a desire to salve their smug consciences.

We give a girl a chance to come back, the booklet read. Come back to what?

I was sent upstairs to the girls again. This time there was a social service worker there who saw that I did no more wandering around.

I sat down beside the intelligent Jewish girl and another girl who stared straight before her. I wanted to talk. The Jewish girl was talking to someone, so I talked to the girl on my other side. She had been here a year and a half, she told me. They had let her out at the end of the six-month period, but she had gone back to her old habits of staying out late and had been confined again. It had happened twice. She did not care. She shrugged her shoulders. I thought of the girls who stayed out late—and did not get confined in reformatories. Why was it an offense in one and not in the other?

This girl was subnormal in intelligence. Why were the normal girls allowed to mix with these, the syphilitic, the subnormal, the prostitutes? One from the last group, the new girl who had come to my room, had tried to teach me the 'trade.' She had wanted to give me the addresses of some 'houses.' Another girl liked to laugh over the dirty words she used. Was she the girl they had cured of bad language?

The next day was Sunday. We all filed into the little chapel room. The Jewish girls were segregated—fully half of them were Jewish—and given to a special minister, a Rabbi. They seemed to be very particular about religion for the girls, if they were not particular about food. They did not know what to do with me. I could not hear the sermon, and therefore would not be benefited, but to get rid of me, or rather to keep me in one place, since, if I was sent to my room I would—as they had found out—not stay there, but would wander all over the place, they segregated me with the Jewish girls.

The Rabbi was talking about sin, the intelligent Jewish girl told me. He was an expert. Expertly he played on the emotions of the girls, expertly he exposed the thin skins of the girls. Pretty soon they were crying. The very pretty girl who had so bewildered me when I had seen her go into the syphilitic bathroom, who was always dancing and laughing—the only one here who laughed often—she was sobbing. Her heart was small, very small, I had judged, as small as her mouth, and she was the last one to be sobbing so, as if the small, the too small, heart were breaking. She was the least able to stand it. Why did not the Rabbi direct his speech to the degenerate with the brutal jaws who cleaned the syphilitic bathroom every day? But the degenerate was beyond the Rabbi, beyond any Rabbi. She was to be envied.

The Rabbi talked on. I shrieked at him in my mind: Get out of here, get out of here, with your obscene slobbering. Get out! Get out with your charity. Go back to your church and preach at the people who can get away with it, who can escape the system, not at these children who land in the system's jaws the instant they stir with life. Go back to your thick-headed, thick-emotioned, people who have the necessary hardness, who are too shrewd to get caught, who listen to you and laugh up their sleeves. Go—get out of here. What do you know of children, of the innocence of children who merely obey their impulses and then are caught? Leave these poor kids alone with their messed up, narrow, poor, unimaginative lives. Leave them alone. Can't you see the innocence behind the bad language, the boasting? Can't you see the uncertainty, the bewilderment?

Talk of sin! Leave them alone, and get hold of their fathers and mothers and the whole unwashed neck of this so-called civilization that made these kids what they are. Talk to the mothers and fathers of their own sins. These children are clean. Leave them alone. They can't answer you back. They have not the unctuous command of words that you have.

Get out of here. Why did you come anyway? Haven't you enough manhood, humanity, to stay away? Or do you come because you enjoy yourself? What's your imagination like? As you talk of sin, are you mentally seducing them? Perhaps the very pretty one who is sobbing her small heart out? Your eye seems to be especially on her. You are calculating the effect of your splendid preaching on her. I hope you're satisfied. I have heard of you and of your reputation for fine speeches. Get out. Get out. You make me sick. You make us all sick, those of us who are not cowed. Get out. You can't reach us. We are wise to you and the system, the more intelligent of us. One of these days we too will be able to do it—and get away with it.

Sunday slipped away. Monday came. When would they let me out? When would they let me out? I must get away from here or I would go mad. I walked up and down the stairs, up and down the staff's stairs. I even aroused the girls from their dead indifference to everything around them. They stared at me as I went, back and forth, back and forth, from one end of the cage to the other, from my room to the toilet, from the toilet to my room.

Monday noon I was called into the doctor's office.

"We are letting you go," she said. "We have no right to keep you, although you deserve it. You have been a bad girl. You have been immoral."

"Like hell I have," I said.

"We've got in touch with your people, and from what they have told us about you, if you were my daughter I'd give you a spanking."

I laughed. "Say, all you can see is their side. I've told the whole damned bunch to go to hell often enough, and I repeat it. I'll always say it. All you people can see is what's straight before you—the surface. You don't care enough to dig down below. You don't want the unusual, anyway. You want everything to fit a pattern."

"I showed your poems to a gentleman friend of mine. He says they are no good," she said.

"He can go to hell," I said, but this time to myself.

They let me go. I had spent five days there. They gave me ten dollars. My father who had never raised his hand to help me before had been prevailed upon to send the money. I wanted to spit on it, I wanted to tear it into bits, but I couldn't afford that satisfaction.

Out in the world again. How wonderful it was to be free! I would never let myself be locked up again. Anything, anything, was better than that. Better to be cold and hungry.

Charcoal drawing of Pauline Leader by Henry Lavarack, ca. 1930.

Afterword
Pauline Leader's Disability Modernism
Rebecca Sanchez

I would tell them that to the few
The word with its assumption of form—
Image implicit only in the known escape of sight and hearing—
Can become meaninglessly too literal.

In "The Mystic Sense," a poetic tribute to Helen Keller published in 1931, Pauline Leader offers a counter-narrative to assumptions surrounding not only the meaning of disability but the ways in which disability experience produces meaning.[1] "To the few"—those like Keller and Leader herself, with non-normative modes of engaging the world—Leader suggests that language can signify differently. Rather than positioning disability as lack, the poem imagines it as a conduit through which the meaninglessness of traditional forms of words can be registered and, by extension, more meaningful alternatives might be constructed. This link between disability embodiment, language, and aesthetics is further developed in Leader's memoir *And No Birds Sing*, in which the author describes and enacts the tensions involved with occupying intersecting types of marginalized identity through formal experimentation. The text's conceptual intertwining of form and identity offers glimpses into the ways that putting the two into conversation enriches our understanding of each.

The Power of Narrative

These dynamics are particularly evident in Leader's imaginative origin story for her deafness, which structurally replicates some of the complexities of both inhabiting a disabled body and of disability itself.[2] Leader creates a fantastical narrative around her hearing loss, personifying deafness as a gnome as a means of explaining both her physiological deafness—"he climbed on the lips of the people and snatched to himself the words that were meant for me, for my ears"—and the social stigma that surrounds it (59).[3] It is the gnome, she explains, who shapes peoples' negative reactions to her: "My mother was seeing the gnome. I saw the gnome in her eyes . . . . she saw only the gnome and his ugliness" (58).

The mythology surrounding deafness that Leader develops in the memoir is infused with this apparent contradiction between the essential and the constructed. The gnome becomes attached to Leader after she descends beneath the cellar, drinking and passing through magical water into another realm. Like Persephone, however, she is not permitted easy egress; the deafness gnome is the price of her freedom. In her fantasy, the king of the gnomes tells her, "'You must take him with you,' . . . pointing to a gnome who laid down his hammer at the King's words. 'Only on that condition will you be allowed to return to your own world'" (56).

On the one hand, Leader acquires the gnome as part of a contract she unknowingly enters into by trespassing in the world of the gnomes. The gnome itself is a separate being, external to her body, something forced upon her. And her later descriptions repeatedly frame her deafness as something outside of her body, imposed by others through social interaction. "But for the people I would not be deaf," she explains over and over. "If it were not for them, I would not be 'deaf'" (105, 62).

On the other hand, according to the logic of the story, it is only because Leader is already different from others that she is able to enter into the gnomes' kingdom in the first place, because she is creative and special, capable of imagining the subterranean world. When she later returns in an attempt to rid herself of her gnome, the king reinforces the idea that it is in some way essentially linked to her— "He was decreed before you were born by an even greater

King. I was merely to deliver him to you at the appointed time" (68). The text cycles between these cognitively dissonant versions of the story, making no attempt to resolve the contradictions.

Leader's characterization of her relationship with the gnome similarly vacillates between divergent poles. Repeatedly, she describes her identity as being grounded in her interiority and her art, realms into which the gnome does not enter. "My poems . . . conspire[d] to save me from the gnome," she writes, because "the gnome had no meaning and no reality for them, my thoughts and poems" (62). Becoming "*really* deaf," capitulating to the gnome, would in this version of her narrative involve losing something vital about her inner world, a process she resists: "They had not succeeded in making me really deaf. My individuality was intact." (129, italics in original).

In other moments, however, the gnome is explicitly linked to Leader's artistic creativity, something she very much associates with her interiority and individuality. The figure emerges from her fairy tale and provides an imagined physical form to the differences between herself and her community, which she describes from the first pages of the book. *And No Birds Sing* opens with an account of Leader's nonconformant behavior, how she is perceived as "a bad girl" who, unlike "respectable people," wanders off and daydreams. The book's first sentence—"This is i, very small i, walking home from the market at night, walking through the dark, apparently limitless streets"—ties that rebelliousness with explicit artfulness, the lower case "i" in which the narrator locates her sense of self (1, 2, 1). While the gnome will frequently bear the weight of Leader's sense of alienation in the narrative, her outsider status precedes her hearing loss.

Moreover, at times Leader describes the gnome as being a vital part of her. "During the six years he had had possession of me," she explains, the gnome "had indeed permeated my whole being" (159). She also uses it as an explanation for her rebelliousness: "'Go to hell,' I said to my mother. 'Go to hell,' I said to the authorities. . . . I would go my way, the gnome's way. For it seemed to me that I had become him. There were no longer two of us, the gnome and myself. There was one: the gnome, and the gnome was myself. If I addressed the gnome, I also addressed myself" (110).

Rather than constituting problematic loose ends, the unresolved tensions between these diverse, often contradictory, ways of describing Leader's deafness contribute to the psychological realism of the book. Self-narratives are not always (or often) internally consistent. The impressionistic structure of the first chapter in particular, with its repetitions and juxtapositions, captures something of a mind at work, in the process of navigating fraught issues surrounding identity, individuality, and community, rather than a narrator who, having come to a particular political or ideological conclusion, filters earlier memories through that lens.

The same is true of Leader's description of her sense of alienation more broadly. She distrusts "the people," the masses, who she perceives to represent conformity and cruelty, and from whom she tries to distance herself through the development of a unique identity as an artist. But she is also uncomfortable with aspects of alterity, particularly her Jewishness, and is desperate to fit in, to have "a house with a hallway in it" like her classmates, and a fancy hat for church on Sunday (13). "I did not want to stand out," she declares, and her relationship to her parents is shaped by the extent to which she views them as both cause and symbol of her otherness (5). "Mixed in with my hatred of my father was shame," she notes. "I looked at him with the eyes of the Americans. . . . he was ridiculous compared with the American men, who all looked alike, who did not stand out. I wanted that kind of a father" (34).

Reconceptualizing Disability

This sense of the narrator's negative capability, of simultaneously craving and despising otherness, of describing identity as both essential and constructed,[4] is particularly significant within the context of Deaf and Disability Studies. Written decades before the advent of either field, Leader's narrative is, therefore, independent of any sense of group identification around disability. It offers an alternative model for thinking about the relationship between embodied and social aspects of deafness, which became problematically bifurcated in some early attempts by Disability Studies scholars to reframe perceptions of embodied difference.

Following the rise of institutionalized medicine in the eighteenth and nineteenth centuries, a medical model of disability developed that identified physical, intellectual, and psychiatric differences as deviations from the norm. The ideology of the norm, Lennard Davis notes, "pushes the normal variation of the body through a stricter template guiding the way the body 'should' be." [5] Throughout much of the twentieth century, it was widely believed to be the function, and indeed responsibility, of medical science to correct such deviations. This attitude toward difference was transferred to non-normative subjects themselves. Under the medical model, disabled people were dehumanized, perceived as problems in need of a cure. The ideology was carried to its most horrific conclusion as part of the Nazi T4 program, which sought to remove disabled individuals from the gene pool through a process of systematic mass murder, and it was also behind the compulsory sterilization laws in the United States.

Part of the political intervention of Disability Studies as a field has been to challenge this account of embodied difference as a threat to the health of the national body politic. One of the most successful ways this has been accomplished, both conceptually and politically, has been the re-description of disability as socially constructed. According to the social model, all bodies vary in their capabilities. Disability occurs when a body encounters a social or built environment that is inaccessible; a wheelchair user, for example, is disabled by a flight of stairs. The social model allowed disability to be framed as a valuable form of minority identity, one that could be protected under civil rights legislation.

Despite the importance of this paradigm shift and the concrete political gains it has enabled, more recent work in Disability

Studies has highlighted the ways that pitting the medical against the social model ultimately fails to capture the complex interplay of these dynamics in the lived experiences of disabled people. Strong versions of social constructionism ironically displace the body from conversations about disability and leave little, if any, space for discussions of pain or trauma. In order to account for these elements, Tobin Siebers argues, "the next step for disability studies is to develop a theory of complex embodiment that . . . raises awareness of the effects of disabling environments on people's lived experience of the body, but . . . emphasizes as well that some factors affecting disability . . . derive from the body." In a similar attempt to move beyond the medical/social binary, Alison Kafer proposes "a hybrid political/relational model . . . that builds on social and minority frameworks but reads them through feminist and queer critiques of identity."[6]

At a moment in which Disability Studies is working to develop such hybrid models, Leader's account of deafness is particularly significant. Predating the medical/social split, the story of the gnome incorporates aspects of both and suggests an alternative approach to talking about disability. Critically, the memoir also enacts a form of thinking about disability through the juxtaposition of competing narratives that gesture toward the complex ways disabled individuals (indeed, all individuals) perceive their bodies and identities. Leader does not attempt to resolve the logical inconsistencies in the descriptions of her deafness (or her Jewishness, or her relationship with her parents). These relationships are all depicted as context and time dependent, moving away from the idea of disability as singular and stable, either as biological fact or identity category, and capturing something about the flux and flow of inhabiting an intersectional identity.

Avoiding the tropes of many disability memoirs, *And No Birds Sing* is not structured by a narrative arc in which the author learns to make peace with his or her non-normative body. Instead, it draws on formal techniques associated with literary modernism, including indeterminacy and contradiction. Its first chapter is particularly playful, providing a juxtaposition of impressionistic moments of significance to the narrator, moments that fold back on one another, challenging previous perspectives. Subsequent chapters maintain more subtle structural experimentation by incorporating competing narratives, dramatizing the process of trying out different versions of self-narrative and explanation. In this, it is more closely aligned with fictional (or fictionalized) coming of age stories such as James Joyce's *Portrait of the Artist as a Young Man* (1916) and Henry Roth's *Call it Sleep* (1934), both of which deploy aesthetic experimentation as a means to capture the experience of navigating marginalized identities.

Assimilation and Resistance

Beyond the specific context of disability, Leader's account of negotiating intersectional experiences of otherness—as a working-class Jewish girl, as a disabled woman, as an artist—is significant as part of a larger conversation about the relationship between formal experimentation and assimilationist discourses at the time of its publication (1931). Anxieties over America's cultural and linguistic heterogeneity had been rising since the mid-nineteenth century in response to both the Civil War, which had raised questions about the ultimate viability of a nation comprised of so many disparate cultures and peoples, and the increase in immigration around the turn of the twentieth century.[7] Reactionary responses to this diversity and the growing sense that America needed a more unified body politic came from multiple directions. The government passed a series of laws—the Page Act of 1875, the Chinese Exclusion Act of 1882, the Naturalization Act of 1906, the Emergency Quota Act of 1921, and the National Origins Act of 1924—aimed at reducing the ethnic, cultural, racial, and linguistic diversity of the population. In 1919, Theodore Roosevelt wrote, "we intend to see that the crucible turns our people out as

Americans, of American nationality, and not as dwellers in a poly-
glot boarding-house."[8]

In the private sector, efforts were undertaken to "Americanize"
immigrants and ethnic minorities. Henry Ford, for example, established a language school at his plant specifically designed both to
standardize the speech of his largely immigrant workforce and to
regulate their personal hygiene, which he perceived as lacking. As
Sarah Wilson describes, the school's graduation ceremony

> required immigrants to act out their abandonment of dis-
> tinct ethnic origins for an undifferentiated "Americanness." In
> this drama workers wearing various national costumes pro-
> cessed from a steamship into the "Ford English School Melting
> Pot" and emerged all identically attired in "American clothes"
> and waving American flags.[9]

This sense of the need to norm the population carried over into
policies directed at disabled citizens. One of the clearest examples
of this can be found in the treatment of deaf Americans. While
the early nineteenth century had witnessed the flourishing of
schools that educated children in a mixture of what would become
American Sign Language (ASL) with spoken and written English,
by the late nineteenth century, the idea of instructing American
children in a language other than English was deemed unaccept-
able. Difference, according to the zeitgeist, was to be eliminated
and, where that was not possible, to be made invisible. Following a
conference for educators of the deaf in Milan in 1880, most schools
across the United States banned the use of ASL and fired deaf
instructors. Jonathan Sterne posits that oralists set out to eradicate
"the cultural problem of deafness" by training pupils "to pass as
hearing people through their speech." Alexander Graham Bell, the
leading proponent of oralism and advocate of eugenic philosophy,
firmly supported homogenizing models and vocally opposed the
formation of a unique deaf cultural identity, a "deaf variety of the
human race."[10]

While struggling to find one's sense of identity and weighing the costs and benefits of striking out on one's own as opposed to attempting to "fit in" are perennial issues for writers of memoirs and *bildungsroman*, the years depicted by *And No Birds Sing* drew into particularly sharp focus the political and personal stakes that attended them. The book registers these stakes at a narrative level through the frame of the threat of "corrective" institutionalization—first when Leader's mother threatens to send her to a reformatory if she does not behave, and later when she finds herself confined to a home for girls after she mistakenly believes she has become pregnant out of wedlock—making it a significant historical record of the effects of normativizing ideology.

By making explicit the power of narrative through her creation of the gnome story, Leader also, and even more significantly, models forms of writing back to such ideology. One way critics have explained the difficulty, indeterminacy, and multilingualism that characterize experimental modernist writing is as a direct response against the calls for conformity and standardization that dominated the modern political landscape. And through its technique of providing readers with multiple contradictory and irreducible versions of the stories Leader tells about herself, *And No Birds Sing* contributes to this project. The edges of the stories don't all line up. The fragments, to paraphrase T. S. Eliot, don't always cohere. And it is precisely in that failure to offer a singular, coherent argument about the questions it raises that the text remains most relevant to us today.

Notes

1. Pauline Leader, "The Mystic Sense," in *Double Blossoms: Helen Keller Anthology*, comp. Edna Porter (New York: Lewis Copeland Company, 1931), 37.

2. Many culturally Deaf people do not consider themselves to be disabled, but rather to be members of a linguistic and cultural minority. This distinction postdates Leader's writing, however, and does not reflect

the way she describes her deafness. Moreover, the disidentification can itself be problematic insofar as it establishes a new hierarchy in which *Deaf* emerges as a privileged term over *disabled*. A great deal of stigma remains associated with the term *disabled* in common parlance, from which it may make pragmatic sense to distance oneself. The deployment of the term within Disability Studies, however, attempts to overturn such biases, emphasizing the productive force of the concept in ways that often apply to Deaf, as well as other kinds of disability, experiences. It is in this spirit that I use the terms and, at times, permit them to overlap.

3. Unless otherwise noted, numbers in parentheses refer to pages in this volume.

4. *Selected Letters of John Keats,* ed. Grant F. Scott (Cambridge: Harvard University Press, 2002), 60. In "Letter to George and Tom Dec. 1817," Keats defined negative capability as the capacity "of being in uncertainties." His 1819 poem "La Belle Dame sans Merci" provides the title of Leader's memoir.

5. Lennard J. Davis, *Enforcing Normalcy: Disability, Deafness, and the Body* (London: Verso, 1995), 34.

6. Tobin Siebers, *Disability Theory* (Ann Arbor: University of Michigan Press, 2008), 25; Alison Kafer, *Queer, Crip* (Bloomington: Indiana University Press, 2013), 4.

7. Sarah Wilson, *Melting-Pot Modernism* (Ithaca, NY: Cornell University Press, 2010), 2. Between 1891 and 1920 alone, more than 18 million people migrated to the United States.

8. James Crawford, *At War with Diversity: US Language Policy in an Age of Anxiety* (Clevedon, UK: Cromwell, 2000), 8. Crawford quotes from Theodore Roosevelt's letter to the president of the American Defense Society, January 3, 1919.

9. Wilson, *Melting-Pot Modernism,* 15.

10. Jonathan Sterne, *The Audible Past: Cultural Origins of Sound Reproduction* (Durham: Duke University Press, 2003), 40; Alexander Graham Bell, *Memoir Upon the Formation of a Deaf Variety of the Human Race* (Washington, DC: National Academy of Sciences, 1884).

Appendix

The flap copy on the original Vanguard edition of *And No Birds Sing* (reprinted below) described the memoir as the story of resilience in the face of physical, class, and ethnic "handicap."

For Pauline Leader the birds will never sing again, the ocean will never roar, the wind never sough through the trees. Young, tensely alive, at twenty-two she is condemned to live in a world of eternal silence, denied even the sound of her own voice.

To those whose hearing is normal, this may seem a minor handicap. Actually, it is nearly as effective as blindness in cutting one off from the ordinary ways of humanity.

But deafness was only one of the tremendous handicaps this writer faced. She grew up alone, friendless, the butt in school of brutal pranks and even more brutal taunts: her father was a butcher and the smell of the butcher shop remained with her; she was an alien and the representative of the despised race. Then, at twelve, the final blow: a long illness and at the end blank and utter silence.

Yet this girl refused to permit the silence to stifle her. She would not sink back and take her place as a nonentity in the ranks of the deaf—a cipher among ciphers. Against the opposition of her parents and with no help from them, she determined to win a place for herself in the world. She could perform only the coarsest labor, and to get even such work she was compelled to accept less than other applicants—this, the penalty of deafness. At times she actually starved; seldom did she have enough to eat. She had strange experiences;

at one time she was detained in a home for wayward girls. Through it all she never lost her faith in herself. "Stand up! Stand up!" she told herself. Now, like the late D. H. Lawrence she can say, "I have come through!"

This simple, poignant story, of mingled beauty and terror, ranks with the great autobiographies of all times. It is the revelation, intense and unashamed, of a human soul. No one will read it unmoved.